D0753635

Complaint Management
The Heart of CRM

Bernd Stauss
Wolfgang Seidel

Australia · Canada · Mexico · Singapore · Spain · United Kingdom · United States

Complaint Management
Stauss/Seidel

ISBN: 0-324-20264-4
Printed and bound in the United States of America by Phoenix Color Corporation.
1 2 3 4 5 6 7 8 9 07 06 05 04

For more information, contact Texere at Thomson Higher Education, 5191 Natorp Boulevard, Mason, Ohio, USA 45040. You can also visit our website at www.thomson.com/learning/texere.

This publication is designed to provide accurate and authoritative information in regard to the subject matter covered. It is sold with the understanding that the publisher is not engaged in rendering legal, accounting or other professional services. If legal advice or other expert assistance is required, the services of a competent professional person should be sought.

Composed by: Navta Associates, Inc.

Stauss, Bernd.
Complaint management : the heart of CRM / Bernd Stauss, Wolfgang Seidel—
1st ed.
     p. cm.
   "American Marketing Association."
   Includes bibliographical references and index.
   ISBN 0-324-20264-4 (alk. paper)
   1. Consumer complaints. 2. Customer relations--Management. I. Seidel, Wolfgang, 1935- II. Title.
   HF5415.52.S83 2004
   658.8'12--dc22

                                                                2004022189

The names of all companies or products mentioned herein are used for identification purposes only and may be trademarks or registered trademarks of their respective owners. Texere disclaims any affiliation, association, connection with, sponsorship, or endorsements by such owners.

This book is printed on acid-free paper.

TABLE OF CONTENTS

Complaint Management in a Customer-Oriented Firm

1.1 COMPLAINTS AS A CHALLENGE TO THE FIRM

Everyone in business hates complaints. Employees dread situations in which they might be abused by angry customers. Employees from all levels of decision-making authority feel that they are being criticized unjustly. They are also annoyed because they have to put time for which they had not planned into handling customers' problems. Then the employees' own schedules are thrown into disarray. Members of top management find themselves more and more frequently confronted with customers who direct their complaints directly to them and who also expect a personal answer. Indeed, top management's time has already been allotted for handling strategic problems. Moreover, members of top management do not see it as part of their responsibilities to grapple with the detailed problems of unknown customers. Therefore, they tend merely to give instructions that a solution should be found. Complaints are then passed down through the hierarchy, although the primary goal of complaint processing is usually to fend off customer concerns as much as possible and/or to find someone to blame within the firm.

Many firms still make it difficult for their customers to register complaints with them. Neither product packaging nor advertisements give any indication to whom dissatisfied customers can turn. If the customers do manage to contact the firm successfully—for example, by phone—they are often unable to find anyone who will take responsibility. It is not uncommon for them to be transferred a number of times to unaccountable or incompetent employees, without getting any closer to solving their problem. Such experiences can result in negative consequences for customers. They make a decision to sever the business relationship and choose a competing product the next time they make a purchase. For the firm, then, future potential business is permanently lost. In especially serious cases, the customers turn their case over to an attorney or they turn to the media. Based on the customers' actions, firms are then forced to react. Usually, though, it does not matter how this turns out. The "opponent" customer usually is not won back, and the costs of complaint processing and problem solving for the firm are higher than they would have been had the firm reacted earlier.

The barriers erected by firms to deter dissatisfied customers from complaining frequently have an even more direct effect: Customers shy away from the exasperation and effort that accompany the search for a

I

responsible contact person and do not complain but instead switch immediately to the competition. Since firms often know nothing about this or only find out indirectly and with a significant time delay, they often come to incorrect conclusions. They refer to low rates of complaint and to the high level of satisfaction that is reflected in the corresponding results from customer surveys. They thus falsely equate low rates of complaints with customer satisfaction and overlook that in these customer satisfaction surveys, they only poll customers who have not yet switched at the time of the survey.

On the basis of this faulty assessment, firms often see no need for action. Even when they do perceive the need, goal-oriented activities remain undone because many firms have not yet recognized that dealing with complaints is a top-level management problem and that complaint management is of strategic importance for any type of customer-oriented corporate policy.

In a tightening buyer's market with an increasing level of international competition during recent years, almost all firms have increased their efforts to become more market-oriented and get greater access to their customers. Today it is difficult to find top managers who do not declare their public support for customer satisfaction as the primary corporate goal. Proclamations like these remain merely lip service, however, as long as they have no effects on the experiences of dissatisfied customers. If firms are actually striving for customer satisfaction, then the minimal requirements for management include avoiding customer dissatisfaction as much as possible and, when it is already present, to put all their efforts into eliminating it. Customers cannot make their discontent any more clear to the firm than they can in complaints, and firms cannot express that they are not interested in customer satisfaction any more clearly than by their disinterested or cool reactions to complaints. Or conversely, anyone who has recognized customer orientation as a prerequisite for the long-term survival of the firm and takes customer satisfaction seriously will regard complaints not primarily as a problem to be warded off, but rather as an opportunity, and complaint management as the core of a customer-oriented corporate strategy.

1.2 COMPLAINT MANAGEMENT AS THE CORE OF CUSTOMER RELATIONSHIP MANAGEMENT (CRM)

For years, it has been clear that in a time of intensive and global competition, a customer-oriented corporate policy is a critical success factor for firms. Nevertheless, considerable strategic-conceptual and information-technology deficits have long existed and have prevented this insight from being translated into consistent action. In the meantime, however, this situation has definitely changed. In the conceptual sense, customer relationship management that focuses on customer relationships offers fruitful insights that lead to a new way of structuring customer-related management functions. In addition, modern information technologies offer new ways of performing these functions with precision and efficiency.

1.2.1 CRM AS A CONCEPTUAL FRAMEWORK

At present, a number of different conceptual understandings are associated with the term "Customer Relationship Management (CRM)." These understandings range from IT-driven programs designed to optimize customer contact to comprehensive approaches for the establishment and design of long-term relationships. The effort to establish a meaningful relationship with the customer is characteristic of this last understanding (Barnes 2003). The aim is a relationship of trust between the seller and the customer that leads to loyal behavior and to a commitment in the sense of an inner bond. Trust and loyalty can, however, be neither forced nor bought; they must be won based on positive experiences. Only when customers actually learn through the various situations of the business relationship that the firm is behaving in a customer-oriented manner and thus has earned their trust can it be expected that the customers will hold on to the business relationship. This understanding of relationship development forms the basis for the following discussion and characterizes the future use of the term "CRM."

A conscious turning away from the traditional perspective of conventional (transaction) marketing is also associated with placing the emphasis on the customer relationship. This conventional type of marketing was primarily focused on the acquisition of new customers and the execution of isolated individual transactions. The fundamental basis for the move toward relationship orientation is the knowledge that winning new customers is associated with extraordinarily high investments in mature markets with minimal growth rates and that the loss of customers weakens the firm itself and also strengthens competitors. For this reason, what is important is not simply to win the customers over in the prepurchase phase, but rather to accompany them through all the purchase and use phases and to bind them for as long as possible by offering solutions to problems that are tuned to their various needs.

The Concept of the Customer Relationship Life Cycle

The conceptual basis for customer relationship management is the customer relationship life cycle. This life cycle is a matter of an ideal typical depiction of the progression of a business relationship from the initiation through to the termination. A business relationship, like a personal relationship, goes through different phases that are associated respectively with varied rates of growth in the intensity of the relationship and requires phase-specific customer relationship management tasks. Figure 1.1 shows a simple variant of such a progression. The intensity of the relationship is expressed through the value of the customer, for instance, through the individual customer's contribution to the profit margin.

During the customer relationship life cycle, three groups of customers can be differentiated with respect to the business relationship. Each group presents management with a completely different set of challenges. Potential ("not yet") customers are addressed by acquisition management, current customers make up the target group of retention management, and the activities of regain management are directed toward lost ("not anymore") customers.

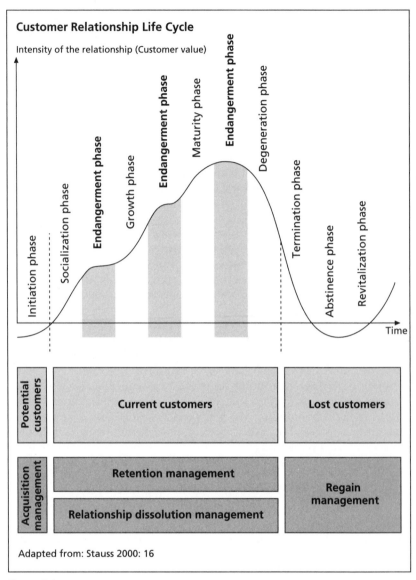

Figure 1.1

The goal of acquisition management is to arouse interest in potential customers during the initiation phase and to induce leads to make an initial purchase. With the help of retention management, firms strive to bind the "attractive" customers that they already have in an ongoing and sustainable manner and to make sure that the respective business potential continues to grow. The various phase-specific tasks of retention management will be addressed in detail in the next chapter. Regain management is aimed at winning back attractive customers who have

4

explicitly announced their intention to break off the business relationship or have actually terminated it (Stauss and Friege 1999; Griffin and Lowenstein 2001). If customers are in the phase of giving notice, the task of termination management is to make an attempt to convince the customers to continue the business relationship by using dialogue and offers designed to win them back. When customers have abandoned the business relationship some time ago, the basic goal of revitalization management is to revive a severed business relationship after a certain abstinence phase.

1.2.2 RETENTION MANAGEMENT AS A CENTRAL ELEMENT OF CRM

The importance attached to customer retention has been growing for a number of years. This is because important security, growth, and profitability goals with regard to current sales-generating customers can be reached with the help of customer retention measures.

Opportunities for growth through customer retention result primarily from a better exploitation of the customer-specific turnover potential of previous customers. This exploitation effect refers to the possibility of increasing purchase intensity and to the initiation of purchases in other business areas (cross buying). Its meaning is especially clear when one relates the penetration potential to the entire duration of the business relationship, rather than looking at a specific period. General Electric, for example, has found that customers buy fifteen major appliances in their lifetime, and therefore the company invested heavily in the GE Answer Center (Tax and Brown 1998). Figure 1.2 contains estimates of turnover potential for the entire duration of a customer-specific business relationship (lifetime turnover).

Growth can be achieved through the reference effect of customer retention, that is, regular customers serve as sources of information and purchase stimulators for customer segments that have not been previously developed. Empirical studies provide specific indications as to the

How Much Are Customers Worth?

Industry	Time Period	Customer Value
Loyal coffee shop customer	1 Year	$ 1,400
Typical supermarket shopper	10 Years	$ 50,000
Pizza restaurant patron	Lifetime	$ 8,000
Loyal credit card customer	Lifetime	$ 12,000
Typical automobile purchaser	Lifetime	$ 150,000
Loyal luxury car owner	Lifetime	$ 320,000

Adapted (with changes) from: Intelligent Intuition 2001: 1

Figure 1.2

scope of this reference potential. Figure 1.3 depicts the corresponding values in relation to customers of banks. While 58 percent of the "totally" or "very satisfied" ("convinced") customers are prepared to "definitely" recommend the provider further and another 25 percent of these customers would "probably" do so, the corresponding values for customers who are simply "satisfied" are 23 percent and 29 percent, respectively. This also makes it clear to what extent the reference potential depends on the customer's level of satisfaction and consequently can be enhanced by measures that increase that satisfaction.

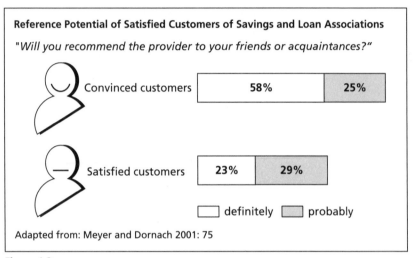

Figure 1.3

On the basis of security- and growth-enhancing effects, profitability goals are also achievable by means of customer retention. This effect leads to greater proceeds as a result of repeat and additional purchases and to cost reductions as a consequence of acquisition costs that have been saved and efficiency advantages in business development. A series of empirical studies verifies that increases in profit resulting from customer retention are quite considerable. Reichheld and Sasser (1990) report that firms can increase their profits by 100 percent when they lower the switching rate of their customers by 5 percent.

1.2.2.1 CUSTOMER RELATIONSHIP MANAGEMENT TASKS

In order to realize the greatest possible economic benefit from customer commitment, several different management tasks must be accomplished. These can be differentiated according to how long the customer relationship has been established, the level of stability or degree of danger that can be seen in the relationship, and the level of attractiveness the customer holds for the firm.

New Customer Relationships: New Customer Management

The deciding factor regarding the duration of the customer relationship is whether the customer is a first-time buyer or has already engaged in a series of purchases. First-time buyers who enter into a new relationship with the firm are often still unsure if their decision was the correct one and if they want to hold onto it in the future. In this "socialization phase," therefore, it is important for firms to consolidate the business relationship and shape it within the context of new customer management. It is imperative to new customer management to strengthen new customers in their purchase decision through offers of information and dialogue and to build up a relationship of trust with them.

Stable Customer Relationships: Retention Management Narrowly Defined

Customer relationships are stable when customers are basically satisfied or when they do not seriously engage in thoughts of reducing the level of business contact. Relationships with these stable customers should be strengthened. They should be further developed, built on, and deepened. This strengthening takes place during the growth and maturity phases through the implementation of instruments of retention management in a narrowly defined sense. With the help of these instruments, customers are bound to the firm because they experience preferential and individual treatment or because barriers to switching are erected. An extensive array of measures is available to achieve this end. These measures may emphasize either generating commitment toward the firm on the part of the customers or binding them contractually, economically, or on the basis of technical factors. Related activities include customer-contact programs, multiple-user programs, member cards, and customer clubs.

Endangered Customer Relationships as a Result of a Complaint Incident: Complaint Management

Business relationships are endangered when customers are weighing the possibility of breaking off the relationship. This is the case primarily when customers are dissatisfied with products, services, or other activities of the company. Dissatisfaction is one of the principal reasons that customers terminate their loyalty to the firm and become receptive to the competition's offers. Therefore, what matters for firms is discovering and analyzing customer dissatisfaction and transforming it back into satisfaction by means of targeted measures. Complaints constitute a pivotal starting point for this process. Customers who complain voice their complaints directly to the firm. These customers make it possible for the firm to provide a solution for problems within the framework of complaint management, to establish customer satisfaction, and to achieve customer commitment. In this way, complaint management aims for a stabilization of the customer relationships that have been endangered through dissatisfaction.

Endangered Customer Relationships for Other Reasons: Switching-Prevention Management

Customer relationships can certainly be endangered without this endangerment's being expressed in complaints. This is the case, for example, when dissatisfied customers decide to switch without articulating this decision to the firm beforehand. But even customers who have not had an especially negative experience with the provider and who have no occasion to complain may belong to the group of endangered customers. It is conceivable that the feeling of being connected to the firm is lost over time, that the desire for change increases, or that a competitor makes the customer an attractive offer. For these reasons, it is necessary to look for indications of a decrease in the intensity of the relationship, to identify the danger of switching through a proactive monitoring of terminations ("churn analysis"), and to induce affected customers to continue their business relationship by means of switching-prevention management measures (Wei and Chiu 2002).

Customer Relationships That Are Not Attractive: Relationship Dissolution Management

A fundamental reference point of retention management is the attractiveness of a customer relationship that results from the current or future contribution it is expected to make to the firm's economic goals. What is decisive for the firm's investment in customer relationships is the value of the customer, which serves as the standard for determining which customers are attractive and which are not. Customers who are not currently profitable and are not expected to make a positive contribution to the profit margin in the future are not attractive. Also included in this group are customers who require an especially high outlay in terms of support measures or a specific individualization of the firm's performance and thus generate unjustifiable costs. The loss of value that these customers cause increases with the duration of the relationship. It is the task of relationship dissolution management, therefore, to pursue a conscious strategy for the dissolution of the customer relationship. This may occur through active termination or through the sensitive carrying out of restrictions in performance and price adjustments that induce the customers either to modify their behavior or to terminate the business relationship.

Figure 1.4 shows an overview of the varied states in which customer relationships may be observed, as well as the corresponding goals and tasks of customer relationship management.

1.2.2.2 COMPLAINT MANAGEMENT AS THE MOST IMPORTANT FUNCTIONAL AREA OF RETENTION AND CUSTOMER RELATIONSHIP MANAGEMENT

Complaint management occupies a special position within the framework of retention management and customer relationship management:

- Customers who complain do not need to be identified, selected, and contacted according to certain criteria, as occurs with customer segments that are retained in the context of outbound-oriented measures; instead, they become active of their own accord.
- Customers who complain are endangered customers. Because they represent potential turnover and contributions to profit margin that are in immediate danger, they constitute the primary target group of all customer retention strategies.

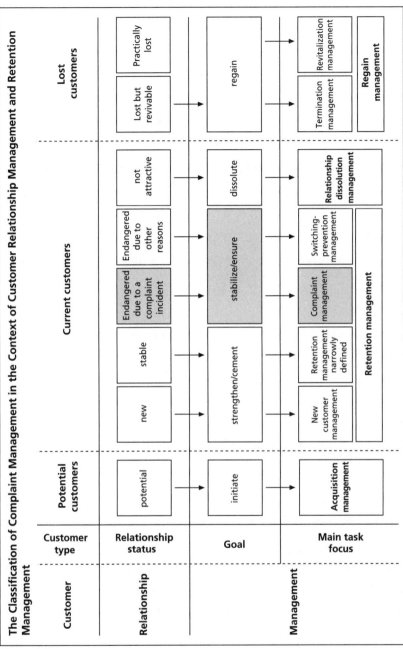

The Classification of Complaint Management in the Context of Customer Relationship Management and Retention Management

Customer	Potential customers	Current customers					Lost customers	
Customer type	potential	new	stable	Endangered due to a complaint incident	Endangered due to other reasons	not attractive	Lost but revivable	Practically lost
Relationship status	initiate	strengthen/cement		stabilize/ensure		dissolute	regain	
Goal								
Main task focus	Acquisition management	New customer management	Retention management narrowly defined	Complaint management	Switching-prevention management	Relationship dissolution management	Termination management	Revitalization management
Management			Retention management				Regain management	

Figure 1.4

- Customers who complain are in a situation in which they have a problem and urgently desire a solution. If firms offer this solution, they show that they too are entering into the relationship along with the customer and that they are taking on responsibility in the relationship. This is an excellent basis for securing trust and commitment on

9

the part of the customer and consequently is the prerequisite for creating lasting customer loyalty.

If firms then set out to introduce customer relationship management, it is essential to use complaint management as a logical starting point. In complaint management, firms must think from customer problems out, firms must secure and strengthen relationships, and firms can achieve a level of commitment that is based on positive experiences in situations where problems are encountered. Complaint management can thus be seen as the heart of customer relationship management.

1.3 COMPLAINT MANAGEMENT AND CUSTOMER CARE

In many firms, complaint management tasks are taken over by departments that are designated "Customer Care." For this reason, it is frequently unclear whether these terms have the same meaning. Similar confusion arises with respect to the relationship between customer care and customer relationship management, as these departments usually do their work using CRM software and follow its understanding of relationship management. It is essential, therefore, to start with the conceptual clarification.

Fields of Activity in CRM, Customer Care, and Complaint Management

In terms of the breadth of the field of activity, customer relationship management, customer care, and complaint management can be differentiated by the type and extent of the respective tasks that must be accomplished.

As described earlier, customer relationship management is the totality of corporate measures for the systematic initiation, development, maintenance, and safeguarding, and even the termination and reinitiation of customer relationships if necessary. Customer retention management stands at the center of the spectrum of activity.

Complaint management is a part of retention management. The target groups of its activities are those customers who have come to the firm with a complaint because they are dissatisfied.

Complaint management communicates solely with the group of customers who have a complaint. The central core is inbound communication, which is restricted to complaints. Outbound communication—the active contacting of customers by the firm—takes place only insofar as it is useful in satisfying the complainant. This applies, for example, to telephone inquiries and to intermediate and final replies, as well as to follow-up actions and contacts.

All the same, customers do not come to the firm only with complaints, but also with other articulations, including primarily orders, terminations, notices of amendment, praise, enquiries, and ideas for improvement. Orders, declarations of intentions to complete a sales contract, and terminations, declarations of intention to terminate a contractual relationship, constitute legally binding and purchase-relevant declarations on the part of the customer. In a notice of amendment, customers inform the firm of changes in their personal circumstances that are relevant to the business relationship. As far as praise is concerned, customers express their satisfaction with the firm's products, services, and course of action, all of their own accord. In addition, it regularly happens that they ask for information that is important to them when they make enquiries or approach the firm with ideas for specific possibilities for improvement.

The planned handling of all these customer concerns constitutes the functional area of customer care that includes complaint management as a central element. The inbound perspective is dominant. What customer care and complaint management have in common is a concentration on communication initiated by the customer and the condition that both seek to achieve customer commitment, not through the marketing of products and services, but through the resolution of concerns that are brought forward by customers. Customer care does, however, have a more extensive spectrum of tasks than does complaint management because of its inclusion of all forms of articulations.

In addition to the primarily inbound-oriented activities of customer care, CRM encompasses all the outbound measures initiated by the firm that are necessary for the consolidation, strengthening, stabilizing, safeguarding, or—in extreme cases—the dissolution of the business relationship. Here once again, the focus is not on sales-oriented but rather on firm-oriented actions that aid in the building and further development of individual customer relationships. Figure 1.5 summarizes these connections.

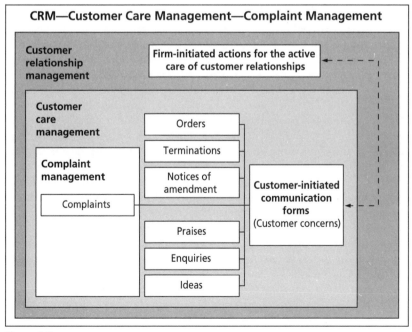

Figure 1.5

Integrative management of the customer relationship requires coordination of these relationship-relevant tasks with the transaction-oriented activities of the marketing, sales, and service functions and in this way, guarantees a consequential integration of and agreement with the sales-oriented measures that are prominent in these areas.

1.4 THE ROLE OF COMPLAINT MANAGEMENT IN QUALITY MANAGEMENT

Complaint management aids in the stabilization of endangered customer relationships and is consequently a fundamental element of the type of relationship management that is oriented toward external customers. But this in no way means that stabilization represents the only goal of complaint management. The analysis of complaints is an important basis for continual quality improvement initiatives, so complaint management is also a fundamental starting point for quality management (Brown, Cowles, and Tuten 1996; Lam and Dale 1999).

Conceptually speaking, the above discussion also makes it clear that complaint management is an integral component of all the current quality management theories.

Complaint Management within the Framework of ISO 9001

In comparison to its predecessors, the ISO 9001 norm is distinguished by a substantially greater consideration of the customer's perspective. As is stated in the norm, it aids in the "development, implementing and improving the effectiveness of a quality management system, to enhance customer satisfaction by meeting customer requirements" (ISO 9001, 0.2).

This idea is also clearly demonstrated in the fundamental illustration of the process model, which shows the customer as the point of departure and orientation for all measures (see Figure 1.6). The starting point begins with the requirements of the customers toward whose fulfillment product realization is directed. The product as output of the value-added process must be evaluated by the customer, and the data regarding the level of customer satisfaction must be ascertained, analyzed, and utilized for improvement measures. Complaint management holds a place of central importance, both in the determination of customer requirements and in the measurement of customer satisfaction. With regard to the requirements, it is necessary to identify the expectation of customers in relation to changes in products and services and their express wishes for new performance offers from complaints and to include these in the product planning process. In reference to the evaluation of products and services, complaints provide unambiguous evidence that customer expectations were not fulfilled. Since complaints also contain concrete descriptions of problems and suggestions for solutions, they often furnish much more valuable clues for the formulation of improvement possibilities than do the results of customer satisfaction surveys, which are mostly presented as relatively abstract average-scaled values.

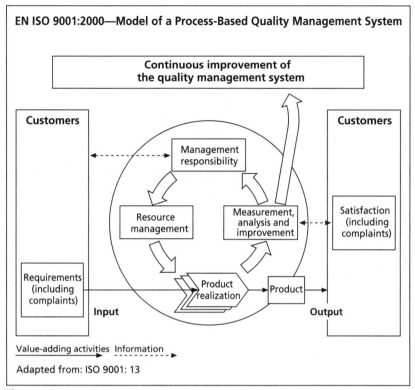

EN ISO 9001:2000—Model of a Process-Based Quality Management System

Figure 1.6

The further explanations within the norm clearly substantiate the ideas of customer orientation and underscore the importance of complaints and complaint management. This occurs when demands that would suggest a prioritized utilization of complaint information are placed on a customer-oriented quality management system. Moreover, the collection and analysis of complaints is once again explicitly required, for example, in Chapter 7.2.3 of the ISO 9001, in which effective arrangements for communicating with customers are required and "customer feedback, including complaints" is specifically listed. In an analogous fashion, Chapter 8.4.2 ("corrective action") demands documented procedures to define requirements for receiving nonconformities ("including customer complaints").

Complaint Management within the Framework of the Malcolm Baldrige National Quality Award Program

Much earlier even than the quality management system that complies with the ISO 9001 norms, the Total Quality Management concept emphasized the customer as the orientation factor of a quality-driven company. The fundamental goal of Total Quality Management (TQM) consists of bringing the firm into line with the expectations of customers and thereby increasing its competitiveness so that an especially high degree of customer satisfaction and commitment is achieved as a result of superior quality.

TQM Awards, such as the Baldrige Award or its European counterpart, the EFQM model, have for years been viewed as the most consistent conceptual realizations of the Total Quality Management approach. This view continues to be applicable, even though the notion of quality in these concepts has been widely replaced by Performance Excellence. The Malcolm Baldrige National Quality Award Program demonstrates that quality is not an isolated phenomenon, but rather can only be implemented within the framework of a corporate-wide concept that encompasses all functions and areas. The seven elements of the Baldrige Model make this clear: Leadership, Strategic Planning, and Customer and Market Focus represent the leadership triad and stress the responsibility of senior leaders for the company's direction and success. Human Resource Focus, Process Management, and Business Results represent the results triad, demonstrating that employees and key processes accomplish the work of the organization that yields the business results. Measurement, Analysis, and Knowledge Management serve as the information foundation for the performance management system (NIST 2003).

The importance of complaint management in the context of the Baldrige Model must be rated highly. Complaints are addressed in the core values. Reducing defects and errors and eliminating causes are viewed as important parts of customer-driven excellence. Added to this is the statement that an "organization's success in recovering from defects and mistakes ('making things right for your customer') is crucial in retaining customers and building customer relationships" (NIST 2003: 1).

The careful handling of customer complaints is of special importance for the criteria Strategic Planning; Measurement, Analysis, and Knowledge Management; Process Management; Business Results; and Customer and Market Focus. In the area of Strategic Planning, it is important that vital decisions be based on information about customer and market needs, thus squarely on analyses of complaints as a fundamental form of customer feedback. Under the criterion Measurement, Analysis, and Knowledge Management is required, among other things, that proof be provided of how relevant knowledge from customers is transferred into organizational knowledge. This includes the recognition of complaint information as a basic element of customer-oriented knowledge management. In the area of Process Management, it is also required that the key value creation processes and support processes are based on the requirements of the customers. Under the Customer-Focused Results as a subgroup of the Business Result category, the organization has to provide information of the current level of customer satisfaction and dissatisfaction, and customer complaints are explicitly mentioned as relevant data. Complaints are most frequently and directly mentioned in the detailed explanations of the criteria "Customer and Market Focus." Here companies have to describe how they use relevant information from current and former customers, including complaints, and they are asked to answer the following questions: "What is your complaint management process? How do you ensure that complaints are resolved effectively and promptly? How are complaints aggregated and analyzed for use in improvement throughout your organization and by your partners?" (NIST 2003: 18). Professional complaint management also touches on other elements of the Baldrige Model. It can be expected that the "Financial and Market Results" are positively influenced through the stabilization of customer relationships. Additionally, an acknowledgment of the problems perceived by customers and the systematic elimination of these problems can have a motivating effect on employees and lead to an improvement in the "Human Resources Results."

Figure 1.7 depicts the Baldrige Model and makes it clear which elements will primarily benefit from active complaint management.

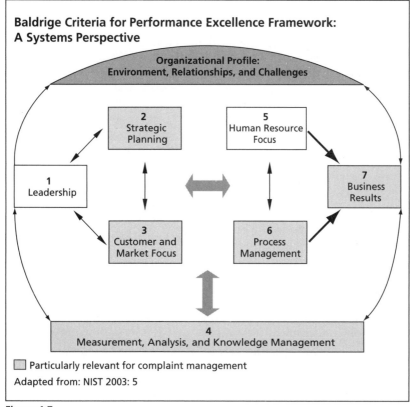

Figure 1.7

2

Complaints

2.1 DEFINITION AND TYPES OF COMPLAINTS

What are complaints? At first glance, this question seems strange, since customers often use the term "complaint" in their letters or begin a conversation with the sentence, "I want to make a complaint." However, customers often avoid this expression, cloak their criticism in a polite request, or even emphasize that they don't actually want to complain, but do expect that a repetition of the incident in question will be avoided in the future. Thus, it is clearly necessary to clarify the concept of complaints.

Broadly defined, complaints are articulations of dissatisfaction that are expressed toward firms and/or third-party institutions with the aim of making a provider aware of a behavior that is subjectively experienced as harmful, receiving compensation for adverse effects suffered, and making a change in the criticized behavior. A relatively broad conceptual understanding, which includes a differentiation of various types of complaints, is expressed in this definition:

- Complaints are a matter of articulations, that is, verbal or written statements.
- From these statements emerges the understanding that the complainant is dissatisfied. This is not, however, dependent on whether the customer uses the term "complaint." The extent of dissatisfaction is also unimportant. All statements that show that the performance or the behavior of the firm does not fully comply with the customer's expectations are complaints as defined here.
- Complaints may be brought not only by customers, but also by members of other interest groups, who, for example, lament damage to the environment from ecologically harmful production processes. Moreover, criticism is not expressed only by individuals but also by institutions, such as associations or the media, who demand a general solution for problems, independent of a specific individual case.
- Complaints place the affected party in direct opposition to the firm itself. Dissatisfied customers can, however, choose an indirect path by turning to a third-party institution (for instance, arbitrators, administrative bodies, or the media) as an "advocate" of their interests. In such cases, the third-party institution approaches the firm in the customers' name or informs the public.
- The dissatisfaction of the affected person does not necessarily have to be related to product deficiencies or other aspects of the market offering (such as price). The sociopolitical behavior of the firm can be a further object of complaints.

A complaint is brought forth intentionally. The customers demonstrate a particular intent in their articulation. In many cases, they turn to the firm in the post-purchase phase because they believe that they have not received the expected level of performance from them such as an auto repair that did not yield the desired result or furniture that was delivered shows signs of being damaged. The customers want either an improved or a completely new performance, the partial or complete restitution of the purchase price, or compensation for consequential damages. If the customers understand this demand as a claim against the firm that they can establish through the legal process, then we can speak of claims. In practice, "complaints" and "claims" are often not differentiated. It is useful, however, to make this distinction in order to point out the special case of legally relevant complaints. In this sense, the concept of "claims" characterizes a subset of complaints in which customers in the post-purchase phase explicitly or implicitly connect complaints about the product or service with a lawful demand that can be established legally if necessary.

In this general sense, complaints are intentional expressions of dissatisfaction by interested parties or institutions with respect to some aspect of corporate behavior. The following considerations will be based on this broad understanding, even if product-related expressions of dissatisfaction that customers articulate directly to the firm take center stage. Figure 2.1 shows an overview of the conceptual determination and the delimitation based on points of emphasis.

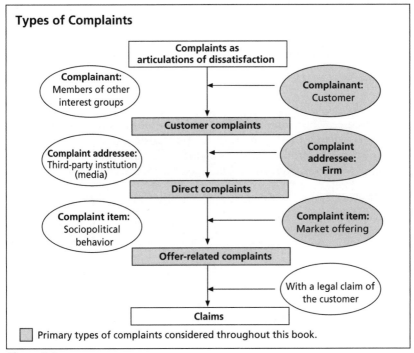

Figure 2.1

2.2 TRUE AND FALSE REGARDING COMPLAINTS

In corporate practice, there are very definite judgments about complaints that are by no means firmly based on information. It is often a question of prejudices that seem to be plausible at first glance. If someone is serious about active complaint management, however, what is true and what is false regarding complaints has to be differentiated, and prejudices in the firm must be dismantled.

In the following discussion, several of the especially long-lived and stubborn prejudices will be listed, and commentary that contradicts them will be introduced.

PREJUDICE 1: "Our customers are satisfied. The low number of incoming complaints proves it!"

COMMENT 1: "Wrong! Low complaint numbers are not a meaningful indicator of customer satisfaction!"

Many firms are convinced that complaint management is not a matter of urgent concern for them, since they receive comparatively few complaints. They infer from the low number of complaints that customers are satisfied. This conclusion is false. Most dissatisfied customers do not complain. Whether a customer complains or not depends on a multitude of factors that are, in part, substantially influenced by the firm. Low numbers of complaints can be the result of higher barriers to complaints or resigned customer behavior. In many firms, very critical expressions by customers are not viewed or documented as complaints at all, for example, because they are given orally. Typical examples of this include auto-repair shops and grocery stores. Complaints are integrated in the context of the normal course of business processes, and customer conversations are overwhelmingly taken care of in conversations with customer contact personnel. Only a fraction of the customers who remain dissatisfied after such contacts complain in writing to management. Concluding that customers are satisfied cannot be justified based on this small number of complaints.

PREJUDICE 2: "The number of complaints should be minimized!"

COMMENT 2: "Wrong! The number of dissatisfied customers should be minimized. The percentage of dissatisfied customers who complain should be maximized!"

In many firms, the goal of minimizing the number of complaints is used as a pretext. Because the number of complaints can be reduced without changing the level of customer dissatisfaction, this goal is pointless. The first priority must be to minimize customer dissatisfaction. The prerequisite for this is, however, that the firm be informed as explicitly as possible about the type and extent of customer dissatisfaction. The firm must therefore pursue an active policy that leads customers to turn to the firm with complaints, rather than saying nothing or going over to the competition. Plymire (1991) stated that the best way to a customer-oriented corporate culture is via an increased number of complaints. A long-term reduction in the number of complaints can only be achieved when the proportion of customers who complain is maximized.

PREJUDICE 3: "Customers who complain are adversaries!"
COMMENT 3: "Wrong! Customers who complain are partners!"

Customers who complain are often immediately categorized negatively. They are considered to be malicious, to be opponents. The firm immediately assumes a self-defensive position, and the basic corporate attitude is oriented toward defense if not toward counterattack. This attitude is wrong. It does not take into account that the complainants are current (and possibly future) customers who have a right to bring forth their views, wishes, and demands. Customers who express their opinion toward the firm show their interest in the firm because they allow a possibility of later improvement. Customers who complain are not opponents, but rather partners in the effort toward continuous improvements in processes and products.

PREJUDICE 4: "The majority of customers who complain are either grumblers or grousers!"
COMMENT 4: "Wrong! The vast majority of customers are not grumblers or grousers!"

Even among firms that accept the value of customer complaints, there is a widespread view that a large percentage of complaints are made by grumblers and grousers. The demand for complaint stimulation encounters a great deal of skepticism because it is feared that the share of those who would inundate the firm with unwarranted complaints, behave in an impudent manner, and make unfounded demands would thereby increase. However, the vast majority of customers are not grousers. Indeed, it is difficult to come by reliable numbers because no generally accepted definition of a "grouser" exists and because it is the firm itself that makes the corresponding categorization in each specific case. But experts warn about overemphasizing the problem of grousers. Blanding (1991) reports a study in which calls to a typical customer service department were analyzed. In this study, fewer than 5 percent of the customer calls were classified as "irate," less than 0.1 percent as "insolent," and none as "unfounded." Therefore, what matters most is seeing a complaint as an expression of a legitimate customer concern, not as objectionable grousing.

PREJUDICE 5: "Complaints only lead to greater costs!"
COMMENT 5: "Wrong! Complaints are not associated solely with costs, but instead provide opportunities for higher revenue and profits. Ignoring complaints, on the other hand, only leads to greater costs, never to higher revenue!"

Complaints are perceived by firms as threats because they are exclusively regarded as a cost factor. Costs are generated during the processing of complaints just as they are when customer demands (such as product returns or reimbursements) are fulfilled. Indeed, these costs must be examined in relation to the benefits that can be achieved. The critical information that is contained in complaints gives firms the chance to identify and remove errors, thereby constantly improving themselves and reducing costs. Since customers express their criticism about the firm and do not immediately migrate to the competition, the firm still has the chance to keep the dissatisfied customer. "Any problem that employees who are close to the customer can discover and resolve is a chance to go beyond duty and win a customer for life." (Hart, Heskett, and Sasser 1990: 149). The costs of processing complaints, then, are investments in future business.

Whoever wants to implement complaint management will be confronted with prejudices such as these. In order to be able to cope with this situation managers need a sound basis of information. For this they can fall back on results of satisfaction research and customer complaining research.

3

The Behavior of
Dissatisfied Customers

If firms want to avoid dissatisfaction or placate dissatisfied customers, they must know how satisfaction/dissatisfaction arises, what keeps customers from complaining, and which aspects of the firm's reaction to a complaint delight and bind customers.

3.1 THE ORIGIN OF CUSTOMER DISSATISFACTION

How the customers judge products or services with which they have had prior experiences is reflected in their satisfaction or dissatisfaction. Satisfaction/dissatisfaction is, therefore, the result of an ex-post-assessment and implies a concrete, self-aware consumption experience.

The process of assessment is usually described in reference to the "disconfirmation paradigm" (Oliver 1980; Parasuraman, Zeithaml, and Berry 1985, 1988; Oliver 1997), according to which satisfaction or dissatisfaction arises as a consequence of a perceived discrepancy between expected and experienced performance. Customers develop more or less concrete expectations regarding offerings available in the market. These expectations are formed depending on respective needs and are greatly influenced by the experiences the customers have had in the past with the same or similar products. Furthermore, information is a factor that fundamentally influences expectations, both information that customers receive by word-of-mouth in their social sphere and information that the firm itself disseminates through the media in the context of provider communication, for example, direct advertising (Berry and Parasuraman 1991).

During the process of consuming or using consumer goods or of utilizing services, the customers experience the actual performance level of the goods and compare the perceived performance with their expectations in a complex weighing process. Satisfaction occurs when the performance substantially exceeds the customers' expectations, while dissatisfaction arises when the performance falls decisively short of their expectations. The fulfillment of their expectations merely leads to a feeling of indifference.

This understanding of the satisfaction construct provides an important indication for an explanation of complaint behavior. Customers complain because their expectations were violated to a great extent. It is this violation of minimum expectations that triggers such great irritation and leads to considerable endangerment of the business relationship.

3.2 CUSTOMER SATISFACTION AND COMPLAINT BEHAVIOR

In many cases that are not especially aggravating, customers will tend to try to rid themselves quickly of the uncomfortable feeling they have when they are disappointed in their expectations and experience dissatisfaction. They are then engaging in a process of dismantling their psychological dissonance by belatedly reducing the expectations they originally had or correcting their original negative impression in a more positive direction. If this kind of belated harmonization of expectation and perception is unsuccessful, the customers face the question of how they should then behave.

Behavioral Alternatives of Dissatisfied Customers

In principle, various ways of behaving are available to the customer, although it is certainly also possible that the customer may resort to several activities at the same time. The customer may:
- switch by changing brands or exiting the market
- engage in negative word-of-mouth communication
- remain inactive despite dissatisfaction, or
- complain to the firm or to a third-party institution

In many cases, customers switch immediately because they view an argument with the firm as time-consuming, irksome, and/or futile. This switch is commonly accompanied by negative word-of-mouth communication, in which the customers recount their negative experiences within their social spheres such as to family members or among friends or acquaintances (Richins 1983). This kind of word-of-mouth communication is particularly effective. Since the people telling the story experienced the event themselves and are not pursuing selfish goals in their depiction of that event, the content of the word-of-mouth communication seems more believable and convincing by far than any type of paid communication methods the provider might employ.

Some customers do not change their behavior despite being dissatisfied, thus making them appear to be inactive. They do not switch because, for example, to them the inconveniences associated with the change (such as closing one bank account and opening a new one) seem at first to be too great. They also do not engage in negative word-of-mouth communication to any appreciable degree. These customers should, however, in no way continue to be regarded as loyal customers. When other negative incidents arise or when a competitor makes an appeal to these customers, they will quickly decide to make a change.

A Majority of Dissatisfied Customers Do Not Complain

Some of the dissatisfied customers will certainly complain. The question then becomes, under what conditions do customers choose this alternative? Complaint research has been occupied with this question for years and can provide some important answers (among others, Singh 1988; Halstead and Droege 1991; Singh and Pandya 1991; Singh and Widing 1991).

A fundamental result of this research is the insight that most of the dissatisfied customers do not approach the firm with complaints. For every articulated complaint, there is a far greater number of "unvoiced complaints." Research by the consulting firm TARP (1997) found that for major problems, about 31 percent of individuals who encountered the problem did not complain, and Nielson found that for small problems, 70 percent of dissatisfied consumers don't articulate their problem. This is of particular relevance because studies indicate that the noncomplainants are by far the least brand loyal (Goodman 1989).

According to the findings of Goodman, O'Brien, and Segal (2000), one can proceed under the assumption that regardless of industry, approximately 50 to 80 percent of dissatisfied customers forego the chance to bring their irritation to the attention of a customer-contact employee or to a decentralized or centralized location of the firm. The number of complaints registered in the firm represents merely the tip of a dissatisfaction iceberg (Goodman 1989).

Determinants of Complaint Behavior

When dissatisfied customers are queried about the reasons for their complaint passivity, they often give answers that provide information about the fundamental dimensions of influence of their behavior. Figure 3.1 shows a compilation of these answers.

Customers' Reasons for Not Complaining in Spite of Dissatisfaction

"No one would listen to me anyway."
"I didn't know to whom I could complain."
"I was partially responsible."
"I wasn't sure how to talk about this situation. It was too personal."
"The last time I complained, nothing happened."
"It wasn't worthwhile."
"The person I wanted to complain about might have lost her job."
"I had a problem last week; they would think I am picky or a whiner."

Adapted (with changes) from: Barlow and Moller 1996: 58

Figure 3.1

As the result of systematic analyses of answers such as these, empirical complaint research shows that it is primarily the following aspects that influence the decision to complain, and should be regarded as determinants of complaint behavior: complaint costs, complaint benefits, product attributes, problem attributes, and attributes specific to the person and to the situation.

COMPLAINT COSTS. Obviously, customers carry out an internal cost-benefit analysis, based on which they make the decision to complain or not. In the context of this calculation, the costs of the complaint itself play an important role (Bearden and Mason 1984; Ross and Oliver 1984). Customers associate complaints with time and costs, and frequently with exasperating arguments, frustration, anxiety, or stress as well (Oliver 1997). These material and immaterial costs to the customer are determined by the firm. If they refuse their customers information about where and how they can complain, firms increase customers' complaint costs. In addition, if they put up barriers to customers' obtaining restitution by demanding that they return an opened package, for example, the costs are increased yet again (Kendall and Russ 1975). If they make it uncomfortable or embarrassing for the customers to make their complaint, their immaterial costs increase. Firms can consequently influence the probability of a customer complaint in the case of dissatisfaction by varying the complaint costs.

COMPLAINT BENEFITS. The costs must be compared to the benefits of the complaint. This comparison is primarily dependent upon the subjective value of the solution to the problem that the customer expects from the provider. The value is, however, weighed against the probability that the complaint will be successful (Jacoby and Jaccard 1981; Richins 1983). Most customers complain only if they believe there is a realistic chance that the firm is prepared to make restitution. Someone who has no hope of a positive reaction will refrain from making a complaint. Firms can influence the perception customers have that a complaint will be successful, specifically by the extent to which customer orientation is practiced and communicated. Paradoxically, the more coldly and inflexibly they conduct themselves with regard to customers, the fewer firms will have to reckon with complaints.

PRODUCT ATTRIBUTES. The relevance of the consumer experience is the foremost product attribute that influences the probability of complaints (Bearden and Oliver 1985; Richins and Verhage 1985). Making complaints is complicated and burdensome. The customers will put up with the process only when they view the damages suffered as being substantial, which is always the case with goods that they deem to be especially important because of their high purchase price or their prestige value.

PROBLEM ATTRIBUTES. Not all the problems perceived by customers are equally likely to become the subject of their complaints. Customers are most apt to choose this approach when the problem at hand can be manifestly proven, when it is a clear-cut problem that can be somewhat objectively described and leaves little room for subjective evaluation. If the circumstances cannot be proven or if the incident could be interpreted differently by different people, customers are less likely to take the risk of complaining, especially in writing (Best 1981). Quality attributes which, like lack of friendliness, for instance, are evaluated subjectively are considerably less often the object of complaints than verifiable circumstances (such as a malfunctioning product), even if the degree of dissatisfaction experienced is the same.

The unambiguousness of causal attribution figures prominently as a problem attribute. Complaints are more likely to be considered as a reaction by dissatisfied customers the more unambiguously the cause of their dissatisfaction can be attributed to the provider. If the customers are firmly convinced that the provider carries sole responsibility for the problem that has occurred, they are more likely to complain than they would be in cases in which they consider themselves to be partly responsible for the problem (Richins 1983; Folkes 1984).

Person-Specific Attributes. Person-specific attributes are also clearly jointly responsible for whether a dissatisfied customer complains or not. The influence of socio-demographic attributes (age, gender, education), psychographic attributes (product knowledge, self-confidence, complaint experience), and behavioral attributes (communicative and interactional behavior) were investigated in various empirical studies. The results are not consistent; however, one can make the general statement that the typical complainant tends to be a young, highly educated male with an average to high income level (Warland, Hermann, and Willits 1975; Morganosky and Buckley 1987; for contrasting results, see Singh 1990). Complainants appear to be distinguishable from noncomplainants in that they have a higher level of self-confidence (Bolfing 1989), in particular, they believe that they are able to manage the complaining situation effectively (East 2000; Susskind 2000).

Situation-Specific Attributes. Last, the conditions of the situation are another factor that has an influence on whether a customer complains. Perceived time pressure can induce customers to refrain from making a complaint, or customers may regard themselves as compelled to express their complaints in an especially dramatic manner due to comments from peers or the observation of the incident by a third party.

These research findings are of extreme practical importance for complaint management. They demonstrate that complaint information cannot provide a complete overview of problems as they are perceived by customers. The analyses of the determinants of complaint behavior show that complaint information should not be seen as being representative because it is highly probable that specific problems of certain customer groups are underrepresented or overrepresented. For this reason, the analysis of complaint information must always be complemented by ongoing customer satisfaction surveys. The results described point out possible actions that can be considered as part of a firm's complaint policy, since some determinants can be influenced through corporate measures. It is possible, for example, to erect or dismantle barriers to complaints and to have an influence on the costs to the customers and on their assessment of whether the complaint will be successful.

3.3 COMPLAINT SATISFACTION AND ITS INFLUENCE ON CUSTOMER BEHAVIOR

The Origin of Complaint Satisfaction

If dissatisfied customers choose the alternative of complaining, they again have certain expectations about the firm's answer and the targeted solution (Oliver 1997). This complaint expectation then becomes the standard on the basis of which the customers assess their actual experience with the firm's reaction (perceived answer to the complaint). If their expectations are exceeded, complaint satisfaction is the result. If they are fulfilled, indifference is the result. Otherwise, complaint dissatisfaction occurs (see Figure 3.2).

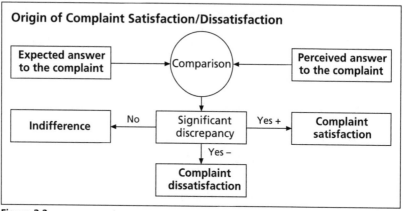

Origin of Complaint Satisfaction/Dissatisfaction

Figure 3.2

Dimensions of Complaint Satisfaction

Knowing which aspects of the firm's reaction the complainants are rating and how important these aspects are in forming complaint satisfaction or dissatisfaction is of great importance in the specific development of complaint management.

Complaint satisfaction research has increasingly taken up this question in recent years (Tax, Brown, and Chandrashekaran 1998; Boshoff 1999; Smith, Bolton, and Wagner 1999; Buttle and Burton 2002; Davidow 2003). Most authors refer to a "justice framework" including "distributive justice" (fairness of the outcome), "procedural justice" (fairness of processes and procedures) and "interactional justice" (fairness of the interpersonal treatment). The attributes of complaint satisfaction named in the various studies vary in the details but are generally consistent. They can be conceptually organized into four dimensions, which customers make the subject of their evaluation of the firm's complaint management.

1) Accessibility: Ease with which a corporate contact person can be found for a customer's problem; knowledge of where complaints should be addressed;

2) Quality of the Interaction: Customer-oriented design of the interaction that takes place during the acceptance and processing of the complaint. This dimension can be further differentiated into individual subdimensions:

   a) Friendliness/Politeness: Courteousness with which the complainant is treated; polite conversational tone/style of language;

   b) Empathy/Understanding: Readiness to see things from the customer's perspective; understanding of the customer's irritation; individualized handling of the case;

   c) Effort/Helpfulness: Recognizable effort to solve the problem in accordance with the wishes of the customer;

   d) Activity/Initiative: Actively seeking contact with the customer; inquiring about the desired solution; notification of delays;

   e) Reliability: Adherence to promises with respect to content and time;

3) Reaction Speed: Promptness with which a confirmation of receipt arrives; promptness of reaction to further inquiries from customers; promptness with which the case is solved;

4) Appropriateness/Fairness of Results: Appropriateness of the solution to the problem; fairness of the restitution offered.

This catalog of dimensions underscores that complaint satisfaction is not solely influenced by the solution the firm offers, but rather by the total experience of the complaint situation.

A study by Stauss (2002) further demonstrates the importance of the total complaint experience for complaint satisfaction. A factor-analytical evaluation of a customer satisfaction survey on complaint satisfaction showed that two factors can be differentiated. The first factor incorporates the attributes "Appropriateness/Fairness," "Reaction Speed" and "Reliability"; the second factor, "Friendliness/Politeness" and "Empathy/Understanding." According to this theory, complainants make a distinction according to factors that can be designated as "cold facts" and "warm acts" when evaluating the firm's answer. The cold facts of the first factor include attributes that the complainant judges on the basis of objective facts (amount of the refund, length of the processing time, keeping of promises) and that therefore are subject to a more factually oriented and rational assessment. The attributes of the second factor—warm acts—are related to the personal treatment of the complainant. Friendliness and empathy determine whether the complainants come away with the impression that their problem was taken seriously and that they were treated with respect. Indeed, the empirical study shows that cold facts complaint satisfaction has a somewhat greater effect on global satisfaction than does warm acts complaint satisfaction. The extent of this effect, however, turns out to be slight. The size of this underscores that the way the customer is treated is just as important as having control over the processes when it comes to the retention effect of complaint management.

Retention Effect of Complaint Satisfaction

Results of studies in complaint behavior research consistently demonstrate that complaint satisfaction or dissatisfaction has an extraordinary degree of influence on the attitude toward or the satisfaction with the business relationship, as well as on the purchase and communication behavior of the complainant (Andreasen and Best 1977; Gilly and Gelb 1982; Smith and Bolton 1998; Durvasula, Lysonski, and Mehta 2000).

Complaint dissatisfaction intensifies the customer's dissatisfaction with the firm and leads to negative word-of-mouth communication and switching. Studies show that the most negative actions were taken by customers previously loyal to the company, who are particularly disappointed (Tax and Brown 1998). In comparison, the sequence of effects for complaint satisfaction targeted by complaint management is that customers who are satisfied with the answer to their complaint regain their satisfaction with the product and the firm. This leads to an increased readiness on the customers' part to express themselves positively within their social spheres with respect to the product and the firm (positive word-of-mouth communication) and to hold on to the business relationship (repeat purchase).

The effect of complaint satisfaction/dissatisfaction on the customer's global satisfaction provides impressive confirmation of the results of the German "Customer Monitor" (Servicebarometer 2003), which records both the satisfaction of German customers with products and services (customer satisfaction) and the satisfaction of complainants with the handling of their complaints (complaint satisfaction) in a variety of industries on a yearly basis. As Figure 3.3 from the home improvement store industry shows, the average value of customer satisfaction in this industry is 2.52 on a 5-point scale (1 = completely satisfied). For those customers who didn't have a complaint (91 percent), the satisfaction value is slightly better (2.50), whereas customers who complained and weren't satisfied with the company's reaction show a satisfaction value way below average (3.23). The satisfaction value of complainants who were just satisfied is also below average (2.98). In contrast, the satisfaction of those complainants who were convinced by the company's reaction is especially positive. The corresponding satisfaction value (2.40) is even better than that of those customers who didn't have a complaint. This so-called recovery paradox is also confirmed in other empirical studies (Michel 2001).

With regard to the communication behavior of the complainant, many studies confirm that complaint experiences are made the subject of word-of-mouth communication (Maxham 2001; Maxham and Netemeyer 2002). Positive as well as negative experiences are repeated on a

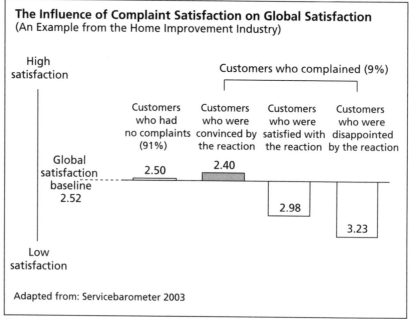

Figure 3.3

large scale and thus have an effect far above and beyond the case itself. It has been proven again and again that the incidents that lead to complaint dissatisfaction are communicated considerably more often than are positive experiences (TARP 1997, Goodman 1999). A study conducted by TARP for Coca-Cola showed that satisfied complainants told an average of 4–5 people about their positive experience, while dissatisfied customers told an average of 9–10 people about their negative experience (TARP 1997: 11).

Not only does complaint satisfaction or dissatisfaction influence communication behavior, but also the intention to make a repeat purchase and the actual repeat purchase behavior (Gilly and Gelb 1982; Andreassen 1999; Liu, Sudharshan, and Hamer 2000; Miller, Craighead, and Karwan 2000). Research by TARP (1997) showed that 70 percent of those customers who articulated a problem and were satisfied remained brand loyal, and more than 95 percent in the case of a satisfactory and quick reaction by the company. Whiteley (1993) reports survey results suggesting that 82 percent of complainants whose problems were quickly resolved would buy again. Studies also confirm that the loyalty of satisfied customers can be even greater than the loyalty of customers who have experienced no problem with the product or the firm (Adamson 1993; TARP 1997). Goodwin and Ross (1990), for example, point out that catalog customers whose complaints were solved in a timely manner were more profitable than customers who had no complaint.

In view of these consistent findings concerning the contribution that complaint management makes to customer retention and thus to the achievement of fiscal goals, it is astonishing that not all firms draw the appropriate conclusions, thereby leaving substantial possibilities for customer retention unexploited. Empirical studies reveal that many complaining customers do not even get an answer to their complaints. A survey among consumers who complained to the Better Business Bureau (BBB) reveals a large proportion of cases in which consumers reported that companies did not offer any type of option to potentially resolve their complaints. In the home-construction industry, for example, two thirds of the consumers reported that the companies offered nothing to resolve their complaints (Fisher, Arnold, and Ferris 1999). But anyone who fails to stabilize otherwise endangered business relationships through the use of professional complaint management is foregoing potentially significant economic success. Specific possibilities for how firms can estimate the extent of this economic potential will be pointed out later. First, however, the conceptual foundations of professional complaint management will be described.

4

Principles of Complaint Management

4.1 GOALS OF COMPLAINT MANAGEMENT

Complaint management encompasses the planning, execution, and controlling of all the measures taken by a firm in connection with the complaints it receives.

The global aim of complaint management lies in increasing the profitability and competitiveness of the firm by restoring customer satisfaction, minimizing the negative effects of customer dissatisfaction on the firm, and using the indications of operational weaknesses and of market opportunities that are contained in complaints. From this global aim the following subgoals relating to turnover and costs can be derived.

Subgoals Relating to Turnover

STABILIZATION OF JEOPARDIZED CUSTOMER RELATIONSHIPS THROUGH THE ESTABLISHMENT OF COMPLAINT SATISFACTION. As the central element of retention management, complaint management targets the restabilization of customer relationships that have been jeopardized as a result of dissatisfaction. This stabilization takes place on the basis of the empirically confirmed finding that complaint satisfaction can be achieved through the rapid and generous settlement of complaints. This complaint satisfaction then leads to a vast improvement in the customer's global satisfaction with the business relationship, to product and firm loyalty, and thus to steady sales and profit-margin contributions.

INCREASE IN PURCHASE INTENSITY AND PURCHASE FREQUENCY, AS WELL AS PROMOTION OF CROSS-BUYING BEHAVIOR. Handling a complaint satisfactorily should increase the commitment of the customers and their willingness to engage in intensified purchases from the firm. This phenomenon may occur by the customers engaging in multiple purchases, increasing their purchase frequency, or expanding their purchasing of other products and services.

IMPLEMENTATION AND CLARIFICATION OF A CUSTOMER-ORIENTED CORPORATE STRATEGY. Customer-oriented complaint management conveys security to the customer and helps to prevent dissatisfaction or to intensify satisfaction. In this way, complaint management provides a fundamental contribution to the development or maintenance of a customer-friendly corporate image. It also gives a clear signal to employees of the seriousness of customer-oriented corporate strategy, since the internal pressure to deal with customers in a customer-oriented manner intensifies as critical customer feedback increases.

CREATION OF ADDITIONAL PROMOTIONAL EFFECTS THROUGH WORD-OF-MOUTH COMMUNICATION. Negative word-of-mouth communication should be prevented and positive word-of-mouth communication should be stimulated by means of complaint management. Since both consumer problems that lead to complaints and the complaint experiences that follow are discussed within the customer's social sphere, this personal communication is an important variable that influences the attitudes of other consumers toward the firm or the product (multiplication effect) and thus on the exploitation of the sales volume of potential customers.

IMPROVEMENT IN THE QUALITY OF PRODUCTS AND SERVICES THROUGH THE USE OF INFORMATION THAT IS CONTAINED IN COMPLAINTS. Complaints contain valuable information about relevant user problems pertaining to products, services, or corporate conduct. This information is important for a system of quality management, as it provides an indication of the adequacy of fixed quality levels and adherence to quality standards. Furthermore, the information offers an abundance of insights into user expectations that, when used in the development of product modifications and innovations, can ensure future sales potential.

Subgoals Relating to Costs

AVOIDANCE OF SWITCHING COSTS. The goal of the stabilization of customer relationships may be formulated as a cost goal in the sense that switching costs can be avoided. If dissatisfied customers choose to switch immediately to a competing product rather than lodge a complaint, the resulting loss of turnover may be regarded as a switching cost.

AVOIDANCE OF THE COSTS OF DISAGREEMENTS. When customers express their dissatisfaction by a complaint directly to the firm, they provide the firm with the opportunity to have an influence and to take corrective action. If they instead choose to complain via a third-party institution (e.g., media, arbitrators, attorneys), the disagreements usually become more time- and cost-intensive for the firm. A system of complaint management that prompts the customer to choose the direct method of complaining to the firm consequently reduces these costs of disagreements.

AVOIDANCE OF OTHER EXTERNAL FAILURE COSTS. Problems that become the subject of complaints commonly lead to instances in which warranties and guarantees are invoked. Warranty costs can be lowered and guarantee claims reduced through a systematic analysis of complaint information with reference to product deficiencies.

AVOIDANCE OF INTERNAL FAILURE COSTS. Complaints not only contain indications of product deficiencies, but also point to process flaws. An appropriate use of this information can lead to a more productive designing of internal processes and an avoidance of mistakes and redundancies.

4.2 FUNDAMENTAL TASKS OF COMPLAINT MANAGEMENT

The goals of complaint management can be achieved only if a series of fundamental tasks that can either be assigned to a direct or to an indirect complaint management process are accomplished.

In "direct complaint" management, the tasks are directly related to the individual case and target the elimination of individual customer dissatisfaction and the establishment of complaint satisfaction. In accordance with the "Moment of Truth" characterization coined by Carlzon (1987) to describe the contact situation between the individual customer and the employees of a firm in the service-building process, the contact situations reflect the "moment of truth in the complaint management process" within the context of these direct tasks. The tasks of complaint management in which the customer is not directly involved are designated as "indirect" complaint management.

Tasks of the Direct Complaint Management Process

Relevant to the direct complaint management process are complaint stimulation, complaint acceptance, complaint processing, and complaint reaction.

In the context of complaint stimulation, dissatisfied customers should be encouraged to bring their perceived problems to the attention of the firm. There are three main subtasks that must be tackled. First, a decision about the complaint channel must be made, that is, the questions must be answered concerning which method (verbal, telephone, written, or electronic) customers should use in making their complaints and to which organizational unit they should bring those complaints. Second, active communication of the complaint channels must take place so that the highest possible percentage of dissatisfied customers chooses to react with a complaint and select the proper complaint channel. Third, accessibility of the organizational units accepting complaints must be assured so that the capacity required within the context of gradual complaint stimulation is provided.

The complaint acceptance phase primarily affects the organization of the complaint input and the documentation of the complaint information. When complaints are made in person or by telephone, the customers experience important aspects of the corporate reaction to their concerns during the initial contact with the firm. In the case of written complaints, by contrast, the initial contact with the complainants takes place in the form of intermediate replies or final answers. How the customers perceive the firm's reaction plays a decisive role in whether their dissatisfaction is reduced or increased even further. For this reason, it is important to organize the receipt of complaints so that clear lines of responsibility are drawn and the employees who will receive the complaints are prepared for what they will encounter.

What is important in the documentation of the complaint is to record the problem brought forward by the customer in a thorough, rapid, and structured manner. Here decisions must be made about the contents of the documentation, the categorization of those contents, and the form that the documentation will take. Basic contents of the documentation include the informational content of the complaint (information on the complainant, the problem itself, and the object of the complaint), as well as the complaint handling information (information on the complaint acceptance, complaint processing, and complaint reaction). A useful scheme of categorization is required for the systematic documentation of complaint information. With respect to the form of documentation, firms may use standardized forms and/or fill-in-the-blanks forms in complaint management software programs. The process of documentation may also be at least partially transferred to customers, such as if they are requested to describe their complaints on a structured opinion card or to enter them on a specific complaint page on the Internet.

What is most important within the scope of duties in complaint processing is the systematic design of complaint settlement. The first step is to identify and model the different types of complaint processing procedures. Next, it must be determined who is responsible at each level: for the entire complaint management process, this is the "Process Owner"; for the processing of an individual case, the "Complaint Owner"; and for the individual steps of the processing procedure, the "Task Owner." Processing deadlines for the various processes and substeps must also be established. A system of reminders and escalations that is developed according to these deadlines aids in monitoring adherence to them. Rules and forms for internal communication of the locations that participate in the processing of a complaint must be stipulated. Finally, all the processing steps with their contents, the locations that carried them out, and the deadlines must be chronologically documented for each individual complaint case in a complaint history.

In the area of complaint reaction, it is worthwhile to define fundamental guidelines and rules of behavior so that the target goals of achieving a calming of the situation and of finding a satisfying solution are not threatened. In defining these rules and guidelines, it is necessary to make a distinction depending on the way in which customer criticism is articulated. Another key subtask in the context of complaint reaction is the decision about which solution should be offered to the customers in view of their complaint. Financial (discounts, money back, compensation for damages), tangible (exchange, repair, another product, gift), or intangible offers of compensation (apology, information) are the principal types considered. In order to make a decision that is suitable for the customers as well as for the problem, informational prerequisites must be either satisfied or established. Included among these are the availability of detailed data about the complainants, their affiliation with certain customer groups, and their economic value to the firm. Within the scope of activity of complaint reaction are decisions about the extent of and time frame for the communication that takes place after the complaint input. On the one hand, it must be determined which acknowledgments (e.g., confirmation of receipt and intermediate replies) will take place and in which form (verbally, by telephone, in writing). On the other hand, clear-cut standards for the maximum period of time in which these communications are to occur must also be set.

Tasks of the Indirect Complaint Management Process

Once the complaint reaction phase has been reached, the direct complaint management process is completed. Complaint analysis, complaint management controlling, complaint reporting, and utilization of complaint information constitute the indirect complaint management process, which is handled in the absence of customer contact.

Complaints contain specific indications of organizational weaknesses in the planning, production, and marketing of products and services, as well as evidence of changes in customer preferences or market opportunities. For this reason, the information contained in complaints must be quantitatively and qualitatively analyzed. The focus of quantitative complaint analysis is the monitoring of the extent and distribution of the volume of complaints and the prioritization of the problems perceived by customers. In terms of qualitative complaint analysis, a systematic causal analysis must be carried out, on the basis of which suggestions for improvement can be developed with the use of various types of planning instruments.

The scope of responsibilities in the category of complaint management controlling encompasses three important subareas: evidence controlling, task controlling, and cost-benefit controlling.

The central concern of evidence controlling is ascertaining to what extent complaint management is in a position to reveal the degree of dissatisfaction present among the customers of the firm, to make this dissatisfaction articulated in complaints evident to management.

Task controlling is concerned with monitoring the extent to which the tasks of complaint management are being successfully accomplished. Quality indicators and quality standards must be formulated with reference to all the subtasks, and these indicators and standards must be continually reviewed for compliance and suitability. Objective standards can be determined for only some of the quality indicators (e.g., time targets to ensure rapid complaint processing). In other cases, the solution is to use satisfaction values as standards and to revise them in reference to complaint satisfaction surveys. Moreover, productivity indicators and productivity standards that reveal the efficiency of task fulfillment should be fixed. The firm-relevant quality and productivity standards should then be collected in a Complaint Management Index (CMI) according to their respective level of importance. This CMI should be seen as the central aggregate control benchmark of task controlling.

The function of cost-benefit controlling is to estimate the cost and benefit effects of a particular system of complaint management. In cost controlling, the costs that arise during the acceptance, processing, and reaction phases, as well as those that emerge in the context of the indirect complaint management process, must be calculated. Benefit controlling quantifies the various benefit dimensions of complaint management (information, attitude, repurchase, and communication benefits). The economic efficiency and the return on complaint management can be computed by comparing the cost effects with the benefit effects.

The information from the complaint analysis and from complaint management controlling must be made accessible to the various internal target groups. Decisions must be made with respect to complaint reporting to determine which analyses (quantitative and qualitative) should be disseminated or provided on demand, at which time intervals, and for which internal customer segments (management, quality control, marketing).

A key goal of complaint management lies in providing a substantial contribution to a quality management system, as complaint management makes sure that the information gathered from complaints will be actively utilized in the development of measures of improvement. The achievement of this goal requires not only regular complaint reporting, but also a systematic utilization of complaint information through the application of specific management measures and instruments. Among these is the application of quality planning techniques in the development of solutions to problems, the inclusion of complaint information in the work of quality improvement teams, the exploitation of complainants' idea potential, and the integration of complaint information in a customer knowledge management system.

Figure 4.1 gives an overview of the tasks of direct and indirect complaint management processes. In addition, this figure alludes to two other fundamental aspects of complaint management. The first is its strategic involvement in customer relationship management. The second is that optimal task fulfillment is associated with the structure of the organizational, human resource, and information technology frameworks.

All the tasks of the direct and the indirect complaint management processes and the necessary frameworks will be described in detail in subsequent chapters.

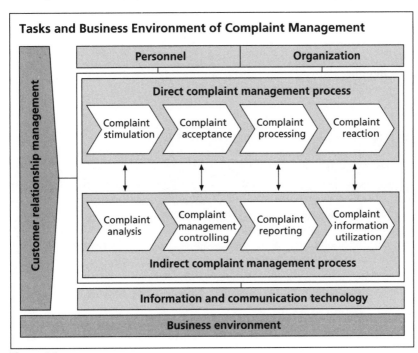

Figure 4.1

5

Complaint Stimulation

5.1 COMPLAINT STIMULATION RATHER THAN COMPLAINT MINIMIZATION

The Problem of "Unvoiced Complaints"

The goal of many firms is to minimize the number of incoming complaints. This goal only makes sense, however, if one proceeds based on the assumption that all dissatisfied customers complain, which in turn would mean that a low number of complaints was a clear indicator of a low level of customer dissatisfaction.

Empirical complaint research has shown, however, that this is not the case. The majority of dissatisfied customers do not complain. It is true that the respective percentages of unvoiced complaints vary depending on the product segment and the type of problem, but it is also the case that more than 50 percent of dissatisfied customers do not complain. In a study done by TARP, the percentage of "non-complainers" was 69 percent for airlines and 82 percent for car rental companies (Adamson 1993). Instead of complaining, dissatisfied customers choose to react in a different way. They talk about their negative experiences with friends, relatives, or co-workers, or they immediately switch to another provider. A low number of complaints should not, therefore, be interpreted as an expression of a high level of customer satisfaction. It could be that customers have a resigned attitude, because in their experience, complaining is not "worth it." A low number of complaints may also be the result of defensive measures implemented by the firm that make complaints expensive, difficult, and uncomfortable for customers (Fornell 1978).

If a firm really takes the goal of achieving customer satisfaction and customer loyalty seriously, it is more productive for them not to pursue an across-the-board minimization of complaints, but instead a minimization of customer dissatisfaction. This requires that the firm be informed as extensively as possible about the type, extent, and causes of customer dissatisfaction. Only then can meaningful starting points for quality improvements be identified. Complaint management can only develop its retention goals with respect to customers who complain. It is thus necessary to maximize the percentage of those dissatisfied customers who choose the "complaint alternative."

Complaint Maximization as the Goal of Complaint Stimulation

Complaint stimulation includes the complaint management task area that is concerned with encouraging dissatisfied customers and making it easier for them to express dissatisfaction in a complaint. The central goal of complaint stimulation could be described using the term complaint maximization, which is often misunderstood. Complaint maximization in this sense does not mean that customers should be given greater cause for complaint. Complaint maximization means that the greatest possible percentage of dissatisfied customers should be encouraged to come directly to the firm when they have a complaint.

Firms are faced with the challenge of removing the barriers that would prevent disgruntled customers from filing a complaint. Important tasks include the reduction of the customer's material and time costs, as well as the establishment and communication of proper channels of complaint. Firms must unmistakably signal that they are willing to take responsibility for all the causes that could give rise to dissatisfaction, as well as their desire to eliminate these causes to the customer's satisfaction.

In particular, customers must be motivated to bring forward any type of dissatisfaction they might have experienced, not merely instances in which a problem has occurred and customers could invoke a legally enforceable solution. It is a fact that it is not only serious performance deficits that cause customers to be irritated and to switch to another provider, but it is often "smaller" incidents such as an unfriendly remark, an arrogant gesture, or insufficient or false information. Incidents such as these only rarely become the subject of complaints, with the result that the firm hears nothing about these problems and does not have the chance to retain the dissatisfied customer or to eliminate the cause of the problem.

With the help of complaint stimulation, as many dissatisfied customers as possible are to be prompted to come to the firm with all their problems. In this way, the share of unvoiced complaints will be minimized or, stated another way, the share of complaints of dissatisfied customers will be maximized. On the basis of the acquired complaint information, the firm can subsequently carry out a careful diagnosis of the problem and eliminate its cause. In this sense, complaint maximization and complaint minimization represent not conflicting goals, but complementary ones. The success of complaint stimulation measures is the number of customers who complain, expressed as a percentage of the total number of dissatisfied customers. The success of complaint management itself can be seen primarily in the avoidance of mistakes and in the reduction of customer dissatisfaction, as well as in the resulting decline in the number of complaints.

Increased Complaint Volume as an Indication of Success

It is to be expected that the volume of complaints will initially increase substantially with the implementation of complaint stimulation measures. This increase in the volume of complaints should not be interpreted from the outset as an expression of rising defects in quality and increasing customer dissatisfaction. An increase in the rate of articulation (the ratio of complainants to dissatisfied customers) after the implementation of stimulation measures should be chalked up as a success for complaint management. If, however, the number of complaints rises but the rate of articulation remains the same, the firm has merely experienced an increase in the number of problems causing customer dissatisfaction.

5.2 COMPLAINT STIMULATION MEASURES

A firm has at its disposal a number of ways to stimulate complaints. Primary among these are the establishment of complaint channels and the active communication of complaint stimulation measures. Other activities such as the simplification of problem-solving processes, customer- and complaint-satisfaction surveys, and product and service guarantees have an indirect influence on complaint stimulation.

5.2.1 ESTABLISHMENT OF COMPLAINT CHANNELS

The fundamental task of complaint stimulation is the establishment of complaint channels that make it easy for the customers to express their dissatisfaction. Customers have several complaint channels at their disposal: verbal, written, by telephone, and electronically. The establishment of complaint channels implies that organizational units for each complaint channel are clearly defined and communicated to the customer. In this context, complaint stimulation has two interconnected functions that must be performed: It must make it possible for the customers to articulate their complaint in the way that they desire, and it must make sure that the processes and responsibilities specific to each complaint channel are internally defined and established.

The Verbal Complaint Channel

The verbal complaint channel is primarily relevant for service companies that create their "product" in the presence of the customer (e.g., hotels or auto-repair shops). A similar situation exists for companies that market their products through wholesalers and retailers or through their own sales representatives.

Since customers communicate directly with employees, the barriers to complaints are especially low, and dissatisfied customers are able to articulate their dissatisfaction immediately during the interaction. However, customers take advantage of the chance to express their complaints verbally to varying degrees, depending on the reaction they expect and how they perceive their own role in relation to the person with whom they are interacting. In particular, customers will choose to forego a verbal complaint and instead switch to another provider when they dread an uncomfortable argument or think that they won't be able to win in a verbal dispute with trained employees. The same applies to situations in which customers feel that they are in an inferior position of power, relative to the respective contact person (for example, toward health-care workers or physicians in hospitals), and even worry about negative sanctions if they were to make a complaint.

In order to reduce barriers to complaints such as the above, firms must communicate clearly and unmistakably that critical expressions from customers are desired. An excellent example of such communication is the saying that is posted in many small customer-service firms: "When you are satisfied, tell your friends. When you are dissatisfied, please tell us!" It is further necessary to make sure that there are a sufficient number of employees available who will react positively and encouragingly to complaints. In particular, they must be capable of demonstrating cooperative behavior and not evoking feelings of inferiority.

Setting up a service or an information area (Customer Relations Desk) as a specific contact point for customer concerns (as in hotels or retail establishments) constitutes a facilitation of verbal complaint articulations. In this way, customers receive a clear signal from the firm that they have the chance to clear up any questions or problems in a personal conversation, and they are told which person can handle their concerns.

Another way that the firm can use verbal communication as a feedback instrument for customer dissatisfaction is to inquire actively about problems that have been experienced, as opposed to waiting passively for complaints. Instead of hoping that customers will take the initiative, it is worthwhile for the firm itself to become active and to approach customers. After each transaction, a simple question can be asked: "Was everything okay?" Then information about the customer's perception of quality can be obtained (Hart, Heskett, and Sasser 1990). A variation of the above has, however, proven to be a better way to phrase the question: "Could we have done anything better?" or "What should we do better in the future?" These questions make it easier for customers to answer candidly because they are able to disguise their criticism in the form of a suggestion for improvement. Moreover, the answers can be more easily used for specific corrective measures.

The Written Complaint Channel

Letters (including faxes) represent the classic form of written complaints. The written, formally correct presentation of the case demands much time and effort on the part of the customer. For this reason, many customers take the firm up on its offer of registering their complaints by telephone or on the Internet. There are, however, situations in which the customers prefer to make their complaint in writing. Such is primarily the case when it is a question of liability, or when the complainants would like to approach management personally or to establish a permanent proof of their articulation. A complaint-stimulating effect for letters and faxes can be achieved when the firm clearly communicates to the customers to whom they should direct their written complaint.

A specific form of written complaint stimulation are comment cards, which are used especially in the customer-service sector (hotels, restaurants, banks). These comment cards are preprinted answer cards on which customers can describe in their own words either what has upset them or what they have found to be positive.

Figure 5.1 shows an excellent comment card from the coffee shop chain Starbucks Coffee Company. The company's desire to listen to and get advice from the customer is expressed most convincingly in the greeting ("We'd love to hear your thoughts"). The introductory sentences also clearly express how much the company is interested in customer feedback in order to make the Starbucks experience the best it can be for the customer.

Figure 5.1 Part A

This comment card is also noteworthy for other reasons:

- The card does not restrict the possibilities for feedback to a few pre-determined attributes, but rather gives the customer a great deal of room to describe positive or negative experiences thoroughly. In this way, customers have the opportunity to express their view of things and their specific experiences in their own words. This underscores the company's interest in having feedback about specific customer experiences and not just average values on a satisfaction scale.

- The card refers customers to other channels of feedback, namely the possibility of contacting the company by telephone, electronically, or in writing. The verbal channel is explicitly addressed. The customer is informed that helping is one of the employees' (partners') central

We want to do everything possible to make your Starbucks Experience the best it can be. So please tell us what we are doing that makes you really happy, or if there's anything else we could be doing better. Your feedback and ideas about your experience at Starbucks are very important to us.

OTHER WAYS TO CONTACT US

→ *Call* us at [number].

→ *E-mail* us at [email address].

→ *By mail:* [Address line 1—Company name]
[Address line 2]
[Address line 3]

SPECIFICS ABOUT YOUR VISIT

Which store did you visit? _____

What was the date of your visit? ___|___|___
MM   DD   YR

What time of day did you visit us?
☐ Morning   ☐ Afternoon   ☐ Evening

MAY WE CONTACT YOU?

Please leave your name, address, phone number or e-mail address if you want us to respond to your comments.

_____

_____

_____

_____

PLEASE SHARE YOUR THOUGHTS WITH US:

_____

_____

_____

_____

_____

_____

_____

_____

_____

_____

_____

MOISTEN, FOLD, SEAL AND MAIL.

Our partners (employees) are here to help.
If for any reason you are not satisfied, please let them know.

Thanks for your time!

Figure 5.1 Part B

tasks. And the customers are asked to let the company know if they are not satisfied for any reason.

• In addition, Starbucks offers customers the opportunity to be addressed by the company itself. They may leave their contact data if they would like a response to their comments. In the case of a complaint, the company can actively attend to reestablishing customer satisfaction.

• It is recognized that the customers are providing a service to the company by providing feedback. Accordingly, they are asked for suggestions and advice and thanked for investing their time ("Thanks for your time!").

The comment card of Starbucks can be seen as an excellent implementation of an active policy of stimulating customer feedback.

Comment cards can be placed either in a "feedback box" at the firm itself or sent to a specifically named person or department. If the firm intends for the cards, as it is done in the case of Starbucks, to be mailed, it should provide addressed and postage-paid cards in order to avoid time and financial barriers for the customer.

The Telephone Complaint Channel

The telephone complaint channel exhibits substantial advantages when compared with the written complaint method, both from the customer's and from the firm's point of view.

For the customer, these advantages are primarily the reduced complaint costs and faster resolution of the problem; for the firm, they consist mainly of the cost advantages and the possibility of addressing the customer individually:

- **REDUCED COMPLAINT COSTS FOR THE CUSTOMER.** By choosing the telephone channel of complaint, the customers usually reduce their costs. This is especially true with regard to financial costs when the firm establishes an 800 number for complaints. It is usually much easier for the customers to express their problem verbally than in writing, so their time and psychological costs are also reduced.
- **FASTER RESOLUTION OF PROBLEMS.** It is frequently possible to reduce customer dissatisfaction with the implementation of dedicated complaint phone lines. The firm is able to react immediately and in many cases can solve the problem over the phone or can transfer the customer directly to the person responsible and initiate the complaint processing procedure without delay. With the establishment of their 24-hour hotline "Your Comments Count," the fast-food chain Burger King was successful in answering 95 percent of all calls right away, or solving incoming complaint cases to the customer's satisfaction during their first contact (Marketing News 1990).
- **REDUCED COMPLAINT-PROCESSING COSTS FOR THE FIRM.** In comparison to the written method of complaint, the firm can save substantial processing costs by using the telephone method. Surveys show that the average processing costs for a typical phone conversation amount to approximately $8–$10, whereas they come to approximately $18 for complaints made in writing (Hart, Heskett, and Sasser 1990).
- **ADDRESSING CUSTOMERS INDIVIDUALLY.** Communication with customers can be conducted better and more thoroughly. The associate conducting the conversation has the opportunity to clarify the circumstances immediately, to provide explanations, and to apologize personally. The associate can also make a realistic assessment of the extent of the customer's irritation. In a telephone conversation, the emotions (such as irritation or bitterness) that the problem elicits in the customer become clear. The associate can take this into account in the way he or she conducts the conversation and thus bring about a calming of the situation. In addition, the associate learns details

about the customers' expectations and can work with them to find an appropriate solution (Vavra 1995).

In order to stimulate the articulation of complaints by telephone, an appropriate channel (such as a call center for customers' concerns) must be established. In setting up such a call center, the stimulating effect is greatest when the firm sets up an 800 number for customers. Research conducted in the telecommunications industry showed that seven out of ten consumers who encountered a problem and did not complain would have articulated if the company had maintained an 800 number (TARP 1997).

The Electronic Complaint Channel

The category of electronic complaint channel includes communication by e-mail or the Internet.

In recent years, the articulation of complaints by e-mail has increased dramatically, and substantial growth can also be expected in the future. This is due, first, to the increased diffusion of the Internet, resulting in a growing number of people utilizing e-mail for their personal communications and second, to the many advantages that this channel provides for customers voicing their complaints and the firms receiving them.

From the customer's point of view, it is primarily the following aspects that are important: e-mail is an asynchronous medium—the sender and the receiver of a message do not have to be present at the same time—so that the problem of accessibility is reduced in comparison to the telephone. E-mail is a rapid medium, and even transfers of information that take place over great geographic distances do not take more than a few seconds. Since e-mail communications can be sent online, very little monetary cost exists for the customers, and the amount of effort and time they must expend is much less than it would be for a letter. Customers who do not wish to expose themselves to a direct, critical conversation also experience less psychological cost when they use the e-mail medium. E-mail provides low dialogue barriers and promotes additional complaints that would not otherwise be articulated.

One advantage for the firm can be found in this stimulating effect itself, but there are others as well. The utilization of the e-mail channel promotes the gathering and analysis of relevant information. If customers use an online form to send their complaints, the firm can then specifically ask them to provide certain information that facilitates the classification and evaluation of the data the customers provide.

Figure 5.2 shows an excellent example. The feedback site of the Tide Fabric Care Network gives customers the opportunity to indicate if they wish to address the company with a compliment, a complaint, or a question. Customers can specify the product concerned as well as give a pre-categorization of the problem that occurred by means of pull-down menus. If customers indicate that they have a complaint, they are taken to an online complaint form as a next step, in which the previously given product and problem information is already partly incorporated. A text field is provided so that customers can give the details of the complaint.

Figure 5.2 Part A

The customers also have the opportunity to communicate their emotional mood disposition on a scale in a "quick mood check." In this manner, data are also available to determine whether the dissatisfied customer is, for example, just "annoyed" or "furious." This information is important not only for the complaint reaction, but also for the analysis in setting priorities for problem-solution activities.

It is noteworthy that the communication is already available and does not need further gathering as data so that the firm can refer to the

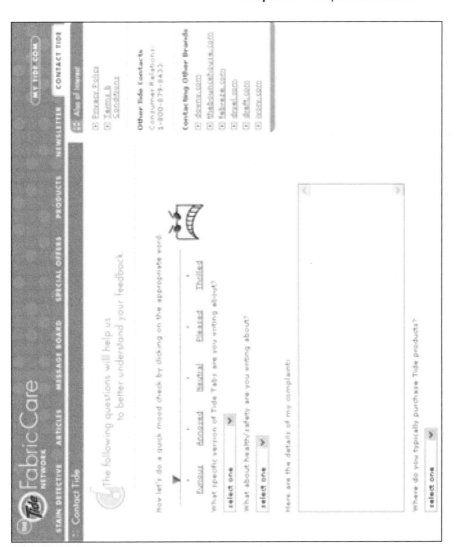

Figure 5.2 Part B

exact wording of the complaint if desired. In terms of costs, it should be noted that a dialogue conducted by e-mail usually requires more processing time and is thus more expensive than a dialogue conducted in person or over the telephone. However, the asynchronism of an electronic conversation means that it is not necessary to maintain processing capacity for short-term peaks in demand so that there are lower idle-time costs for unused personnel capacity. Furthermore, e-mails offer the firm a low-cost way to react to frequently occurring customer concerns in a standardized or automated way.

Two different forms of access or communication for the articulation of customer complaints can be differentiated:

(1) The customers know the e-mail address for the organizational unit that is responsible for handling complaints, and they make a complaint directly from their e-mail system (e.g., MS Outlook). In this case, complaint stimulation can occur only through the communication of the complaint-management e-mail address in other media.

(2) The customer goes to the firm's home page, which then contains a link to a special "complaint site." In order to achieve a complaint-stimulating effect, the link to the complaint site must be conspicuously placed on the home page and must also be available on the firm's other Internet sites if possible. The "complaint site" must be uncomplicated; it must be reachable with one click. A good example for the realization of these requirements is the home page of the Royal Bank of Canada (*http://www.rbc.com*), which is equipped with a category for "Compliments/Complaints," so that dissatisfied customers receive an immediate signal that their complaints are welcome and that they are provided with a fast and uncomplicated complaint channel. Many firms shy away from establishing their own complaint sites and choose a general feedback site instead. If firms really want to stimulate complaints, however, they should address the issue in an upfront manner.

5.2.2 ACTIVE COMMUNICATION OF COMPLAINT CHANNELS

The complaint methods that are established in order to bring about complaint stimulation must be actively communicated to the customer. Only with this type of "Complaint Marketing" can it be guaranteed that customers will use one of these methods when they have a problem and that the volume of complaints from dissatisfied customers will increase.

The invitation to customers to make their complaints to the firm and the information about the complaint channel can be communicated in various ways:

(1) Existing means of correspondence and communication such as form letters, informational brochures, or catalogs can be used to target complaint stimulation in the context of direct customer communication.

(2) A means of communication that is specially developed for complaint management such as business or comment cards, are used as inserts as part of a direct marketing campaign or conspicuously placed and communicated in sales and service locations. Media with a higher level of information use, such as specific informational brochures, give the firm the chance to explain the principles of its complaint policy and to promise a reaction, both of which underscore the credibility of the firm as "complaint-friendly." Figure 5.3 shows a business card from the Hannover utility company in Germany that was specifically conceptualized for the communication of the telephone and fax complaint hotline.

Dialogue cards can be used as an active communication instrument to make the basic dialogue easier for the customer. Figure 5.4

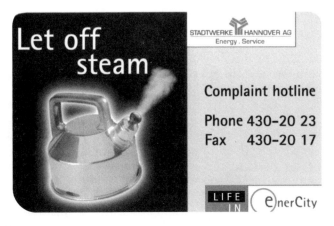

Figure 5.3

shows an SAS Airline dialogue card ("Let's talk"), which is distributed at airports. The card gives customers the chance to articulate their desire for a conversation in a way that is convenient for them. The customers provide their name, address, phone number, and/or e-mail address on the card and put it in the feedback box provided by the firm. To find out the customer's exact cause for concern, the firm must now become active.

(3) Firms can carry out complaint stimulation through the mass media, such as when they request customer feedback in newspaper ads and radio and TV spots and communicate the complaint management phone number, e-mail address, Internet address, or mailing address.

SAS

front

Let's talk

Name_____

Company_____

Address_____

Country_____

Phone_____   **back**

Cell phone_____

E-mail_____

EuroBonus number (if applicable)_____

Please use block letters

Figure 5.4

In their former "We try harder" campaign, Avis asks businesspeople to make a complaint if the ashtrays in their rental cars are dirty: "If you find a cigarette butt in an Avis car, complain. It's for our own good."

(4) In addition to the previous methods, the addresses of complaint departments and the telephone number for complaint calls can be clearly noted on packaging materials, user manuals, or instructional leaflets. General Electric, for example, places its 800 number on all its products and asks customers experiencing problems to contact the company directly (Tax and Brown 1998). Addresses and easy-to-remember telephone numbers can also be displayed on company vehicles.

(5) Firms can achieve complaint-stimulation effects by increasing the utility of complaints or the perceived probability that the complaint will succeed. Product, service, and satisfaction guarantees are the main tools that can be employed. They contain promises about what the firm will do if certain performance promises cannot be kept, products or services fall short of defined quality standards, or customer satisfaction is not achieved. Lands' End, for example, offers to replace any product, regardless of how long ago the transaction took place ("We accept any return for any reason, at any time"). The same applies to the "100% Satisfaction Guarantee" of hotel chain Hampton Inn (Rust, Subramanian, and Wells 1992) or of the Orvis company, which offers country lifestyle products ("We will refund your money on any purchase that isn't 100% satisfactory. Anytime, for any reason"). In view of explicit promises like these, guarantees substantially increase the perceived probability that a complaint will succeed. Since the benefit from the redemption of a guarantee is usually stated exactly (money-back, return if dissatisfied), it is usually simple for the customers to perform a cost-benefit calculation of their complaint. When these guarantees are unlimited and can be invoked with no problem, the complaint costs are also reduced.

5.3 THE REALIZATION OF COMPLAINT STIMULATION MEASURES

Before the firm introduces measures for the stimulation of complaints, it must make sure that an "avalanche of complaints" that would overextend the complaint management system is not set in motion. If the firm does not have sufficiently qualified personnel or the necessary technical system resources available, the incoming calls cannot be processed in a satisfactory manner. The results of this failure are longer processing times and unsatisfactory answers for customers, whose dissatisfaction is thereby increased even further (Vavra 1995).

In order to avoid this danger, it makes sense to implement complaint-stimulation measures gradually and to adjust the required dimensions of the resource endowment accordingly.

During the introduction of complaint-stimulation measures, a series of several activities must be carried out: an analysis of the current situation, a determination of the projected availability and speed of reaction, a prognosis of the prospective complaint volume, planning and provision of the technological and personnel resources required, and the stepwise implementation and communication.

Analysis of the Current Complaint Volume

The first step in the introduction of complaint-stimulation measures is an analysis of the current complaint volume. The number of complaints that have come in and the channels over which they arrived must be documented exactly. The processing times must also be determined in order to acquire clear-cut data of the length of time required for the acceptance and processing of complaints.

Determination of the Projected Accessibility and Speed of Reaction

The next step of the process is to determine what service level and which reaction times should be targeted. Complaint-stimulation measures make sense only if customers can immediately find a contact person when they have a complaint and when they do not have to wait long for a solution to their problem.

A high level of accessibility must, therefore, be ensured for all the complaint channels. This statement applies primarily to complaints that are articulated verbally and by telephone, for which the shortest possible wait times should be planned. With respect to written and electronic complaints, customer-appropriate standards for reaction times (the final answer or confirmations of receipt and intermediate replies) must be established.

Prognosis of the Prospective Complaint Volume

Firms' experience with active complaint management and with the intensive cultivation of dialogues with customers confirms that the complaint volume can increase very quickly. Based on the type of approach planned (verbal, written, by telephone, electronically) and the intended form of stimulation, the firm must estimate the extent to which it can expect an increase in complaints and other customer-initiated communications.

An important basis for the estimation of the additional complaint volume can be found in the results of representative market research studies among all the firm's customers' previous and intended future complaint behavior. Figure 5.5 gives a brief overview of the key questions that are part of a study such as this.

Assuming that in the period to be observed, the number of problems per customer will initially remain constant, one can project the number of problems that customers will experience in the future by considering the expected customer development. On the basis of the complaint willingness stated by the customer, the first clue to the expected complaint volume can be uncovered.

A market research study can, however, provide only a rough prognosis of the expected complaint volume. First, customers are not in a position to predict their future behavior completely, and second, their complaint willingness is also dependent on external factors that cannot usually be influenced, such as a generally increasing level of demand or

Key Questions for the Estimation of the Prospective Complaint Volume (Excerpt)

1. Initial question:
   "Have you had any cause for a complaint in the past 12 months?"

   ☐ Yes ▶ Question 2   ☐ No ▶ exit

---

2. Follow-up question for customers who answered "Yes" to question 1:
   "Did you actually complain?"

   ☐ Yes ▶ Question 2.1   ☐ No ▶ Question 2.2

2.1 Follow-up question for customers who answered "Yes" to question 2:

   2.1.1 "Which channel did you use to complain?"

   ☐ in person   ☐ by telephone   ☐ in writing   ☐ by e-mail

   2.1.2 "Based on your previous experiences, would you complain again if you were ever dissatisfied?"

   ☐ Yes ▶ exit   ☐ No ▶ Question 2.1.3

   2.1.3 Follow-up question for customers who answered "No" to question 2.1.2:
   "Why wouldn't you make another complaint?"

   _____

   _____ ▶ Question 3

2.2 Follow-up question for customers who answered "No" to question 2:
   "What was the reason you didn't complain?"

   _____

   _____ ▶ Question 3

---

3. Follow-up question for customers who answered question 2.1.3 or question 2.2:

   "In the future, you will be able to articulate your complaint by a telephone number specifically set up for that purpose. We plan to publicize this telephone number as part of a special campaign on posters and in other advertising media, as well as through personal letters. We can be reached from 7 A.M. to 12 P.M. Professional associates of our firm are available to accept your complaint and to assist you directly as far as possible. If this is not possible in some cases, we will call back within a day.

   Would you make a phone call under the circumstances described if a problem occurred, and would you articulate your dissatisfaction in the form of a complaint by way of this channel?"

☐	☐	☐	☐	☐
definitely	almost certainly	I can't say for sure	probably not	certainly not
exit	exit	Question 3.1	Question 3.1	Question 3.1

3.1 Follow-up question for customers who answered "No" to question 3 or who cannot make a definite decision:
   "Would you complain by way of another channel?"

   _____

   _____

Figure 5.5

media-technical developments. Therefore, there is every reason to bench-mark the rough data obtained from the study against the results of firms that have already implemented comparable processes of stimulation. An even more precise prognosis can then be made as part of the gradual implementation of complaint stimulation based on experiences in test markets.

The Planning and Provision of Technological and Personnel Resources

The results of the prognosis form the basis for the estimation of any additional technological or personnel resources that may be required. For technological matters, the primary task is to provide the infrastructure that will ensure the projected accessibility and reaction speed. With the telephone complaint channel, this requires a telephone system in the call center that can automatically distribute the incoming calls to employees via ACD-linking (Automatic Call Distribution) and uses CTI (Computer Telephone Integration) to guarantee that employees have immediate, direct access to the customer database as well as to the firm's product and process databases. What is important with the written complaint channel is, among other things, the presence of a document management system based on complaint letters that have been scanned into the system. For electronic complaints, the existence of a proper e-mail management system is of vital importance. In addition, complaint management software with the corresponding hardware must be available, as it will aid in the efficient fulfillment of all the specific tasks that have been defined as part of the firm's system of complaint management.

The necessary employee capacity must be planned at the same time so that the firm will be able to deal with the expected future volume of complaints in accordance with the standards that it has defined. The bases for establishing the necessary capacity come from data about the amount of time required for handling a complaint—differentiated according to complaint channel—as well as from data relevant to the yearly productive capacity of each employee. Dividing the yearly capacity per employee by the estimated processing time per complaint for each complaint channel yields the complaint volume that can be handled per employee per year. The next step is to divide the projected complaint volume per year by the above figure, and the resulting figure is the number of employees required per complaint channel.

Stepwise Implementation and Communication

Despite careful preparation of complaint-stimulating measures, a degree of uncertainty in the planning remains. The additional complaint volume cannot be predicted with 100 percent accuracy. The supposed processing times are simply projected values based on actual experiences, which could deviate from the real values when new complaint-stimulating structures are introduced. It is also conceivable that new tasks will be introduced in the context of complaint management for which no values based on experience exist.

To avoid the danger of falsely dimensioning the capacity, a testing phase in which the stimulation measures are implemented to a limited extent should first be carried out (Furlong 1993). If customer data are available, the existence of a new complaint channel can be communicated to specific customer groups. It is possible to test acceptance of the channel in a regional test market where information about the complaint channel is disseminated within a limited area. In each case, the test results serve as the basis for the prognosis of the total volume for all customer groups or for the entire geographic area. This allows for a demand-oriented adjustment of the necessary capacity according to the required magnitudes. Spotlight 1 shows how Deutsche Post AG proceeded when implementing its customer call center.

SPOTLIGHT I

Complaint stimulation in small doses at Deutsche Post AG

The Deutsche Post AG has set a goal for itself of creating a central communication channel for its customers that is easily accessible for all kinds of customer feedback: enquiries and complaints as well as suggestions and compliments.

Since it was not initially possible to predict how many calls were expected and since the introduction of the hotline number was not meant to trigger an avalanche of customer requests and complaints, it was gradually activated over a period of seven months for certain area codes: only callers from the activated areas were able to reach the hotline. Accordingly, the service phone number was only communicated in the local media in the activated areas and at the same time it was pointed out that only Post customers with the appropriate area code would be able to contact the customer phone line.

With the nationwide launch, the number was placed at the top of the listing for "Deutsche Post AG" in public telephone directories. Since that time, it has also been advertised in brochures as the central telephone contact of Deutsche Post AG. In addition, special advertising material, such as posters and business cards, has been distributed in the Post's branch offices, on which customers are actively asked to contact the customer phone line with questions or problems.

With the communication of this service channel proceeding in small doses, the number of calls gradually increased as well. Accordingly, the staff capacity was increased from twenty telephone agents in the beginning to currently around 350 at five different locations.

It is clear that customers use this communication channel not only for complaints, but also to request information about the products and services of Deutsche Post AG.

Rainer Anton
Head of the KUNDENTELEFON Branch
Deutsche Post AG

6

Complaint Acceptance

When dissatisfied customers come to the firm with a complaint, there are two fundamental tasks that must be accomplished in the context of complaint acceptance:

- Organization of the Receipt of the Complaint. The receipt of the complaint within the firm must be organized. Clear structures of responsibility must be established, and the associates that will have to take complaints during the course of their contact with customers must be prepared for the situations they will encounter (Chapter 6.1).
- Documentation of Complaint Information. All the relevant information contained in complaints must be documented (Chapter 6.2). In doing so, special attention must be paid to two groups of problems: the development of an appropriate system of categorization (Chapter 6.3) and the determination of the forms with which the complaint information is to be documented (Chapter 6.4).

6.1 ORGANIZATION OF THE COMPLAINT RECEIPT PROCESS

6.1.1 THE PRINCIPLE OF COMPLAINT OWNERSHIP

The responsibility that falls on the employees to whom complaints are articulated must be clarified. Here is where the principle of Complaint Ownership has proved itself. According to this principle, the person in the firm who is the first to be informed by a customer about a problem or is the first to perceive a customer problem is responsible from that time on for the recognition, documentation and processing of this problem as a complaint. This person has consequently acquired "ownership" of the complaint.

The Complaint Owners then have the task of either solving the problem immediately, if it falls within their area of professional competence, or bringing in other employees who have the expertise and decision-making authority needed to resolve the issue.

The concept of complaint ownership has been impressively implemented by The Ritz-Carlton Hotel Company/The Ritz-Carlton Hotel Company, L.L.C. It is unequivocally anchored in the "Ritz-Carlton® Basics," a synopsis of the most relevant guidelines for expected employee behavior. Instant guest pacification is the responsibility of each employee, and all employees who receive a complaint are the "owner" of the problem. They are empowered to break away from their regular duties when a guest has a problem or needs something special and to resolve the problem (Ritz-Carlton 1999: 2). In this way, the hotel aims to achieve the goal of resolving all guest complaints before the guests have departed and to make the dissatisfied customer an enthusiastic customer again.

An important aspect of the principle of Complaint Ownership concerns the question of how long the "Ownership of a Complaint" should be maintained. For complaints that arise in the context of contact-intensive service interactions (e.g., a hotel stay, a restaurant visit, or a bank visit) as well as for product complaints, which can be solved immediately during direct customer contact, complaint ownership lasts until the problem is solved. For complaints that are not immediately solvable and entail a corresponding processing procedure, the "ownership of the complaint" expires when the further processing of the complaint is ensured by the "complaint owner." This also applies to those cases in which the customers direct their complaint in writing, over the phone, or in person to an associate who is not "actually" responsible.

Closely associated with the principle of Complaint Ownership is the decentralization of decision-making authority to the employees who engage in customer contact ("Empowerment"). Every associate at The Ritz-Carlton®, for instance, can spend up to $2,000 to pacify a guest who has complained. The specific design of empowerment in the context of the initial contact with a dissatisfied customer will be addressed in Chapter 13.3.5.

6.1.2 COMPLAINT RECEIPT PROCESSES

Customers do not always choose the channel intended by the firm when they make their complaint. Therefore, clear controls for the complaint input processes, the paths that complaints not directed to the responsible position (such as the Customer Care Department) should take, are needed.

Against this background of targeting consistent and timely complaint handling, it must be noted that all complaints first should be transferred to the person responsible, and from there the processing procedure should be coordinated as far as content and time are concerned. This demands that all employees of the firm be informed of where the central responsibility lies. Employees in the incoming mail department must especially be trained to recognize complaint letters.

6.2 DOCUMENTATION OF COMPLAINT INFORMATION

In the initial-contact phase, it is not only important to behave in a way that is appropriate to the dissatisfied customer's situation, but all the relevant information about the complaint case must be documented. General criteria for the documentation of complaints will be introduced below, after which the fundamental contents of documentation and possible ways of structuring them will be addressed.

6.2.1 CRITERIA FOR COMPLAINT DOCUMENTATION

The three main criteria for the documentation of information that is contained in complaints are completeness, structuredness, and speed.

COMPLETENESS. It is most important that all relevant complaint information be recorded. The focus here is on information about the complainants, the experience they had as customers that gave rise to the complaint, and the object of the complaint. Information that is important for the rapid customer-oriented processing and resolution of the complaint must be thoroughly documented during the acceptance process. Information on the measures undertaken by the firm during this initial contact with the customer must also be recorded. This information has a documentary character, but it also forms the basis for later complaint management controlling analyses.

STRUCTUREDNESS OF THE DOCUMENTATION CATEGORIES. The criterion of the structured recording of the customer's problem demands that the complaint information be ascertained in a certain logical content structure so that all the essential information is in fact documented. It must also be guaranteed that the customers' way of telling the story can be easily followed and that they will be interrupted as little as possible during their account. The forms and software templates used must therefore allow for easy access to the documentation criteria.

SPEED. It is important to make sure that the thorough recording of information proceeds quickly when complaint documentation takes place during direct contact between the customer and the associate, which is necessary for reasons of efficiency. It must be recognized that the situation in which a complaint is articulated is an especially sensitive one, and the customer must not be expected to endure a complicated and time-consuming process.

6.2.2 BASIC CONTENTS OF DOCUMENTATION

As a basic principle, we can distinguish between complaint-content information and complaint-handling information. Complaint-content information is related to the complaint incident experienced by the customer and provides answers to the question: "For whom did which problem with which object occur?" The complaint-content information can be further subdivided into complainant, complaint problem, and complaint-object information.

Complaint-handling information refers not to the incident described in the complaint, but rather to the internal process of dealing with the complaint. This information provides answers to the question: "How was the complaint accepted, processed, and resolved?" Consequently, complaint acceptance, complaint processing, and complaint reaction need to be differentiated from one another.

6.2.2.1 COMPLAINT-CONTENT INFORMATION

Figure 6.1 gives an overview of the informational details and the individual characteristics of complaint-content information.

6.2.2.1.1 COMPLAINANT INFORMATION

Complainant information pertains to the identity of the complainants, their role in the complaint process, and the consequences they have considered for their future conduct in the business relationship, based on the appearance of the problem.

Overview of the Complaint-Content Information

Complainant information
- Identity of the complainant
  - Details about the complainant's person/organization
  - Accessibility of the complainant
  - Internal or external customer
- Complainant's role in the complaint process
- Degree of annoyance and behavioral consequences
  - Extent of annoyance
  - Intentions to act or behavioral consequences

Complaint-problem information
- Type of problem
- Exact conditions of the complaint incident
  - Affected organizational unit
  - Date of problem occurrence
  - Specific situation of the incident
- Cause of the problem
- Initial or follow-up complaint

Complaint-object information
- Products and/or services
- Marketing aspects
- Sociopolitical behavior

Figure 6.1

Information on the Identity of the Complainant

In the context of complaint documentation, data about the person who is articulating the problem to the firm is the first information that must be recorded.

PERSON. All the specific details about the complainant's person and/or organization that are useful for the processing, resolution, and analysis of the complaint itself fall into this category. Important details include the customers' name, their customer number (if available), their affiliation with a particular customer group or line of business (e.g., individual or business customer, membership in a preferred customer group) and other possible personal information.

ACCESSIBILITY. The customers' address, as well as the telephone/fax number and the e-mail address where they can be reached, must be recorded. It is also useful to note the times at which the customers can be reached at each address or number so that they can be contacted immediately in case further inquiries are necessary.

INTERNAL OR EXTERNAL CUSTOMER. For the most part, complainants are not members of the firm itself, but customers who purchase the firm's products or services in the marketplace (external customers). In recent years, however, more and more internal processes have been modeled as customer-supplier relationships and implemented using internal performance standards. Therefore, an increase in complaints from internal customers can also be expected. For this reason, then, there must be a way to identify the complainant as an internal customer during the complaint acceptance process so that the processing routines that were specially developed for such cases can be initiated.

Information on the Role of the Complainant in the Complaint Process

RELATIONSHIP TO THE COMPLAINT INCIDENT. Usually, the person making the complaint is the same person who is actually affected by the problem. It sometimes happens, however, that complaints are brought forward vicariously, such as when a son comes to the firm on behalf of his mother or attorneys approach the company on behalf of their client. In cases such as these, the name and contact information of the person making the complaint, as well as of the person actually affected by the problem, should be recorded. The communication during the processing procedure naturally takes place with the complainant; it may, however, be advisable to get in touch with the affected person as well, for example, in order to apologize directly.

Information about the Degree of Annoyance and the Future Behavioral Consequences of the Complainant

EXTENT OF ANNOYANCE. In order to react appropriately, to estimate the risk of losing the customer, and to obtain an informational basis for the prioritization of any corrective measures that may be required, it is necessary to determine the importance that the dissatisfied customer attaches to the incident in question. This may take place during the acceptance of the complaint when the complainants use wording of their choosing to express the extent of their annoyance about the problem. Typical examples are as follows: "That sort of thing does happen sometimes, but I hope that this won't come up again in the future!" or "I'm furious!" In order to facilitate later analysis, it makes sense to utilize a scale of annoyance and to assign the most appropriate scale value to the respective verbalizations used by customers (see Figure 6.2). This assignment of values demands a high degree of empathy on the part of the employees accepting the complaint, since they must perform the evaluation themselves and cannot ask the customer to do it.

INTENTIONS TO ACT, OR BEHAVIORAL CONSEQUENCES. There are a number of future intentions to act that can be taken from customer statements. The customers may make threats related to the business relationship ("You won't see me here again!"). They may announce their intention to carry out other activities, by which they are attempting to assert their rights, for example, bringing in the media or consumer-rights organizations. It is equally possible that they will point out decisions and

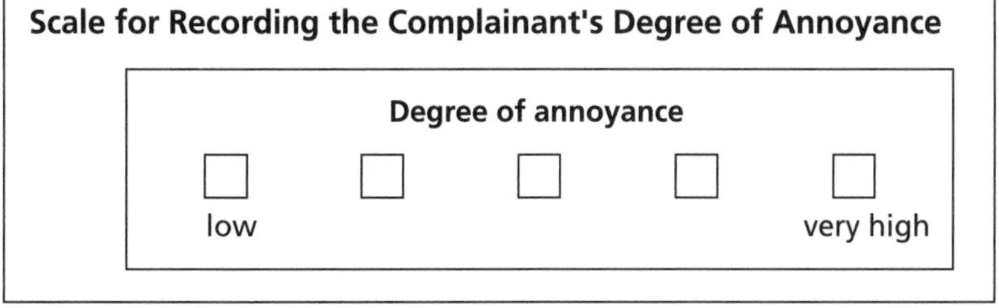

Scale for Recording the Complainant's Degree of Annoyance

Degree of annoyance

low | | | | very high

Figure 6.2

57

consequences that have already taken place ("That's the reason I gave notice").

Such statements related to behavior can either be documented separately or considered in the context of correspondingly modified scales of annoyance. An example of a scale that measures the extent of the annoyance and the repurchase intention at the same time is shown in Figure 6.3.

Scale for Collectively Recording the Degree of Annoyance and the Assumed Consequences of the Complainant's Repurchase Behavior

Degree of annoyance and relevance for the repurchase behavior

☐	☐	☐	☐	☐
Even though I was annoyed, I paid no more attention to the problem.	I was quite annoyed, but I didn't seriously consider a change.	I was very annoyed, and I toyed with the idea of switching my provider.	I was so annoyed that I haven't purchased from this provider for a long time.	I have changed or will change my provider because of this problem.

Figure 6.3

Information on the extent of the subjectively experienced irritation and the intentions to act that result from it constitute an indication of the urgency of removing the problem from the customer's perspective.

6.2.2.1.2 COMPLAINT-PROBLEM INFORMATION

Complaint-problem information is concerned with the type of problem, the exact conditions of the complaint incident (place, time, situational aspects), the cause of the problem, and the classification of the complaint as a first or follow-up complaint.

TYPE OF PROBLEM. The exact documentation of the problem that represents the actual content of the complaint is of decisive importance for the successful accomplishment of complaint-management tasks. Each individual error must be assigned to one of the defined complaint objects (e.g., to a product or a service) during the complaint acceptance phase of each specific case.

EXACT CONDITIONS OF THE COMPLAINT INCIDENT. In order to have an exact explanation of the circumstances, a deeper causal analysis, and a differentiated evaluation of the frequency of the problem, the location of the incident or the affected organizational unit must be recorded. This is especially necessary in the case of a decentrally organized firm with multiple business locations (branch offices or franchise partners). If complaints about unfriendly behavior on the part of employees are more common for one particular branch office, discussions about combating the causes of the unfriendliness and eliminating the problem can be held with that particular unit of the organization.

The same principle applies to the recording of the date on which the problem appeared. This is important for the clarification of warranty questions, the determination of the cause of the problem, and the discovery of the frequency of occurrence of the problem per unit of time (day, week, month, season, year).

It is also useful to record the specific situation of the incident when it has led to especially problematic experiences for the customers. For instance, the situation may be perceived differently by the customers if a problem with their car came up in the middle of a cold and rainy night while they were on the way to a long-awaited vacation with the entire family or whether the incident occurred under less dramatic circumstances. Such information is very valuable in order to be able to design an individualized complaint reaction.

CAUSE OF THE PROBLEM. If the customer's descriptions of the problem contain statements or speculations about possible causes of the problem, they should be recorded, as they may contain important indications for later internal analysis processes.

INITIAL OR FOLLOW-UP COMPLAINT. It frequently happens that customers who lodge a complaint must broach the subject several times and in doing so, express their irritation about certain aspects of the complaint acceptance and complaint processing procedures. The original dissatisfaction they had, which was based on the actual problem, then escalates as a result of the unsatisfactory handling of their complaint. As this mishandling represents further grounds for complaint, it is important to differentiate between an initial complaint and a follow-up complaint. While the initial complaint is related to a specific problem with a product or a service, a follow-up complaint is always a complaint about how an original complaint was handled.

6.2.2.1.3 COMPLAINT-OBJECT INFORMATION

The subject of the problem articulated by the customer is the complaint object. This object is usually a product or service offered by the firm. In addition to these firm offerings, other aspects of the market offering (e.g., the price) or the firm's overall sociopolitical behavior (e.g., measures that are harmful to the environment) may also be the object of complaints.

PRODUCTS AND/OR SERVICES. For cause analysis and corrective measures, it is necessary that the object affected by the complaint (product or service) be clearly identified and recorded. The categorization that is applied should be fundamentally oriented toward the standard product classification (in the form of product lines or model ranges) used by the marketing and sales departments.

As far as services are concerned, the possible customer-contact situations should be described in more detail in order to be able to substantiate better the problem that has arisen. The customers experience many services as a sequence of situations in which they come into contact with some aspect of the service offering and gain an impression of the quality of the service. In the case of a hotel stay, for instance, this contact may include the check-in, the room stay, the restaurant visit, and the check-out.

Therefore, it is not only important for hotel management to find out that the customers are complaining about unfriendly behavior on the part of an associate, but also at what customer-contact point (check-in, room service, restaurant) they experienced this behavior. Only on the basis of such information can targeted corrective actions be introduced.

MARKETING ASPECTS. Customer dissatisfaction can result from the use of marketing instruments. Customers may complain that the provider's products are too expensive or that an advertisement was misleading. Such information is important for a customer-oriented modification of the marketing mix (for example, the "4 P's" of marketing: Product, Place, Price and Promotion). For systematic recording of this information, it may be convenient to use the traditional catalog of marketing instruments as a basis.

SOCIOPOLITICAL BEHAVIOR. Consumers do not restrict expressions of their opinion to the firm's market offerings, but instead take up sociopolitical topics as well and criticize corporate behavior that violates ethical norms or sociopolitical positions (breach of weapons-export restrictions, violations of environmental laws, discriminatory treatment of women). A firm can recognize consumer- and sociopolitically relevant problems in a timely manner and take them into consideration in its organizational planning if it undertakes a targeted documentation of critical statements such as these.

6.2.2.2 COMPLAINT-HANDLING INFORMATION

Complaint-handling information is not derived from the depiction of the case, but is related to the internal handling of complaint acceptance, processing, and reply (see Figure 6.4).

Overview of the Complaint-Handling Information To Be Gathered

Complaint-acceptance information
- Time of receipt
  - Articulation date
  - Time of receipt in the firm
  - Time of receipt in complaint management
  - Date of record
- Complaint channel
- Employee accepting the complaint
- Addressee of the complaint

Complaint-process information
- Processing procedures
- Responsibility for processing
- Processing steps

Complaint-reaction information
- Aspects significant for the firm's response
  - Expectations of the customer with regard to the response
  - Classification of the complaint as warranty or goodwill case
  - Urgency of reaction
- Information about the corporate reaction
  - Promises to the complainant
  - Implemented problem-solving/payment of compensation

Figure 6.4

6.2.2.2.1 COMPLAINT-ACCEPTANCE INFORMATION

Complaint-acceptance information documents the time of complaint receipt from various perspectives, the complaint channel selected by the complainant, the employee who took the complaint, and the addressee chosen by the complainant.

TIME OF RECEIPT. The date of the complaint receipt in the firm is the basis point in terms of complaint settlement. From this point on, the firm is aware that it has dissatisfied customers who are awaiting an answer and a solution to their problem.

To be able to verify the observance of reaction times and to follow the time needed for the processing procedure within the firm, it is necessary to document the receipt of the complaint by the different organizational units that deal with that complaint. On the basis of these different receipt times, the processes can be more precisely understood, and the respective idle times and internal transport times in particular can be identified. This is required for the determination and verification of standard reaction times, for example, "Initial contact with the dissatisfied customer in the case of written complaints within 48 hours."

The postmark of the letter (articulation date) should be recorded separately in the case of written complaints, because the customer has been waiting for a reaction since that time. Longer postal delivery times may also be a possible cause for a delayed reaction. When complaint-management software is being used, the date on which the complaint was entered into the system (date of record) must also be documented. Between the time at which a complaint case reaches the appropriate department and the time at which the case is entered into the system for processing, a period of days can elapse, such as because of lower entry capacity compared to the incoming complaint volume.

On the basis of differentiated documentation of the various receipt times, the firm can carry out, in the context of complaint analysis and complaint management controlling, a targeted analysis of which stations a written complaint in particular passes through, what processing times are associated with the complaint's path through the firm, and what in the end stands in the way of a quick reaction to customer complaints.

COMPLAINT CHANNELS. For each complaint, the communication channel chosen by the customer (in person, in writing, by telephone) should be recorded. Indications about the type of answer the complainant might desire can be drawn from the above information; familiarity with and acceptance of the established complaint channels can be verified.

EMPLOYEE ACCEPTING THE COMPLAINT. The employee accepting the complaint is the person who is the first to be informed by the customers about their dissatisfaction. The name of this employee should be documented so that the first person who talked to the customer can be asked follow-up questions in case anything in the complaint case is unclear, or so that this employee can be immediately named as a contact person in case of further inquiries by the customer.

ADDRESSEE OF THE COMPLAINT. Dissatisfied customers either direct their complaints to the firm in general or name a specific person or department as the addressee. This information is important in monitoring the utilization of complaint-entry channels. If complainants frequently select complaint channels that were not intended by the firm, this is an indication that the established channels are not sufficiently well-known to customers or are inappropriate.

6.2.2.2.2 COMPLAINT-PROCESSING INFORMATION

Complaint-processing information includes information about the processing procedures put in motion by a complaint incident and about those in charge of the complaint case, as well as specific information about the individual processing steps.

PROCESSING PROCEDURES. The various processing procedures are defined based upon the object of the complaint, the type of problem, and the urgency of the reaction. The employees taking down the complaint must note which processing procedure they have initiated and to which person or department they have forwarded the case. This information is required for monitoring and optimizing complaint processing.

RESPONSIBILITY FOR PROCESSING. For complaint cases that cannot be resolved during the initial direct contact with the customers, the employees responsible must be specified in the complaint-acceptance phase. The persons accepting the complaint must then record the name of the responsible associate and at the same time, forward the complaint case directly to that person.

PROCESSING STEPS. If processing steps are introduced or carried out during the acceptance process, these steps should be documented so that transparency in processing is maintained at all times.

6.2.2.2.3 COMPLAINT-REACTION INFORMATION

Complaint-reaction information refers to clues for response decisions and information about the solution to the problem that the firm promised or that it actually implemented.

Information about Aspects Significant for the Response Decision

If certain aspects that will be significant for the firm's response are recognized during the acceptance of the complaint, they should be documented at this time. The following items are included in this group in increasing level of importance: the expectations of the customer with regard to the firm's reaction, the classification of the complaint as a warranty or goodwill case, and the urgency of the reaction.

EXPECTATIONS OF THE CUSTOMER WITH REGARD TO THE RESPONSE. The complainants frequently associate their depiction of the problem with a specific idea of the resolution to the problem or the reparation they desire. These expectations should be recorded during the acceptance process, as they facilitate the search for a need-oriented response by the firm.

CLASSIFICATION OF THE COMPLAINT AS A WARRANTY OR GOODWILL CASE. For legal-liability and processing reasons, it must be recorded during the complaint acceptance whether this is a warranty or goodwill case.

If it is clearly a warranty case, the solution to the problem—according to the guidelines of the warranty—is already decided so that the necessary processing steps can be introduced immediately. If it is evident that the warranty period has just expired or a goodwill solution comes into play for other reasons, this must also be documented in order to introduce an appropriate processing routine.

URGENCY OF THE REACTION. Fundamentally, all customer complaints are equally important for a firm and should also be handled equally. The preferred processing and resolution of a complaint then appears to be justified, or necessary, for two reasons: first, if massive problems that have negative effects on a large number of customers can be uncovered through complaints—perhaps effects that would carry a high risk of damage to health or property—(Problem Risk); or second, if the "usual" handling of complaints is associated with the danger of substantial economic losses or damage to the firm's image (Customer Risk).

Examples in the first case (Problem Risk) would be complaints that indicate defects in the product that are so grave that the affected firm feels compelled to recall its products. Car makers might request drivers of a particular model to bring their vehicles in for inspection. In the case of complaints whose content provides evidence of serious product defects such as these, the firm must deviate from the normal processing procedure so that the problem can be eliminated and possible damages can be limited immediately.

In the second case (Customer Risk), it may be a question of complaints in which the complainants link their depiction of a serious incident with a believable threat to introduce legal or public measures if there is no reaction from the firm or if the firm does not react in a satisfactory manner. A comparable situation exists when the complainant is a customer who is of extraordinary importance for the existence and success of the firm. Here again, a greater urgency of reaction and preferred treatment of the complaint may be justified.

Information about the Corporate Reaction

PROMISES TO THE COMPLAINANT. It may be practical to make promises to the customer regarding time deadlines and content during the complaint-acceptance phase. In the case of promises regarding deadlines, an exact date is perhaps named, by which time the case should be closed. In an unequivocal case diagnosis, promises regarding content are also possible, with a view toward the resolution of the problem or an exact compensation amount.

In order to avoid further irritation later on, all promises made to the customers must be recorded. At the same time, all the firm's efforts must be directed toward making sure that these promises are kept. The customers' doubt in the reliability of the corporate service performance that was triggered by the product defect or service deficit must not be strengthened further in the course of processing the complaint. If keeping the promise is not possible, contact must be made with the customers immediately, and the circumstances must be explained.

IMPLEMENTED PROBLEM-SOLVING/PAYMENT OF COMPENSATION. If the problem can be resolved right away during the complaint-acceptance phase, this response should be documented. In the case of problems that entail further processing, generally held proposed solutions should first be documented with an increasing degree of specification in the course of the processing.

Using the documentation of the solutions, a database can be established, which makes it possible for everyone in a firm that participates in the resolution of customers' problems to react consistently and quickly. Especially with technical product complaints, an expert system for the generation of differentiated answers and suggestions for solutions can be developed based on the documented solutions.

The solutions implemented should not only be documented with respect to content (e.g., money back, exchange, apology), but the costs must also be recorded in order to allow for a permanent analysis of the operational efficiency of the reaction policy.

6.3 CATEGORIZATION OF COMPLAINT INFORMATION

6.3.1 DEVELOPMENT OF A CATEGORY SCHEME

The documentation of complaint information demands a unique and specific assignment to designated categories. A corresponding system of categories must, therefore, be developed.

The development of these categories is one of the most fundamental tasks of complaint management for two reasons: (1) The more precisely the categories reproduce the structure of the problem from the customer's point of view, and the more thoroughly all customer complaints can unambiguously be assigned to these groups, the more the information can be implemented for the continuous improvement of organizational processes. (2) As will be shown later, the correct definition of problem categories is a prerequisite for the differentiated and efficient derivation of corresponding complaint-management processes.

6.3.1.1 REQUIREMENTS OF A CATEGORY SCHEME

For the goals that are pursued through complaint documentation to be achieved, a series of requirements must be fulfilled by the categorization scheme. A good and efficient scheme for the classification of complaints is characterized primarily by action orientation, clear-cut demarcation, completeness, customer orientation, and easy manageability.

ACTION ORIENTATION. Each classification attribute and each problem category in particular must be action-oriented to permit immediate conclusions to be drawn for complaint processing, cause analysis, and the introduction of corrective measures.

CLEAR-CUT DEMARCATION. Each category must be clearly demarcated from the others, which permits an unambiguous assignment of complaints. Only in this way can it be guaranteed that different employees will classify complaints in the same way.

COMPLETENESS. The category system must make it possible for all customer complaints to be documented. An unspecific category called "Miscellaneous Problems" is of little use as it provides no informational content for follow-up measures. If the firm does not wish to eliminate this category, it must be reviewed at regular intervals, and new categories must be created when the need arises.

CUSTOMER ORIENTATION. The problem categories must be formulated from the customers' perspectives and not from the internal point of view. The translation of the customer problems into the "internal" language of the firm should take place in a second step in which technical construction attributes or internally applied error classifications are logically associated with the categories of customer problems.

EASY MANAGEABILITY. The system of categorization must be easily understandable and manageable so that employees can find the correct category when they are documenting the complaint. This requires restricting the categories to a limited number for manual recording on documentary forms. For software-supported documentation, a considerably greater complexity of category systems is possible, although a simple introduction for users must be provided.

It is obvious that the fulfillment of these criteria can lead to conflicts. The requirements of action orientation, clear-cut demarcation, completeness, and customer orientation would seem to indicate a very differentiated system of categories, while the criterion of easy manageability would seem to indicate a simpler system. In this situation, compromise solutions with abstract formulations of customer problems are often tolerated, even though they do not permit exact conclusions to be drawn about the specific problem and its cause or corrective measures. For example, airlines formerly used the category "smoking problems" for all smoking-related problems regardless of whether the customers wanted to smoke but couldn't or were seated in a smoking rather than a nonsmoking section. This kind of generalized complaint categorization prevents the company from identifying the root cause of the problem (TARP 1997). If, however, the criterion of action orientation is violated, it would appear to be more financially viable and efficient to forego documentation completely, since the recorded information cannot lead to any sort of targeted utilization. For this reason, it is part of the specific challenges of software-technical supports both to provide the required number of classification criteria and to guarantee easy manageability on the part of the user.

6.3.1.2 HIERARCHICAL STRUCTURING OF CATEGORY SCHEMES

The requirement for an action-oriented category system can lead to a very detailed catalog of categories, especially in large firms. These categories must be brought into some kind of order that provides for increasing specification over different levels.

The highest demands are placed on the categorization of those complaint objects and complaint problems that constitute the core of complaint information. When firms offer a large number of different products and services in a multitude of variations, and when very different problems may arise in each case, then complex structures for the clear-cut assignment of mistakes to the appropriate category develop very quickly.

In order to keep this complexity under control, a hierarchical structuring of categories is needed so that definite groups and subgroups of characteristics can be set up. Thus, several articles may be assigned to a particular product group or certain problems (e.g., lack of product knowledge) placed in an overarching problem category (e.g., lack of competence).

6.3.1.3 MONITORING OF CATEGORY SCHEMES

In a good category scheme a particular complaint information is always assigned to the same categories, regardless of which associate is entrusted with the documentation. Ensuring this consistency means that greater importance is attached to the monitoring of the category scheme with respect to the freedom to overlap, meaningfulness, and reliability.

In the course of developing the system of categories, the assignment of specific complaints to the individual classification schemes must be carried out by at least two people independent of each other during a test phase. The quality of the categorization results from the degree of consensus between the two assignment processes and is then reflected in the percentage of complaints that are assigned to the same category classes according to both grouping processes. The share of complaints that are classified consistently for each type of complaint information that must be categorized is divided by the total number of complaints for each hierarchical level. The closer the result is to 1, the greater is the level of consensus. If at least 80 percent is not reached, Hayes (1992) suggests verifying and modifying the categories at the respective levels.

The scheme developed must be constantly enhanced, since new products and services are offered or previously unexpected errors arise. The scheme of categorization must therefore undergo a thorough verification process at regular intervals and be adjusted to the changed situation. Only in this way can meaningful results be targeted in the context of complaint assessment.

6.3.2 SUPPLEMENTATION OF CATEGORICAL DOCUMENTATION THROUGH A CLEAR DESCRIPTION OF THE CASE

Each categorization represents a simplification of complex circumstances. The danger of losing information that could provide basic details about the causes of problems and the reasons for customer dissatisfaction thus exists. This point will become clear in the following instance described by Albrecht and Zemke (1985: 119–120).

"A group of passengers sitting on a commuter airplane in Buffalo, New York, got a disappointing message at about 10 one evening. The airplane was parked at the departure gate, during a brief stopover on its trip from Washington, D.C., to Toronto. Just about the time the passengers began wondering aloud why they were so long overdue for take-off, a gruff voice crackled over the intercom: 'Please gather up your belongings and deplane the aircraft. This aircraft has a mechanical problem. It won't be going to Toronto tonight. The gate attendant inside the terminal will tell you what flights are available to Toronto.'

As 60 disgruntled passengers trooped into the terminal, the gate attendant used the public address system to remind them to get in line in front of the desk and be patient. She offered no sign of an apology or any acknowledgment of the inconvenience, just the matter-of-fact announcement that the next available flight on that airline's schedule would depart at 11:15 P.M.

One of the passengers loudly shared the fact that he had quickly called a competing airline and found that that airline's regularly scheduled flight had just left a few minutes ago. He offered the speculation that the gate attendants had delayed the announcement of the equipment problem until they were sure the passengers had no other flights from which to choose. There was a run on complaint forms and some loud discussion about service."

If one wanted to assign this case to a specific problem category, it might be the category of "Flight Delay Due to Technical Problem." Doing so, however, would not adequately document the complexity of the case or the reason that may have been the deciding factor in the customer's dissatisfaction. If efforts toward reducing technical defects are made on the basis of the complaint evaluation alone, substantial deficiencies in the handling of the incident will remain unconsidered (lack of explanation, no apology). The same thing applies to customers' perceptions and interpretations of the incident in question (assumption of an intentional delay of information).

It is important to record the complaint as thoroughly as possible as a narrative of the case. This is relatively easy to guarantee when complaints exist in writing, especially when it is possible to refer to a software-supported archival system. With the aid of systems such as these, complaint cases that are articulated in writing can be scanned and administered. If complaint-management software that is equipped with a corresponding interface to the archival software is implemented, the entire "complaint history" is immediately available and does not have to be documented again separately. In the case of complaints that are taken over the phone or in person, one must manage to record information about specific conditions in the form of key words.

6.4 FORM OF DOCUMENTATION

The documentation of the contents of a complaint may be carried either by employees of the firm or by customers themselves. If documented by employees, either standardized forms or templates in complaint-management software systems are utilized. Customer documentation takes place in the form of opinion cards or forms located on the complaint sites provided on the Internet.

6.4.1 CORPORATE COMPLAINT DOCUMENTATION BY MEANS OF FORMS AND PC-SUPPORTED TEMPLATES

Documentation Using Standardized Forms

Using standardized forms should put the employees accepting complaints in a position to document the complaint information in a thorough, structured, and rapid manner. An example of such a form is reproduced in Figure 6.5. This example takes into consideration complaint-content information (person of the complainant, product as complaint object, type of problem), as well as complaint-handling information (type and

---

Example of a Complaint Documentation Form

Complaint acceptance

Associate who accepts the complaint: _____ Date of receipt: _____

Complaint channel
☐ by telephone ☐ in writing ☐ in person ☐ _____

Addressee of the complaint
☐ Customer care ☐ Sales ☐ Management ☐ _____

Complainant

Basic data
Title: _____
First name: _____
Firm/last name: _____
Contact person: _____
Address: _____
City/zip code: _____
State: _____

Internal/external customer
☐ Internal customer ☐ External customer

Affected person
☐ Complainant herself/himself
☐ Employee of the complainant
☐ Supervisor of the complainant
☐ Relative of the complainant

Annoyance
☐ ☐ ☐ ☐ ☐
low   very high

Complaint object

Product/service
☐ _____ ☐ _____ ☐ _____ ☐ _____

Market offering/marketing mix
☐ Product ☐ Price ☐ Distribution ☐ Communication
☐ Personnel ☐ Process ☐ Physical environment ☐

Sociopolitical behavior
☐ _____ ☐ _____ ☐ _____ ☐ _____

Complaint problem

Case depiction
_____
_____
_____
_____
_____

Type of problem
☐ Problem 1 ☐ Problem 2
☐ Problem 3 ☐ Problem 4

Location of the problem occurrence
_____

Date of the problem occurrence
_____

Initial/follow-up complaint	Reaction urgency
☐ Initial complaint ☐ Follow-up complaint	☐ Urgency level 1
	☐ Urgency level 2
Case resolution desired by the customer	☐ Normal processing
_____	**Warranty/goodwill**
_____	☐ Warranty
_____	☐ Goodwill

Complaint resolution

Resolution of the problem that was actually realized
_____
_____

Promises made to the customer
_____
_____

Time promises
☐ Immediatly resolved ☐ Intermediate reply by _____
☐ Problem solution/compensation by _____

Complaint processing

Complaint Owner	Complaint processing procedure
☐ Complaint Owner 1 ☐ Complaint Owner 2	☐ Process 1 ☐ Process 2
☐ Complaint Owner 3 ☐ Complaint Owner 4	☐ Process 3 ☐ Process 4

Figure 6.5

date of complaint input, data on the resolution/reparation, measures taken, and processing steps).

The categories of documentation are highlighted and furnished with alternative answers, or hints, about which specific information must be recorded in detail. In this way, rapid and thorough recording of data can be guaranteed.

Standardized forms such as these are primarily suited for the documentation of complaint information that takes place during direct contact with the customer such as when the customer makes a complaint verbally or over the telephone. These forms can be reasonably implemented by customer-contact personnel in retail locations, hotels, or banks.

If necessary, complaint information may also be recorded after direct contact with the customer. When a hotel guest complains to a room attendant about a dirty bathroom, the focus then becomes the immediate restoration of the customer's satisfaction. The belated documentation of the complaint information remains important, however, so that they are later available for assessment and controlling purposes and also for continual process improvements.

Documentation Using Software-Supported Complaint-Management Systems

Firms generally employ software-supported complaint-management systems for the systematic documentation and processing of written and telephone complaints in particular. The distinct advantage of these systems is that the criteria of thorough, structured, and rapid documentation of the complaint information can easily be met. Program configuration and control ensure that no fundamental complaint information is omitted. However, the use of these systems presupposes appropriate training for firm employees, in dealing not only with the complaint-management software, but also with the individual documentation contents.

Additional manual complaint-documentation forms must be utilized when software-supported complaint-management systems are put in place if not all subsidiaries or customer-contact personnel have a workstation equipped with the software system or cannot refer to it while a complaint is being made (e.g., in a retail location). The information recorded on the form can subsequently be entered into the complaint-management system and made centrally available for further processing. The firm may also plan for the forms to be scanned into the system, which minimizes the amount of subsequent documentation required.

6.4.2 CUSTOMER COMPLAINT DOCUMENTATION USING OPINION CARDS AND INTERNET COMPLAINT SITES

The use of opinion cards or Internet complaint sites causes part of the information recording to be transferred to the customer (customer complaint documentation).

The design of opinion cards or complaint sites may range from a single text field to the free articulation of the complaint story to a structured layout with predetermined entry fields. In designing the opinion cards and complaint sites, the firm must be careful to use the predefined fields to inquire only about information that the customer can easily provide. Auto makers or dealerships should, for example, avoid insisting that the customer provide the Vehicle Identification Number, since many customers do not have this information handy. Default categories must be worded in such a way that the customer can easily understand them. The following data especially can be requested of customers with no difficulty: address, type of problem, complaint object, location where the problem arose, date when the problem arose, description of the incident as free text, and expected resolution of the problem.

On Internet sites, categories, which are consistently part of a complaint, can be provided as classification criteria so that customers get to choose complaint information from the corresponding lists appropriate to them. For example, the customer might choose the complaint object from the range of products or the location where the problem occurred from a list of all bank branches. Choosing categories facilitates the input of the customer's statements and at the same time supports a consistent documentation. Part of the effort to document the complaint is transferred to the customer, and information can be processed directly if an interface between e-mails and complaint-management software exists.

A good example of a structured inquiry of relevant complaint information on the Internet is shown in Figure 6.6. Depicted is the complaint site of the New York City Taxi & Limousine Commission (TLC). This

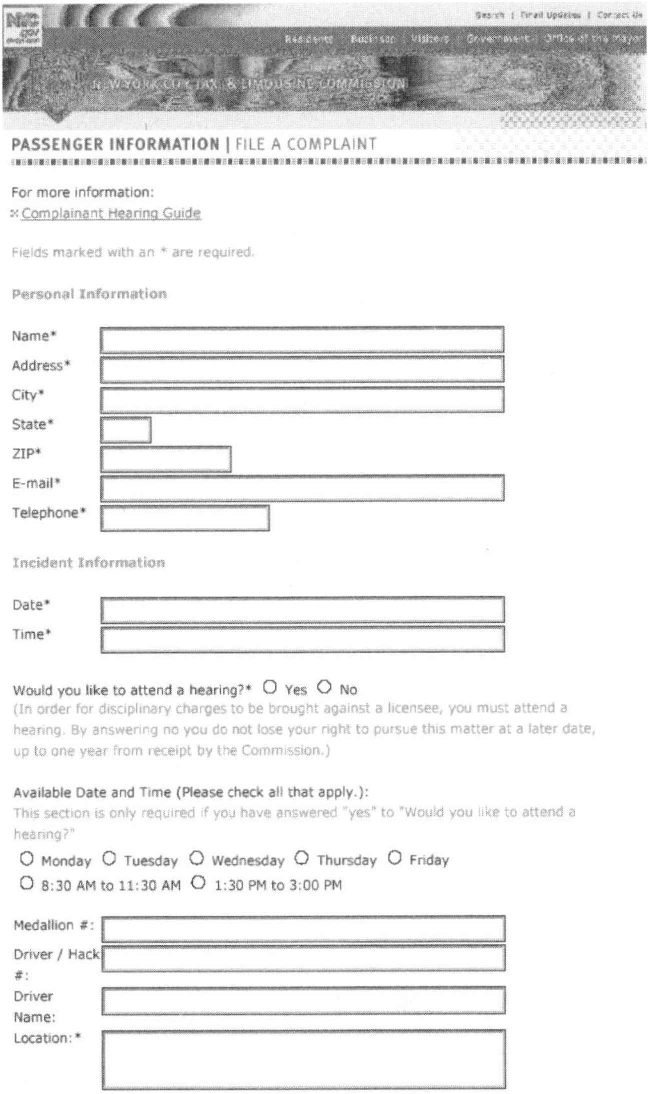

Search | Email Updates | Contact Us

Residents | Business | Visitors | Government | Office of the Mayor

NEW YORK CITY TAXI & LIMOUSINE COMMISSION

PASSENGER INFORMATION | FILE A COMPLAINT

For more information:
Complainant Hearing Guide

Fields marked with an * are required.

Personal Information

Name*
Address*
City*
State*
ZIP*
E-mail*
Telephone*

Incident Information

Date*
Time*

Would you like to attend a hearing?* ○ Yes ○ No
(In order for disciplinary charges to be brought against a licensee, you must attend a hearing. By answering no you do not lose your right to pursue this matter at a later date, up to one year from receipt by the Commission.)

Available Date and Time (Please check all that apply.):
This section is only required if you have answered "yes" to "Would you like to attend a hearing?"

○ Monday ○ Tuesday ○ Wednesday ○ Thursday ○ Friday
○ 8:30 AM to 11:30 AM ○ 1:30 PM to 3:00 PM

Medallion #:
Driver / Hack #:
Driver Name:
Location:*

Figure 6.6 Part A

commission is responsible for the licensing and regulation of New York's 50,000 taxis and limousines, as well as their approximately 100,000 drivers. By going to *http://www.nyc.gov/taxi* and by clicking on "Contact/Visit TLC" and then "File a Complaint," the Internet users have the opportunity to articulate their complaint electronically. The complainants are first requested to provide information about themselves and the time of the incident. Then the complainants can decide if they would like to present their complaint at a hearing and to specify the date and time when they are available. After that, the complainants can give informa-

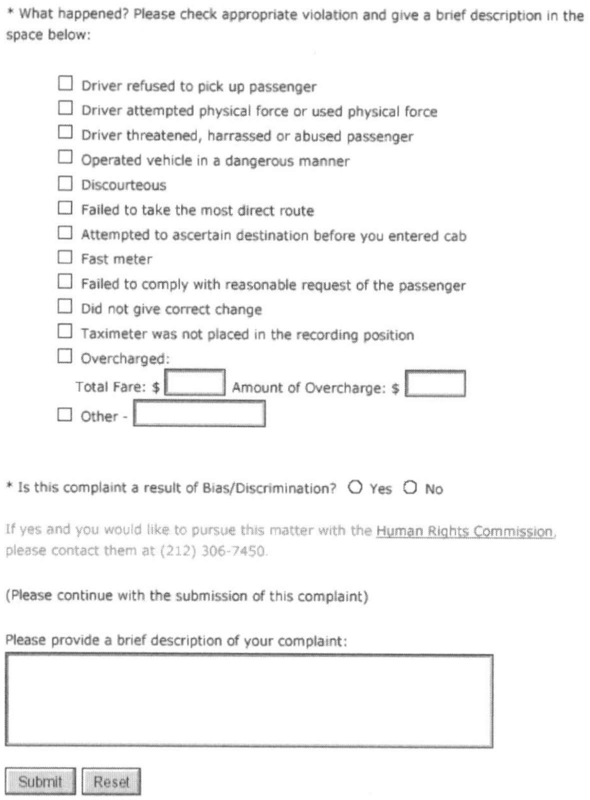

* What happened? Please check appropriate violation and give a brief description in the space below:

☐ Driver refused to pick up passenger
☐ Driver attempted physical force or used physical force
☐ Driver threatened, harrassed or abused passenger
☐ Operated vehicle in a dangerous manner
☐ Discourteous
☐ Failed to take the most direct route
☐ Attempted to ascertain destination before you entered cab
☐ Fast meter
☐ Failed to comply with reasonable request of the passenger
☐ Did not give correct change
☐ Taximeter was not placed in the recording position
☐ Overcharged:

Total Fare: $ [＿＿] Amount of Overcharge: $ [＿＿]

☐ Other - [＿＿＿＿]

* Is this complaint a result of Bias/Discrimination? ○ Yes ○ No

If yes and you would like to pursue this matter with the Human Rights Commission, please contact them at (212) 306-7450.

(Please continue with the submission of this complaint)

Please provide a brief description of your complaint:

[＿＿＿＿＿＿＿＿＿＿＿＿＿＿＿＿]

[Submit] [Reset]

Figure 6.6 Part B

tion about the taxi they took, the driver, and the location where the incident occurred. They are also asked to mark the problem they encountered on a problem list and finally to describe it briefly in their own words. They are also asked to pursue the matter with the Human Rights Commission if they have experienced discrimination.

7

Complaint Processing

At the center of complaint processing lies the question "Who does what, when, and in what order?" To answer this question, the logical sequence of the processing procedures must be defined, the responsibilities at each step of complaint processing determined, the processing deadlines fixed, mechanisms for the monitoring of complaint processing installed, internal communication between the processing locations ensured, and complaint processing documented in an appropriate history.

7.1 THE COMPLAINT-PROCESSING PROCEDURE

7.1.1 IDENTIFICATION OF VARIOUS COMPLAINT-PROCESSING PROCEDURES

7.1.1.1 FUNDAMENTAL CHARACTERIZATION OF COMPLAINT-PROCESSING PROCEDURES

On a rather abstract level, the complaint processing procedures can be uniformly defined and the procedural limits clearly determined. The process begins with the documentation of complaints made either over the telephone or in person or after the receipt of written complaints in the firm. Complaint processing ends with the resolution of the problem and/or a written answer to the customer, or communication in person or by telephone that the complaint case has been closed and, when it is successful, creates a customer who is once again satisfied and loyal.

Upon closer observation, it becomes clear that complaints can be differentiated in many ways, so one cannot proceed based on the assumption that complaint processing is more or less uniform. Some examples from the automotive industry will illustrate this point:

- Customers complain in person to the owner of a car dealership about repeatedly having to wait for a long time when they brought their cars in for service. During the conversation, they could be satisfied with an apology and a small discount as compensation for the inconvenience they experienced.
- Customers complain in writing to the manufacturer's central customer service department that disturbing noises in the engine block have not been fixed, despite a number of trips to the garage. In this case, the responsible associate first informs dissatisfied customers that their complaint has been received, explains to them the processing measures that will be introduced, and forwards the case to a sales unit for the final resolution of the problem. The sales unit then makes an appointment for the customers with the garage and attempts to

eliminate the problem during a more thorough inspection by one of their experts.

- Customers complain to the manufacturer by telephone about a technical problem associated with a fundamental safety risk. Due to the potential danger of the situation, an immediate diagnosis of the problem must take place.
- In a written complaint that is personally directed to the chairman of the board of the manufacturer, large corporate customers threaten to break off the business relationship if a problem is not immediately solved to their satisfaction. First, care should be taken to make sure that the letter is answered by the board member to whom it was addressed; second, in view of the customers' importance to the firm, urgent processing of the case again appears to be called for.
- Customers complain in writing to their dealership about damage that appeared after their warranty expired and demand a goodwill solution. The dealership does not have the authority to decide on its own how to resolve this problem, so it forwards the case to the manufacturer, and the central customer-service department may have to bring in other departments (e.g., the legal department) or sales and marketing units in order to resolve the goodwill case.

These examples make three things clear: (1) Every complaint received initiates an internal processing procedure. (2) The requirements of the processing procedure can be very different, depending on the product affected, the type of problem, the complaint channel, the addressee of the complaint, or the urgency of the reaction. The measures taken and the people or departments included in the process can also depend on whether it is a warranty or goodwill case, or a first or follow-up complaint. (3) It must be determined which basic processing procedures must actually be differentiated and which conditions can be seen as comparable so that a uniform definition of the process can take place.

7.1.1.2 INDEPENDENT, COOPERATIVE, AND TRANSFER PROCESSES

At an intermediate level of abstraction, fundamental key processes of complaint processing can be differentiated.

Definition of Independent, Cooperative, and Transfer Processes

The first classification takes place from the perspective of the department responsible for operative complaint processing. Depending on the extent to which the division responsible for complaint processing can manage the complaint processing alone or requires the help of other organizational areas, three basic types of complaint processing procedures can be differentiated:

(1) Independent Processes. The division that is responsible for operative complaint processing may process a complaint alone (without including other divisions) all the way until its final stage.
(2) Cooperative Processes. In order to resolve the case completely, the complaint department must refer to information or to the expertise

of other departments. These departments will then be requested to take a stand on a certain circumstance or to clarify a legal position. The closure of the complaint case takes place through the complaint management department itself.

(3) Transfer Processes. In this case, it is necessary that the complaint case be transferred to another division. The "Complaint Ownership" goes completely over to a new unit within the organization, which then resolves the case with regard to the customer.

Factors Influencing the Choice and Further Specification of the Three Process Types

The question of which of these processes should be chosen is dependent upon a series of influencing factors. Among these are the costs of the solution desired by the customer, the know-how that is present in the complaint management department, the categorization of the complaint as a first or follow-up complaint, or warranty or goodwill case, and the complaint channel and addressee chosen by the customer. In addition, the product and the type of problem also play a role.

An important prerequisite for the creation of an independent processing procedure is the definition of a maximum amount that can be spent to resolve the complaint, up to which point an extensive investigation of the individual case is not required. Also decisive here is the specific know-how required to diagnose the problem. The more the employees who are responsible for the operative complaint processing have the appropriate expertise or the immediate access to the database of problem solutions, the more feasible become the independent processing procedures.

The decision between first and follow-up complaint is also relevant to the process, because the complaints are related to different types of problems. While first complaints deal with a product-related concern, follow-up complaints deal with an additional problem perceived by the customer in connection with the complaint processing. First complaints are thus to be processed with the inclusion of specialist departments if the problem implies a certain cost amount or technical complexity, while follow-up complaints are mainly to be handled in the context of independent processing procedures by the complaint management department alone.

Warranty or goodwill cases are "classic" transfer or cooperative procedures, since the presence of legal or otherwise specified requirements usually has to be reviewed. It is also possible, however, to make the review requirement dependent on the cost of the solution so that an independent processing procedure for a clearly defined subset of these cases can be determined.

To a certain extent, the customers' articulation behavior also determines the necessary processing procedure. Complaints can reach the firm through very different ways. Organizational units that, from the firm's perspective, should not be the primary units entrusted with this task are also included in the complaint-receipt process. In order to assure rapid and correct processing, all units that accept complaints must be recorded as process starting points. Further, clearly defined transfer processes must be determined, and the organizational units receiving the complaints must be connected with the responsible processing stations by way of specific forwarding guidelines.

In articulating their complaints, customers may turn to a given addressee in the firm with their concern, perhaps to a member of company management that they know by name. In this case also, it is necessary to determine transfer procedures that will guarantee that the incident is forwarded in a way that is appropriate to the problem. For such cases, cooperative procedures may be defined through which the addressee is integrated in the response activities. In that case, they would, for example, sign the receipt confirmation or conclude the case with a personal answer.

The specific character of the processing procedures depends upon other factors as well. In the cooperative procedures, it is highly dependent upon which product or service is affected as to which organizational units must be brought in, since different responsibilities in research and development or production, for instance, may be at issue in each case. Additionally, the type of problem often determines the processing requirements, because different technical expertise is required each time and because different organizational units are affected (e.g., the order acceptance department in the case of a delivery mistake and the deliverer in the case of shipping damages).

7.1.1.3 ROUTINE AND NONROUTINE PROCESSES

A second classification of processing procedures is based on the criterion of reaction urgency, which suggests that a differentiation be made between routine and nonroutine procedures.

The processes that can be characterized as routine processes are those that refer to the vast majority of "normal" complaints with no special sense of urgency. Complaints with a great sense of urgency demand nonroutine processes. For cases in which the safety of customers is jeopardized or particularly high property losses could occur, preferred attention and handling are required. The same applies to the complaints of especially important customers who threaten to switch to the competition or bring in official bodies or the media. In such cases, it is necessary to institute nonroutine procedures that, for defined levels of urgency, provide for the immediate notification of specific decision-makers in the firm who have the professional competence to apply the appropriate case solution and processing. This may occur by linking certain types of problems to different levels of reaction urgency through software. When such a problem arises, the processing employees receive a message on the screen that they must inform a particular person immediately. This person then handles the situation. A comprehensive definition of the behavior is neither possible nor practical for these cases.

Spotlight 2 shows how Thomas Cook Airline is prepared to ensure a quick and effective complaint processing and complaint reaction, even if customer problems that are hard to predict lead to a high complaint volume.

SPOTLIGHT 2

A Fast and Effective Reaction to Events with a High Expected Complaint Volume at Thomas Cook Airlines

Dramatic incidents in the airline industry—massive flight delays, for example—lead to a situation in which a large number of passengers are affected by the problem at the same time. As a result, airlines can anticipate a high volume of complaints about this problem.

In order to counteract an escalation of customer dissatisfaction in cases such as these, in order to prevent duplicate investigations, and especially in order to ensure uniform trouble-shooting and rapid complaint processing, the airline division of the Thomas Cook Group in Germany has established a special processing procedure. The main features of this procedure are that it is initiated at the earliest possible moment after the problem appears and that it ensures fast, consistent processing when massive numbers of complaints are expected. The following case example illustrates the way that this process works.

Because of a defective cockpit window, the flight from Punta Cana (Dominican Republic) cannot take off on schedule and reaches its Munich (Germany) destination only after a 25-hour delay.

The first phase of complaint management is already initiated at the airport in Punta Cana. By providing catered meals and suitable accommodations, the employees on site do everything they can to make this unplanned stay in Punta Cana as comfortable as possible for the passengers.

At the same time, the second phase of the systematic handling of the problem with the delayed flight is initiated by forwarding all the relevant information about the incident and about actions that have already been taken to the central customer service department of Thomas Cook Airlines in Germany by telex. There, one employee takes over central responsibility for the ongoing investigation into the incident and the processing of expected complaints regarding the flight delay. The investigation is based on information from the Operations Control Center (OCC), the Cabin Report, and the Handling Irregularity Report, which contains a brief description of the problem and the actions taken.

With respect to the complaint reaction, the employee makes a decision regarding compensatory payments on the basis of a predefined scope of goodwill provided for flight delays. The employee also prepares a letter that informs the passengers about the reasons for the flight delay, specifies the compensatory payment, and clarifies potential legal claims.

If problem situations that affect a large number of travelers and thus can lead to massive numbers of complaints are dealt with in this preventative form, a series of positive benefits can be achieved:

- An active effort to reduce the dissatisfaction of affected customers takes place already at the moment the problem occurs, when they are offered adequate support services.
- Naming a centrally responsible employee for such incidents ensures that the event can be thoroughly investigated and the reaction processes initiated before any complaints are received, an approach that permits a faster and more effective process without time-consuming and cost-intensive multiple investigations.
- All complainants experience a uniform reaction to the same problem; the same scope of goodwill is thus reliably applied. The firm can therefore avoid a situation in which complainants receive unequal treatment and have new cause for dissatisfaction.
- Since the complaint management system is used by all Thomas Cook, Inc., providers, every employee can trace the compensatory payments that customers have already received. Consequently, expensive double payouts can be prevented—for instance, in cases in which affected passengers file a claim with the airline directly and with their tour operators as well.

Colette Rueckert-Hennen
Vice President Customer Management/Customer Services
Thomas Cook AG, Germany

7.1.2 ANALYSIS OF COMPLAINT-PROCESSING PROCEDURES

The starting point for a systematic design of complaint processing procedures is an analysis of how the current procedures are designed to achieve both efficiency and complaint satisfaction among customers.

Analysis of the Current Complaint-Processing Procedures from the Perspective of the Firm

The first step is the analysis of the current organizational procedures of complaint processing. The basis for a differentiated analysis is the consultation of a representative sample of complaint cases that were received within a certain time period (e.g., one year). These cases must be analyzed with differing degrees of detail. First, the fundamental process phases of each complaint processing case should be identified (e.g., internal transfers, case examination, intermediate reply, decision, final answer). Then, upon evaluating the available documents, it must be determined which organizational unit has been active to what extent in the individual phases (e.g., sales force, central customer service department, management). The length of time spent by each organizational unit on each of the various activities must also be recorded.

This view of the internal processes of complaint processing will be complemented by an analysis of the corresponding customer processes of perceived complaint resolution.

Analysis of the Complaint-Processing Procedures from the Perspective of the Customer

This may occur by undertaking a contact-point analysis of the complaint processing procedure on the basis of representatively chosen complaint cases. In doing so, all customer contacts up to the final resolution of the problem are ascertained and visualized in a flowchart, the intervals between the individual contact points are documented, and interviews with complainants are carried out concerning their experiences at the respective contact points.

In the context of the first process step, contact point identification, all the interactions must be documented: starting with the complaint articulation and continuing with the confirmation of receipt, intermediate reply, and any follow-up inquiries by telephone or in writing, all the way until the final answer is provided.

A variation of the flowchart representation, variously designated as "Service Blueprinting" (Shostack 1987) or "Service Mapping" (Kingman-Brundage 1992), provides a suitable instrument for the systematic visualization of the processing procedures as the customer experiences them. What is special about this technique is that the sequence of the experienced complaint case is documented from the perspective of the customer affected and that it is made known through a "line of complaint evidence" which areas of the complaint management processes are visible to the customer ("onstage actions") and which take place "backstage" (see Figure 7.1).

On the basis of this visualized customer process, former complainants can then be consulted about their experiences at each contact point and about their assessment of the acceptability of the reaction time in the context of contact-experience measurement.

The results of the contact-point analysis form the starting point for the new conceptualization of the complaint processing procedures from the perspective of the firm.

7.1.3 SPECIFICATION AND VISUALIZATION OF COMPLAINT-PROCESSING PROCEDURES

Specification of Complaint Processing Procedures

The first level of specification in the complaint processing procedures is reached when the procedures are assigned to general classes of participating organizational units (independent, cooperative, or transfer process) or to levels of urgency (routine or nonroutine procedures).

Following this assignment of the procedures, the next level of specification consists of defining the basic activities, the corresponding responsibilities, and the processing times. This involves processing steps such as "Prepare Confirmation of Receipt/Intermediate Reply" or "Forward for Comment" or decision nodes such as "Resolution within X

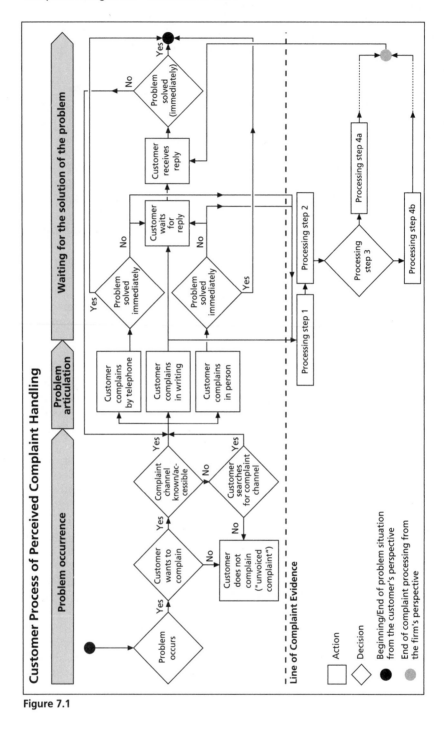

Figure 7.1

Hours Possible?" or "Comment Arrived?" upon which the different processing methods and their corresponding activities are dependent. This process specification also includes the identification of interfaces at which the output of one organizational unit represents the input of another organizational unit at the same time. This determination should take place as much as possible in interdepartmental teams, whose members represent the participating business units. In this way, a consensus can be reached on a process sequence that is efficient and transparent and that takes into consideration the perspectives of those affected by that process.

Visualization of the Complaint-Processing Procedures

In order to ensure a quick overview of the processing procedures, it is recommended that the processes be visualized in a flowchart. The phases of a process with the appropriate inputs and outputs, as well as the interfaces, can be immediately identified. One can recognize whether the subsequent activities can be dealt with simultaneously—process phases run parallel to one another—or which phases are dependent upon preceding subprocesses and process steps. In this way, it is possible to uncover sources of potential errors and to determine corresponding control points in the process (Bhote 1991). Responsibilities as well as scheduled dates for individual processing steps can then be determined and visualized (see Figure 7.2).

In this simple example, only the rather rough visualization of a single (cooperative) processing procedure occurs. Normally, however, it is necessary to depict special and detailed processes for complaints that reach the firm by way of different complaint channels (e.g., in person, over the telephone, in writing, or electronically).

7.2 RESPONSIBILITIES DURING COMPLAINT PROCESSING

From the standpoint of customer-oriented complaint processing, three relevant responsibilities result from the structure of the direct complaint management process:

- On the overall management process level—the Process Owner
- On the individual case processing level—the Complaint Owner
- On the level of the individual phases of complaint processing—the Task Owner

7.2.1 THE PROCESS OWNER

Complaints are frequently articulated to different people or departments in the firm. Consequently, employees from different departments must be trained to deal with dissatisfied customers and must be informed of the person to whom the complaint should be forwarded. In many cases, one organizational unit, for example, the customer-service department, cannot manage the processing of a complaint by itself. It is often necessary to include other departments or sales units in order to reach a targeted solution to the problem. In addition, interdepartmen-

Example of a Complaint-Processing Procedure for Written Complaints

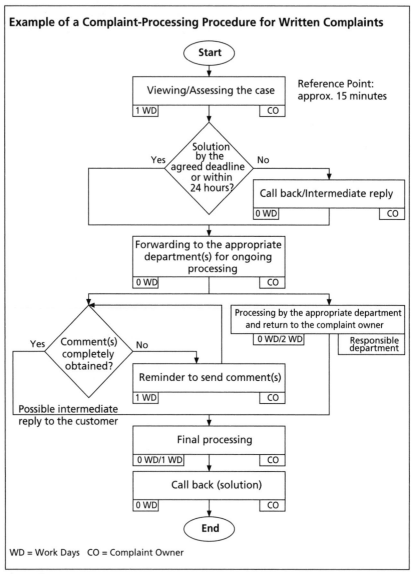

Figure 7.2

tal management tasks arise from the dissemination and use of complaint analysis and controlling information.

The position within the firm that has the inclusive responsibility and accountability for the procedures that arise as part of complaint management, or the person that assumes this position, is designated as the Process Owner. This Process Owner directs and coordinates all the complaint-management task areas—across task-area and departmental boundaries. In firms that have a central "Complaint Management" or "Customer Care" department, the function of the Process Owner usually falls to the decision-maker responsible for this area.

7.2.2 THE COMPLAINT OWNER

As has been previously described in connection with the complaint-acceptance procedure (Chapter 6.1.1), the person who is first to be informed by a customer about a problem is responsible for recognizing, documenting, and processing the problem as a complaint. This person has ownership of the complaint and is designated as the Complaint Owner.

It is principally the task of the Complaint Owners to solve the problem immediately if it lies within their area of competence. Should their competence be exceeded, but an immediate resolution is possible in principle, they have to inform the responsible party, introduce troubleshooting procedures, and make certain that an arrangement desired by the customer takes place. Consequently, the "Complaint Ownership" in this case ends with the resolution of the problem.

For complaints with problems that make the inclusion of other people or departments necessary, the respective Complaint Owners are responsible for the smooth and timely coordination and handling of the processing procedure. They must make sure that promises to the customer are kept or deviations from agreed-upon arrangements are communicated and elucidated without delay. The line areas participating in the process perform a coordinating function and see to it that the measures that have been agreed on are observed properly and within the time limits. They also have the function of the "Team Leader" within the team of employees participating in the process and as such initiate common efforts toward continuous improvements in efficiency and effectiveness. In their relationship to the Process Owner, the tasks of the Complaint Owners consist of monitoring the outcomes of the processing procedures and presenting the results, as well as suggestions for improving the process.

In complaint cases that must be turned over to other units within the organization for processing and final replies, the question of whether Complaint Ownership is also given up may be asked. The situation can be regulated in this manner, but this solution cannot be recommended for all cases. If, for instance, bank customers complain to their account executive at the local branch, they do so because they expect that their addressee will assume responsibility for their case. In complaint cases in which the addressees turn the processing over to the central customer service department due to a lack of decision-making authority, they should remain informed of how things are progressing, especially about the solution offered to the customer, and should maintain contact with the customer. At the same time, a Complaint Owner in the central complaint management department is then responsible on this organizational level for seeing that the procedures of complaint processing are carried out according to available principles and serves as the contact person for the Complaint Owner at the branch level.

7.2.3 THE TASK OWNER

In addition to the structures of responsibility for the complete complaint-management process (Process Owner) and the respective individual case processing (Complaint Owner), the responsibilities for the individual steps in the course of complaint processing must likewise be determined.

Employees who are occupied with carrying out the individual tasks during the complaint processing (examination of the case, preparation of intermediate replies) are Task Owners. A corresponding task profile exists with specific case-handling instructions, time limits, and clearly regulated competencies. The Task Owners must be informed of which input the preliminary process step will provide them, what added value they contribute to the solution of the problem, and which output is expected of them. At the same time, the determination of the task extent and authority will also regulate which problems necessitate that they get in touch with the Complaint Owner or when they can introduce measures independently.

7.3 DETERMINATION OF PROCESSING DEADLINES

Studies confirm that the speed with which firms react to a complaint significantly influences the satisfaction of the customer. A survey of callers to a service hotline showed an unmistakable connection between the percentage of fully satisfied customers and the reaction time of the firm. Seventy percent of customers who received a callback within a time span of four hours were very satisfied, whereas the corresponding percentage of customers who did not receive an answer until after four hours was 31 percent (Adamson 1993).

Clark, Kaminski, and Rink (1992) arrived at similar results in their experimental studies. It was shown that those persons who received an answer to their written complaints relatively quickly were substantially more satisfied than those whose complaint reply took longer to arrive. If there was no reaction at all to the complaint by the firm (which occurred in 23 percent of cases), the attitude toward this firm significantly declined on all image dimensions. The complainants were convinced that the firm did not care about dissatisfied customers and did not treat customers fairly. The majority expressed their intention to switch to a competitor in the future.

This proves that active complaint management also means deadline management. Firms that take customer problems seriously must react to complaints immediately, by seeking direct contact with the dissatisfied customer—even if the problem itself cannot be resolved immediately. It is also important to make sure that the processing of the complaint takes place quickly and within a previously fixed time frame, and that contact with the customer is reestablished, especially when deadlines are exceeded. It is assumed, of course, that clear deadlines exist for all identified complaint processing procedures, as well as for their subprocesses and processing steps.

In order to schedule the deadlines, two types of time indicators must be determined and related to each other: (1) Processing times that affect external customers and thus exert a decisive influence on their complaint satisfaction. They apply to the entire time span from the complaint articulation to the final reply. Also included under this type of time indicator are time limits, by which time a confirmation of receipt or intermediate reply in the case of longer processing times must be sent to the customer. (2) Processing times for individual process phases as targets for the Task Owner.

The external, customer-oriented time targets depend to a great extent on the internal processing times. Therefore, every scheduling has to use them as a starting point. For the individual processing procedures, the entire processing time must be defined as the period of time from the receipt of the complaint in the firm until the resolution of the problem. Then the amount of time must be calculated and assessed for the individual process phases ranging from processing times and idle times before and after processing to internal transport times associated with the transfer of the complaint incident from one processing unit to another.

On the basis of this time analysis, the Process Owner and the Complaint Owner can engage in joint considerations about the reduction of ineffective time components and establish phase-related periods as internal time standards. In doing so, various factors must be taken into consideration. Besides the extent and complexity of the work to be carried out, these factors include the personnel and technological resources available, as well as the complaint volume and the expectations of the complainants regarding the firm's reaction speed. In any event, it depends on the fixing of time standards that represent feasible targets for employees and departments participating in the processing. If unrealistic processing times are set, exactly the opposite of what should be achieved with time scheduling will occur. Delays in meeting deadlines that lie outside the immediate sphere of influence of the Task Owner become the rule. The standards set are not taken seriously. The employees become unmotivated. Customers are promised unreliable deadlines, which contributes to an increase in their dissatisfaction.

When the planned processing times for all process steps have been defined from the internal perspective of the firm, the customer-related time targets for intermediate replies and final answers can be determined.

Another step is reached when time targets such as these are communicated to the customer as a universal standard and promise of performance, such as "We'll solve your problems within seven days!" The indispensable prerequisite for an official publication of standards like these is the fact that they have proved their worth over a long period of time. If this is not the case and the standards are missed to a considerable extent, the firm can count on a massive increase in customer dissatisfaction and corresponding internal problems and de-motivation.

In determining internal standards and external temporal performance promises, different measurement categories are usually applied. The internal time targets are commonly given in workdays, while the customers base their understanding on calendar days when they are given temporal performance promises. For this reason, the internal targets that are calculated must be adjusted for external communication to consider nonwork times (weekends, holidays).

7.4 INSTALLATION OF MECHANISMS FOR THE MONITORING OF COMPLAINT PROCESSING

Since the reaction speed and the observance of promised deadlines substantially influence the complaint satisfaction of the customer, the firm must install systems that provide the on-time processing of complaint cases according to the standards that have been set and call attention to time delays that represent deviations from those standards: an employee-oriented reminder system and, coupled with it, an escalation system that spans all hierarchical levels.

7.4.1 THE EMPLOYEE-ORIENTED REMINDER SYSTEM

If the deadlines that have been set are exceeded during the course of processing a complaint, the respective Task Owner must be made aware of this fact and reminded of it. Manual administration of internal reminders hardly seems possible when the complaint volume is high, since the Complaint Owner cannot have a complete overview of the status of all the complaint cases and the respective deadlines that have been scheduled. The utilization of a software-supported complaint-management system, in which the time standards are clearly set down and which allows for automatic reminders, proves to be nearly indispensable.

If the time delay can be attributed to their own inattentiveness, the reminded employees must then process the case immediately, or "preferentially." Reasons for exceeding the processing deadline may, however, also lie outside the Complaint Owner's sphere of influence. This is the case, for example, when a specific product defect leads to an unexpectedly large increase in complaint volume and causes the complaint capacity to be exceeded. When such a development arises, the Task Owner should inform the Complaint Owner early so that a remedy can be found through short-term corrective measures.

If, in the course of complaint analysis, it is discovered that processing deadlines have been exceeded numerous times by certain Task Owners or in specific problem areas, the delays must be systematically analyzed for their causes and appropriate measures must be devised, either to adjust the standards or to change the procedures so that the standards can be observed in the future.

7.4.2 THE HIERARCHY-SPANNING ESCALATION SYSTEM

In the case of a reminder system, the employees themselves are informed of the delays in their processing of complaints. In the context of an escalation system, however, the complaint cases for which the processing deadline has been exceeded are transferred to higher levels in the hierarchy, all the way up to the CEO, at set time intervals.

Three main goals are associated with the establishment of this type of escalation system:

- Direct pressure is exerted on the Task Owner and the Complaint Owner to keep the performance promises that have been made to customers in terms of content and deadlines. For those affected, it is embarrassing to have to answer repeatedly to the person in the next higher position about why the processing deadlines have been exceeded for no good reason. The escalation process thus serves as an internal medium for more discipline in complaint processing.

- Numerous messages regarding noncompliance with deadlines in the context of complaint processing force Process Owners to deal with the structural causes of process deficiencies and to develop appropriate corrective measures.
- Managers at higher levels of the hierarchy are immediately signaled through the escalation about the danger that existing customer dissatisfaction is substantially increasing. They must, therefore, see to an immediate resolution of the problem and verify that the customer has already been informed of the delay and its causes. Senior staff is also personally confronted with customers' problems and must take up the task of dealing with questions about the proper handling of dissatisfied customers and the relevance of complaint management. This can lead to a greater sensitivity to problems on the part of top management and promote the willingness to accord complaint management the attention and support it requires.

In order to determine the specific design of the escalation process, the number of reminder days must first be generally determined, after which time the complaint case escalates. At the same time, it must also be determined: (1) the number of levels of escalation, (2) the people responsible at each of those levels, and (3) the number of days allowed before a complaint case is turned over to the next level of escalation (Figure 7.3). The practical execution of the escalation system presupposes the utilization of a software-supported complaint-management system in the case of substantial complaint volume.

Spotlight 3 shows an example from Xerox, Inc., of how an escalation system can be successfully used to promote speedier complaint processing.

Example of the Design of an Escalation System

Escalation level	Exceeding of the time standard in workdays	Responsible person
1	2	Line manager
2	4	Department manager
3	7	Division manager
4	10	Board of directors

Figure 7.3

SPOTLIGHT 3

The Escalation System of Xerox

Since 1991, the German subsidiary of Xerox has been working with a computer-supported complaint management system that permits the decentralized acceptance of claims and ensures their transference to the appropriate responsible employee. The priority placed on complaint management in this company is shown by the levels of escalation that reach all the way to management.

Since March 2000, the firm has been using a new SAP/R3-supported software program that was specifically adapted to its internal processes and given the name Xecure (**Xe**rox **Cu**stomer **Re**lationship) by the Customer Satisfaction Management Division, which is in charge of this complaint-management system.

The procedure of claims processing is primarily supported by two main targets, and noncompliance with these targets triggers escalation processes: (1) The first goal consists of contacting the customers within 48 hours after the claim is received, discussing the resolution with them, and agreeing upon a deadline for settlement. (2) This settlement deadline is then recorded in the complaint-management system, and its observance is monitored.

The basic path taken by a claim is illustrated in the following example: A customer turns to the responsible salesperson for an incorrect invoice. The salesperson identifies the customer in the Xecure System via the invoice number and, by selecting the claim type "Invoice Claim," initiates the forwarding of the claim to the competent associate in the accounting department who is informed about the incident via an automatically generated e-mail. This associate gets in touch with the customers, informs them about the approach that will be taken, agrees on a settlement deadline with them, and records the relevant information in Xecure. Only after the customer has received a credit or a corrected invoice is the process concluded and the solution and the cause of the problem documented in the system.

If the associate has not contacted the customers within 48 hours or the agreed-upon settlement goal has not been achieved, the escalation system goes into effect and transfers the process automatically to the manager of the Collection Department. This person can intervene in the processing or else discuss the problem with the subordinate and clarify the reason for the delay. At this escalation level, what is important is not to exert pressure on the subordinate to observe the procedures, but rather to react as quickly as possible with regard to the customer. If no additional activities related to the incident in question are registered by Xecure in the status of this first escalation level within another 48 hours, the incident escalates directly to the Vice President of Customer Administration.

This escalation process is the same for all divisions of the company and always ends at the highest executive level, or with top management, in the second step. Multiple transfers of an incident between different employees and repeated delays in settlement dates also lead to escalations.

The so-called "Closed Loop Process" was introduced in order to optimize the process and achieve record satisfaction with the claims processing: Every week, an external agency receives 10 percent of the closed cases recorded in the Xecure system and asks the customers whether the claim was resolved satisfactorily. If the situation was not fully resolved, the Customer Satisfaction Management Division is informed. This division then gets in touch with the processor who closed the case, as well as with the supervisor, in order to bring about a final settlement.

With the implementation of the escalation process, Xerox Inc., found an effective way to manage complaints to their customers' satisfaction. This is demonstrated in particular by average processing times of five days with a claims volume of approximately 1,000 incidents per month.

Esther Brottinger
Customer Satisfaction Management
Xerox GmbH

7.5 DESIGN OF THE INTERNAL COMMUNICATION BETWEEN THE PROCESSING UNITS

Firms that practice active complaint management must determine to which information the processing units should refer and which paths the communication should take place. The Complaint Owner and the Task Owner concerned should undertake these considerations together. It is also their common task to make these communication processes known within the firm in order to ensure smooth processing of complaints.

With respect to the information required, the specific data that are recorded for each individual case must be available at each step in the processing procedure to the extent required. In addition, the processors must receive information about the results of each preliminary step in the processing procedure. If new insights arise during the course of the complaint processing regarding the cause of the problem, for instance, or if the customer submits new documentation, the proper procedure for the forwarding of this information to the appropriate stations must be regulated.

The communication between the units can occur in writing, by telephone, in person, or by e-mail. Principal consideration should be given to those communication media that allow a rapid transmittal of information and minimize idle or transport times. This is the case primarily with electronic mail systems, especially when they are integrated into a software-supported system of complaint management that directly assigns the mail messages to the appropriate case. If it is not possible to fall back on systems like these, contact in person or by telephone, as well as by faxes, represent suitable media.

Independent of which media are used, all processing steps must be thoroughly documented, along with their results, and made accessible to the associates. This is quite possible in the context of a software-supported system of complaint management because the processing activities are entered into the system and the database is available to all those participating in the process. Spotlight 4 provides an impressive example of how online information use is possible with the help of this kind of system and how the processing procedure can be accelerated and improved in this way.

SPOTLIGHT 4

Optimization of the Processing Procedures Via Online Transparency at DaimlerChrysler AG, Global Service & Parts

In the claims management system, the responsible processors are informed via online information about any similar incidents that already exist. In this way, duplicate or repeated processing of claims and inquiries can be prevented. This means that all the persons who are involved in the processing of a claim are automatically and promptly informed as to processes, measures, and insights that are available for or were undertaken in like or similar claims cases. Redundancies and parallel searches can thus be avoided. The way in which the active informational use of online information can accelerate the processing procedure of a claim and improve the quality of the processing is shown by the following example:

A wholesaler complains about the wrong delivery of spare parts. The claim is recorded in the system. The processor responsible clears up the problem by checking the inventory level of the replacement part in question. The investigation shows that all the parts from a particular batch were incorrectly labeled by the supplier, and the wrong goods were delivered due to the incorrect labeling. The inventory level is corrected as soon as possible, and the goods with the correct labels are provided.

As soon as the cause of the error is known, it is recorded in the database system, as is the removal of the error. If another claim on the same replacement part comes in to a different employee at some later point in time, an online reference appears in the system to the effect that in the case at hand a supplier error arose, but the problem has been eliminated in the meantime and the correct goods are now deliverable. Thanks to this information, every employee who accepts and processes a claim can immediately give the customer specific details about the cause of the mistake, the corrective measures that were introduced, and the resolution of the problem. An investigation with a second verification of the inventory level, as would be necessary without the information from the database, is unnecessary.

Peter Diehsle
Global Service & Parts
DaimlerChrysler AG

7.6 THE COMPLAINT-PROCESSING HISTORY

In order to maintain the transparency of the measures that have been implemented and carried out for the employees as well as for the complainants and to ensure target-oriented communication with the customer, the individual processing steps must be documented in the context of the complaint-processing history, along with their results, for each individual complaint case. If all the associates who deal with customer complaints can refer to these histories, they are in a position to provide the customer or internal conversation counterparts with information about the status of the processing. In this way, clarity is brought about and errors are avoided, such as would be the case if the customers received different information from different people about the status of their concern.

The following information in particular must be chronologically documented:

- date/time on which the processing activity should be completed pursuant to the time standards defined
- date/time on which the processing activity is actually completed pursuant to the time standards defined
- going over/under the time targets
- the responsible employee (Task Owner)
- the respective processing result (e.g., intermediate reply sent or result of a judicial assessment of the case)
- processing status of the activity (not yet in process, in process, completed)
- type of reaction to the complaint as well as the individual case resolution.

8

Complaint Reaction

The term "Complaint Reaction" encompasses all the complaint management activities that the customer perceives during the complaint handling process and that have a direct effect on the customer's complaint satisfaction. Among these activities are the immediate handling of complainants, the realized solution to the problem, and all the communication with the customer during the processing of the complaint. All these aspects will be addressed in this chapter. It will also be shown to what extent a differentiation of the complaint reaction that is based on the customer's value can prove useful and how the interaction with the complainant can be documented in the complaint history.

8.1 BASIC RULES OF BEHAVIOR FOR HANDLING COMPLAINANTS

Many customers can completely sympathize with mistakes and errors occurring. This understanding very quickly changes to nonunderstanding and indignation, however, when employees show no willingness to eliminate the problem or make up for the damage. Customers are still turned away, put off, transferred, or even suspected of wanting to cheat the firm. Typical statements by employees include the following: "I can't do anything about that, either!" "I'm not responsible for that!" "My colleague does that!" "You must have used the product incorrectly!" "Are you sure you purchased that from us?" Reactions like these are sure to drive away the customer for good.

In order to avoid this danger and ensure appropriate behavior on the part of employees during communication with the complainant, fundamental rules of behavior are required, both for the direct conversation and for the answering of written complaints.

8.1.1 RULES OF BEHAVIOR FOR THE DIRECT CONVERSATION WITH COMPLAINANTS

Situations involving a direct confrontation with complainants in person or on the telephone represent a great challenge for employees. Complainants frequently react emotionally and indignantly, exaggerate and confront the employees with personal reproaches. Under these conditions, it is difficult to control one's own emotions, have a reassuring effect, and work out a constructive solution with the customer. Comprehensive explanation of the correct behavior and systematic training are thus required. For this, the following rules of behavior, which relate to five typical phases of a complaint conversation, can be used as guidelines (Dietze 1997).

Greeting Phase

In the greeting phase, it is decided whether a destructive argument or a constructive conversation will develop. When employees receive a complaint by phone, their voice should sound friendly and open to signal their willingness to talk and make it difficult for the irritated customer to act rudely.

If employees receive customer complaints in person, they also must approach the customer in an open and friendly manner. The employee should maintain eye contact and focus his attention on the customer. It is especially important that the conversation be conducted in a calm environment if the problem is a difficult one. By retiring to appropriate premises and offering the customer a seat, the customer receives the message that the employee wants to take time for him and his problem and takes his complaint seriously. This shifting of the complaint dialogue to a separate conversation area would seem to be especially necessary if extremely irritated customers attempt to use this opportunity to achieve effects by their behavior with the other customers who are present, by raising their voices, or by making certain statements (Dietze 1997; Haeske 2001).

Aggression-Reduction Phase

After the greeting, the customer should be given the opportunity to depict the incident from his point of view. The employee must express her care and attentiveness through her facial expressions, eye contact, and body language. What is important verbally is to express regret to the customer for the unpleasantness that has arisen or to apologize officially. This gesture is often difficult for employees, especially when they see the incident differently or have not caused the problem. Nevertheless, such an expression of regret or apology is necessary because it is perceived as the instrument through which understanding for the customer's annoyance is expressed and because it represents a key requirement for building a personal relationship with the customer that will be important as the conversation progresses.

In the aggression-reduction phase, what is of primary importance is to allow the complainant to have a chance to speak. He must be given the chance to let off steam. It is possible that an error caused by the firm has put him in a very uncomfortable situation, and strong resentment has been building up. Outbursts of anger during complaints lead to feelings of relief (Bennet 1997). Only when the customer has had the opportunity to express this irritation will it be possible to bring the conversation down to a factual level and to have a constructive discussion about possible solutions. Accordingly, the employee must first allow the customers to have their say—without interrupting them—and must listen attentively in order to be able to record the specific circumstances of the problem correctly. While she is doing so, she should make notes. The fact that his personal conversation is being recorded in writing pushes the customer to describe the incident more carefully and realistically. During telephone conversations, short affirmative remarks should be made to demonstrate to the customer that he is being listened to attentively and that the problem has in fact been understood.

The most common error that is made in this phase consists of interrupting the customer, whether it is with counterclaims and instructions, or with hypotheses for the possible causes of the problem or hasty offers of solutions or compensation. The employee may be completely in the right, but in this phase, interruptions like these prevent reduction of the aggression and development of a constructive conversation. Instead, they cause the customer to react even more angrily and cause the situation to escalate.

In this part of the complaint conversation, a situation may arise in which extremely annoyed customers personally insult the employee. Verbal attacks such as these are not to be taken personally, and certainly not to be answered in like fashion. It is necessary to maintain an inner distance from the criticism and react calmly to accusations of guilt, exaggerations, and insults. This does not mean that all attacks have to be taken completely. Especially rude insults should be calmly rejected in the subsequent phases of the conversation.

Conflict-Settlement Phase

After the customer has been given the opportunity to express his annoyance and present the problem situation from his subjective point of view, it is then important to bring the conversation to a factual level. In order to do this, it is necessary to clarify the facts precisely by asking a series of specific questions. It is vital that all circumstances that are meaningful from the customer's point of view and for further processing be thoroughly addressed.

This factual dialogue contributes to conflict reduction in the conversation. This applies especially when understanding for the customer's individual situation and for the extent of his irritation is expressed in a believable manner and with empathy. Even while showing sensitiveness toward the customer, however, the employees should avoid further admissions of guilt or assignments of guilt to other employees or departments in the firm.

Problem-Solution Phase

If the conversation can be successfully continued on a factual level and the situation explained clearly during the conflict-adjustment phase, the basis for talking about a suitable problem solution with the customer has been established. Demands articulated by the customer during the first phases may be seen in a different light and modified after the facts have been clarified. Solutions offered by the employees are now perceived as logical conclusions of the factual analysis and thus have a much greater chance of being accepted than would have been the case at the beginning of the conversation.

Many times a suitable solution cannot be reached in the first conversation, since the causes and possible solutions must be investigated. Here it is advisable to offer the customer a callback or an additional conversation, making an exact promise about the time of the call or conversation. It is imperative that the appointment given be kept. If this is not possible despite every effort being made, the complainant is to be informed about the reason for the delay in a timely manner.

As a matter of principle, the postponement of the immediate problem solution is not the best solution, neither for the customer nor for the firm, as other time- and cost-intensive steps must then be undertaken. If, however, such a postponement cannot be avoided, it at least has the positive effect that the search for a problem solution is less stressful than it would have been had it taken place in the presence of the customer, who leaves the provider with the feeling that someone is taking care of his problem now.

Conclusive Phase

In the conclusive phase of the conversation, the suggested solution is again repeated, and the customer must have understood it as well as accepted it. If the customer declares himself to be in agreement with the stipulated approach or with the problem solution offered, the farewell to the customer takes place. The conversation should be ended with a positive verbalization in which the employee expresses her satisfaction that she was able to solve the problem in accordance with the customer's wishes or to initiate the solution process.

Figure 8.1 summarizes in the form of a checklist the recommended activities for the direct conversation with complainants.

8.1.2 RULES OF BEHAVIOR FOR RESPONDING TO WRITTEN COMPLAINTS

For written complaints, the reaction situation looks different. The lack of direct customer contact means that less pressure exists in this situation than in a direct conversational situation with a complainant. Where the causes of complaints lie and which problem solutions are suitable can be clarified internally. This is, however, made more difficult because immediate follow-up inquiries to the customer are not possible.

Rules of behavior similar to those presented for complaints made by telephone and in person also apply to responses to written complaints.

Initial Wording

Just as in a complaint conversation conducted on the telephone or in person, it is important to choose an open and friendly introduction when responding to written complaints. Bureaucratic, unemotional, legal, or cold wordings such as "We confirm the receipt of your complaint and advise you as follows" should be avoided. Sentences like this generate an inner resistance in the customer and reduce the likelihood that he will accept the subsequent approach taken.

Checklist for Dealing with Dissatisfied Customers

1. Understand complaints as a **normal part of your job** and as a chance to reduce customer dissatisfaction and to ensure customer retention.
2. Look for a **quiet location** for the complaint conversation. Do not let other customers listen to the conversation. Offer the customer a seat. Address the customer by name.
3. Signal **willingness to talk.** ("Let us talk about this calmly.") Use your gestures, eye contact, and body language to convey that you are paying close attention. Offer an **apology** or at least **regret** that the customer has had a bad experience. Use the **first-person form** when formulating your responses. ("I am really sorry that you had this inconvenience" or "I apologize for the trouble caused")
4. Listen carefully. Do not interrupt the complainant. Let her/him speak first **without interruption** even though she/he may bring up unfounded statements.
5. Conduct the conversation in a **calm and courteous manner**. Respond calmly to exaggerations and personal accusations. Respond to insults calmly and bring the conversation back to the factual level. Do not argue with the customer and do not engage in a power struggle. An argument with the customer is always won by the customer.
6. **Take notes.** The activity of writing down what she/he says demonstrates to the customer that you are taking the complaint seriously and encourages her/him to explain the circumstances more accurately. Furthermore, the notes are valuable in complaint handling and analysis.
7. Avoid **immediate diagnoses** and listen to all the information without confessing that you were at fault.
8. Ask **questions regarding the contents until the situation becomes completely clear.** Pose questions in a courteous manner. ("Thanks for the hint. One more thing I would like to know is . . .")
9. Put yourself in the **customer's place.** ("I can easily imagine that you are annoyed"). Avoid wordings that increase the level of annoyance. ("You've got that totally wrong!" or "But this is your fault!")
10. If a mistake actually happened, **do not blame** a colleague, other departments, or the firm in general ("That happens all the time" or "They never get it right")
11. Initiate the handling of the complaint **immediately**. Offer a fair solution.
12. Ask if the customer **agrees** with the settlement.
13. If a **prompt solution** is not possible, promise the customer that the case will be thoroughly reviewed and indicate how long it will take before she/he receives a notice. **Observe this deadline**. If this is despite your best efforts not possible, inform the complainant in a **timely manner** and **explain the reasons**.
14. If you are not responsible or you cannot do anything, **forward the complaint** and see to it that the receipt and handling process is continued according to the customer's wishes.
15. Conclude the conversation **positively**. ("I'm pleased that we could satisfy you like this")
16. **Analyze** the complaint case and notify the responsible manager so that the source of the error can be quickly eliminated.

Adapted from: Brymer 1991; Zemke 1993

Figure 8.1

Problem Repetition

It is important to communicate clearly to the customer that his problem has been understood correctly and to the fullest extent possible. In the next section of the response letter, therefore, the problem that the customer described in his complaint letter should be summarized again. This problem repetition is the foundation of the subsequent sections of the letter in which the conflict settlement takes place and the problem solution is explained.

Conflict Settlement

In a written response, it must be candidly signaled to the customer that the employee can put herself in the customer's place. The individual case should be addressed and understanding for the customer's irritation should be shown. Along with an expression of regret or an explicit apology, this makes it possible to reduce negative emotions in a customer and to move him to a factual level as he is reading the response letter. The basis for a rational examination of the suggested solution can then be created.

Problem Solution

The description of the problem solution that is offered to the customer lies on a factual level. It is important that the customer understand this solution clearly and can definitely establish an immediate connection to his problem. If the customer's expectations can be met or exceeded, the advantages and benefits that result from the solution should be emphasized. If the customer's expectations are not met or claims are denied, well-founded explanations must be provided.

Concluding Wording

The concluding formulation depends upon whether the customer's problem has been solved in accordance with the customer's wishes or whether a refusal must be communicated to the customer. In a positive decision that corresponds to the expectations of the customer, reference can be made to the hoped-for reestablishment of the customer's satisfaction and the continuation of the business relationship. In refusals, it is advisable to express once again regret about the incident or to ask for understanding of the decision.

Style of Language and Orthography

In a written response, it must always be considered that the customer has no opportunity to pose follow-up questions directly if he has problems understanding. Escalating dissatisfaction can arise if text passages are worded incompletely, incomprehensibly, or inconsistently. This verbal quality of written reactions to complaints is very commonly undervalued and neglected.

The same applies to spelling concerns and aspects of grammar and punctuation. Errors of this kind are taken by the customer as indicators of careless handling of his concern. Therefore, great care should be taken with the automatic generation of confirmations of receipt, intermediate replies, or final reply letters that the complainant's name and other details are written correctly in the address as well as in the salutation of the letter.

8.2 APPLICATION OF THE RULES OF BEHAVIOR TO SPECIFIC TYPES OF COMPLAINANTS AND COMPLAINTS

The rules of behavior were previously presented as a function of the complaint channel chosen by the customer, without addressing the specifics that individual complainants or complaints may exhibit. Among the special groups of complainants are repeat or multiple complainants and grumblers or grousers. Specific complaints exist when customers take their complaints to different units within the firm at the same time (scattered complaints), complain about individual employees, or announce action consequences in their complaints (threats).

8.2.1 SPECIAL TYPES OF COMPLAINANTS

8.2.1.1 REPEAT AND MULTIPLE COMPLAINANTS

If customers complain about the same problem several times within a certain time period, one is dealing with "Repeat Complainants"; if customers repeatedly complain about different problems, one can speak of "Multiple Complainants." Both groups are to be identified and to be treated specially, since the business relationship is highly endangered because of the repeated occurrence of a problem. In repeat complainants, this applies even when the customer experienced a satisfactory problem solution or compensation. Customers do not simply want to be treated appropriately in a complaint case; they also want to be able to assume that the firm is taking measures to preclude a repetition of the same occurrences in the future. If this is not the case, customers' trust in the seriousness of the firm's customer orientation will be significantly impaired.

Repeat and multiple complainants require special attention. The principles of listening and of sincere regret addressed under the rules of behavior apply here to an even greater extent. It must be explained to repeat complainants especially which measures were introduced in order to ultimately eliminate the problem that has arisen. It is further recommended that they be contacted after the complaint case has been closed and informed of the success of the measures that were carried out.

The especially sensitive attention given to repeat and multiple complainants is advisable so long as they are not clearly identified as grumblers or grousers.

8.2.1.2 GRUMBLERS AND GROUSERS

In principle, companies should assume that their customers are honest and that their claims are legitimate. Another basic assumption will take the company farther away from the customer (Andreassen 1999). Nevertheless, there are customers among the complainants who have no understandable reason for a complaint, present untenable demands, or even consciously want to damage the firm with their complaints.

It is not easy to identify this small group that frequently influences the internal organizational picture of complainants very negatively. It would be wrong to designate a customer who complained repeatedly within a certain time period as a grumbler. It would be equally wrong to regard someone as a grouser simply because he doggedly insisted that his complaint case finally be processed after repeatedly broaching the subject.

However, several clues for identification of grousers can be found. Grousers tend to

- invent problems
- falsify the facts considerably and dramatize
- present demands that are not related in any conceivable way to the damage suffered
- make serious threats that go beyond the acceptable forms of action (switching, bringing in attorneys and the media).

Grumblers can be recognized because they

- choose even the slightest cause for detailed complaint articulations
- take a marginal problem as the occasion to criticize many aspects of the firm's range of products and services
- make realistic solutions difficult or impossible by objecting to every alternative
- derive obvious satisfaction from the continuation of the conflict.

The assessment of whether these circumstances are present in an individual case should, however, not be left to the personal opinion of the employee alone. The employee should accept each complaint in an impartial manner. If, however, she begins to have the impression that she is dealing with a grouser or a grumbler, she should undertake a thorough examination of the case. Along with her examination, she should investigate the occurrence of the problem in question and the associated consequences, as well as the previous complaint behavior of the customer, in the customer and complaint database.

If it turns out that definite deceptions on the part of the customer exist regarding the appearance of the problem and the damages, that the customer repeatedly presents extreme demands, and that objective grounds for complaint are not present, then an unjustified complaint exists. Such cases are to be rejected matter-of-factly. In an extreme case, it may be perfectly reasonable to pursue an active farewell to the customer, in which the customer is politely but unmistakably advised that the firm is no longer interested in a continuation of the business relationship under the given conditions. An example of this can be seen in the approach taken by the hotel chain Hampton Inn, which recommends a different hotel in the future to those guests (Tax and Brown 1998).

8.2.2 SPECIAL TYPES OF COMPLAINTS

8.2.2.1 SCATTERED COMPLAINTS

Scattered complaints represent a form of complaints that is encountered again and again. The customer turns to different units in the firm simultaneously with the same complaint, for example, to a regional subsidiary and to the executive board. This behavior can have three causes: (1) In the past, complainants have had bad experiences with making a complaint. In contacting several units simultaneously, they are counting on better chances for an appropriate reaction. (2) They would like to be sure that company management also acquire knowledge of the problem and in this way lend emphasis to their demand. (3) They are attempting to obtain several compensation benefits for the same problem.

If complaint processing does not take place in a coordinated manner, the danger exists that the complaint will be processed multiple times. This is problematic because of the duplicated work alone. An additional problem arises when the complaint is processed by the different units with varying quality and/or different problem solutions being offered. The consequence is that the customer perceives the complaint processing to be unprofessional and at the same time is rewarded for his behavior.

The challenge then consists of identifying scattered complaints such as these. One possibility is to collect all complaints in a central location and sift through them, independent of who received them. If a decentralized access structure exists and a software solution for entering complaints is employed at the participating locations, the possibility exists for recognizing scattered complaints in the context of documentation by comparing them with processes that have not been closed out yet.

If a complaint is identified as a scattered complaint and it is conceivable that the processing will take up a longer time span, it should be communicated to the customers that their complaints have arrived at the various addressees, and the unit responsible for the coordinated processing must be given out to them at the same time. If the problem can be solved immediately, the processing is to be initiated and closed by the internally coordinating units. In the final reply, the employee must document that the individual complaints arrived at the different addressees, but the processing was taken over by just one responsible unit.

8.2.2.2 COMPLAINTS TO TOP MANAGEMENT

Special attention must be given to complaints that are directly addressed to the firm's top management. Two reasons in particular are responsible for this treatment. First, customers do not know who the competent contact person in the firm is. Consequently, they turn to the head of the firm, hoping that the complaint will then be processed or forwarded to the correct department. Customers also deliberately write to management when they personally would like to call attention to a serious problem, or when they have previously tried in vain to achieve success in another way or were dissatisfied with the previous complaint handling (Follow-Up Complaint).

The principle that the addressee of the complaint should answer the customer also applies to top management, even when the problem solution and case processing can or must be undertaken by another unit. Customers turn to executives because they expect the executives to take personal care of their problem. If this is not the case, disappointment sets in, and the customer orientation and commitment to customer satisfaction that have been publicly proclaimed by the firm's management become unbelievable to the customer.

A special problem arises when customers turn to management with the request to review rebate or goodwill demands that have already been refused. In order not to undermine the credibility or decision-making authority of complaint management or of the customer-contact personnel, well-founded decisions made by the responsible employees should only be corrected in exceptional cases. If this cannot be avoided, modified decisions should be passed on to the customer by the affected employee and not by the executive himself. If customers perceive that they achieve more when they turn to top management, they will increasingly use this method in the future for their first complaints.

8.2.2.3 COMPLAINTS ABOUT EMPLOYEES

A sensitive form of complaint—both for the customer and for the firm— are complaints about the behavior of individual employees.

The rules of behavior that have already been introduced are also to be applied in this case. Since it is not clear at the time of a personal articulation of such complaints who has made an error (the employee or the customer), either admitting that the customer is right or standing up for the employee should be strictly avoided in the first contact with the complainant.

It is also necessary to listen to the customer initially, to calm him down and to lead him over from an emotional conversational level to a factual one. Many times, it is advisable to offer the customer a callback or a second conversation so that a consultation can first be held with the affected employee.

If it turns out that the mistake is the fault of the employee and that this employee must continue working with the customer, the employee should apologize to the customer personally with an appropriate offer of compensation. Internally, the situation must be used for feedback by discussing better ways of reacting with the employee. If similar cases accumulate with the same employee, an urgent need for training exists. If there are still no changes in behavior, it should be decided whether the employee should be active in customer contact in the future, since the firm will have to accept uncontrollable customer losses otherwise.

If it turns out that the mistake is clearly the fault of the customer, the supervisors should seek out a conversation with the customer and clarify the situation. It is also appropriate for the supervisors to explain the employee's position and give reasons why they will also support appropriate patterns of behavior in the future. If there are repeated similar cases in which clear-cut misbehavior on the part of the customer is suggested, it stands to reason that consequences analogous to those presented earlier for employees—here, in the form of active dissolution of the customer relationship—should be contemplated. In doing so, however, the negative economic consequences of losing the customer must be weighed against the negative consequences that result from the conflicts and their accompanying de-motivating effects for employees if the relationship is retained.

8.2.2.4 THREATS ASSOCIATED WITH COMPLAINTS

Many customers associate the articulation of their complaints with the threat of consequences that they want to invoke if the complaints are not processed as the customers expect. They announce the severance of the business relationship or the introduction of legal action or publicity measures. There can be several reasons for tactics like these. Customers threaten

- because they want to emphasize their demands
- when they have the feeling that their problem is not being taken seriously enough
- because they have the feeling that no one wants to help them further, or
- when they have the feeling that they are being cheated.

Studies show that 75 percent of customers who threaten that they want to end the business relationship at the next opportunity in fact intend to carry out this reaction (Dietze 1997).

Customers who threaten to switch should therefore always be openly confronted and asked what can be done in this particular situation to deter them from their intention. If realistic expectations are named, the firm must take advantage of the opportunity to bind them further to the firm. If customers who are threatening to switch cannot be deterred from their intention, however, the business relationship is to be terminated with a positive farewell (Good-bye Management). Doing so increases the chances that the customer can be won back to the firm after some time has passed.

A further threat made by dissatisfied customers is to introduce legal means or bring in the media. The rules of behavior are also to be applied in these cases. The firm should strive for conflict settlement, especially when the customers are candidly asked how the problem can be eliminated from their point of view. If the demands appear to be unrealistic upon assessing all the circumstances and the customers' value, the customers must be informed in a matter-of-fact way that the firm would like to have avoided the circumstances described, but is now prepared to advocate its position actively in court or in the media.

Another means of putting pressure on the firm that is often used by customers is the threat to decrease the amount paid on current invoices or not to make upcoming payments. This threat is most often expressed when exaggerated performance promises are made by the firm that cannot be kept, and the customer feels cheated. If it turns out that the performance promise in fact is a substantial deviance from the performance rendered, rectifications should take place, or concessions to the customer in the form of rebates or goodwill benefits should be made. If performance deficits such as these are not discovered, this should be calmly explained to the customer, and his demand should be refused. It may be practical to deviate from this rule if specific circumstances exist or if an otherwise successful customer relationship is in great danger.

8.3 DECISION ON THE CASE SOLUTION

The decision on the case solution constitutes an essential part of the complaint reaction. Since this decision must take place on a firm-specific and case-specific basis, only rather rough guidelines for decision-making can be established. In establishing these guidelines, answers to the following questions should first be found:

- Which solution possibilities are available?
- Which factors determine the choice of the appropriate reaction form for each case?
- Up to what amount demanded should the firm forego an extensive investigation of the individual case?
- How should one behave in the case of unjustified complaints?

8.3.1 SOLUTION POSSIBILITIES AND INFLUENCING FACTORS FOR THE CHOICE OF REACTION FORM

Basic Solution Possibilities

There are three groups of measures that are available as basic solution possibilities: financial, tangible, or intangible reactions (Figure 8.2). Among the financial reaction forms are money back, price reduction, and compensation for damages. In the case of tangible solutions, the compensation takes place in the form of a payment in kind (exchange, repair, another product, gift). All customer-oriented forms of communication that target a decrease in the complainant's dissatisfaction (information, explanation, apology) are numbered among the intangible reactions.

The choice of the reaction form in each case is restricted by goods-specific conditions and led by cost considerations. Exchange and repair are thus not available as options where services are concerned. Repairs lend themselves primarily to durable consumer goods, whereas exchange and money back are especially suited for low-value consumer goods for which an individual case investigation would be too costly. The offer of a replacement product is only possible when it offers customers the same benefit as the product that they originally desired. In contrast to

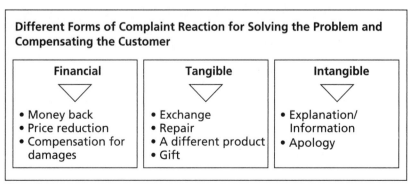

Figure 8.2

exchange, repair, and the offer of a replacement product, gifts as a tangible reaction form represent not a real solution of the initial problem, but rather a gesture of compensation. For this reason, they are primarily considered when—as is frequently the case in the service sector—later elimination of the problem is not possible. They can also be used in addition to the other alternatives in order to increase the complaint satisfaction by providing a positive surprise. Intangible reactions are always advisable, regardless of whether the actual problem solution makes yet another reaction form necessary. With an apology, the firm takes on the responsibility for the problem that has arisen and contributes to the reduction of dissatisfaction on an emotional level. Through targeted information and explanations, many problems can be solved immediately, misunderstandings cleared up, or future problems prevented.

The choice between financial or tangible reaction forms and intangible reaction forms is also determined by the type of error. Chase and Dasu (2001) recommend that behavior-oriented intangible reactions such as apologies should be applied to process-based behavioral problems, and outcome-based financial or tangible reactions should be applied to outcome-based errors and problems (see Spotlight 5).

SPOTLIGHT 5

The Right Remedy

How do you make up for a service-encounter error? Research on what customers perceive as fair remedy suggests that the answer depends on whether it is an outcome error or a process error. A botched task calls for tangible compensation, while poor treatment from a server calls for an apology. Reversing these recovery actions is unlikely to be effective.

Imagine being a copy store manager faced with two complaining customers. One says that the job was done right but the clerk was surly. The other says that the clerk was pleasant but when he got home, he realized that his report was missing two pages, and he had to take it to a competitor near his house to get the job done right. What should you do?

In the case of the rude clerk, don't give the customer some tangible compensation, such as a coupon for his next visit. All the customer really wants is a sincere apology from the clerk and the manager. In the case of the botched job, you can apologize all over the place, but that won't satisfy the customer. He wants the job done right, and he wants some compensation for his inconvenience. Thus, while apologies are appropriate in both situations, behavioral research clearly indicates that process-based remedies should be applied to process-based problems and outcome-based remedies should be applied to outcome-based problems.

(Adapted from: Chase and Dasu 2001: 84)

Reaction Forms and Their Influence on Complaint Satisfaction

When choosing the appropriate reaction form, one should pay attention to whether the solution offered will be judged to be adequate by the customer and that the goal of high complaint satisfaction can actually be reached. Estelami (2000) analyzed consumer reports of delightful and disappointing complaint solutions. In goods markets, the customers desired most a replacement of the product and a prompt response. Also expressions of empathy, "no questions asked," and politeness by the employees handling the complaint were among the top mentioned categories. Goodwin and Ross (1989, 1990) investigated which forms of compensation are favored by dissatisfied service customers and found, too, that the complaint dissatisfaction depends not only on the form of solution (tangible or intangible compensation), but also on the experience of the total processing procedure.

Customers prefer tangible and financial compensations. Even when they are of relatively low value, they have a substantial positive influence on the complaint satisfaction. However, the degree of complaint satisfaction varies with the extent to which the complaint process is perceived as fair.

Complaint dissatisfaction is greatest when the demander's perspective is blatantly disregarded in the complaint processing and the customer is put off with just an apology. But even the customer who is initially listened to with understanding is dissatisfied or even very dissatisfied with the complaint situation when he has the impression, based on an absent tangible and financial problem solution, that the firm simply gave him the opportunity "to let off steam," without taking him or his concern seriously.

It thus becomes clear to what degree the customer's complaint satisfaction is dependent upon the extent to which the complainants have the feeling that they are being treated "justly" or "fairly" (Goodwin and Ross 1990; Blodgett, Granbois, and Walters 1993). The fairness or unfairness of the treatment is judged by the customer on the basis of various aspects of the firm's reaction (Goodwin and Ross 1990):

- First, the complaint processing procedure must fulfill certain conditions so that it is perceived as fair. Among these conditions is that the customers can present their view of things and that they also have the impression that the special conditions of their case are fully appreciated. The perceived fairness in the procedure also includes that they are not treated in an unfriendly manner when making their complaint, that no bad intentions are attributed to them, and that they are not made responsible for the problem.

- Second, the outcome of the complaint procedure must be considered to be fair. From the customer's point of view, his own performance and the counterperformance of the firm must be balanced against the solution offered. In this respect, overly generous financial compensations or gifts are neither necessary nor reasonable. They will no doubt be accepted, but regarded as inappropriate and consequently as a blatant attempt to influence the customer and engender reactance—that is, psychological resistance—rather than enthusiasm. What matters is not wanting to buy the customer's satisfaction with exaggerated gifts, but rather solving the problem brought forward by the customer.

If the problem solution is missing, the assessment of this negative result is dependent upon whether the customer is of the opinion that the provider does not want to and/or cannot solve the problem. These connections are clarified in Figure 8.3 with a "Willingness Matrix" of complaint reaction (Cottle 1990).

Case 1 is unproblematic ("Able and willing"). Since firms are both prepared to solve the customer's problem and are in a position to do so, complaint satisfaction is achieved. High complaint dissatisfaction is to be expected in Case 4 ("Unable and unwilling"), since firms express an attitude with their reaction that is received by the customer in the following way: "I can't help you, but even if I could, I wouldn't."

Cases 2 and 3 are more interesting. In Case 2 ("Willing but unable"), the provider recognizes the problem and tries to solve it, but is not in a position to do so, either at all or at the present time. It is thus conceivable that hotel guests complain about chilly room temperatures or noisy fellow guests, but it is not possible for the hotel manager to see to it that the heat is repaired immediately or that the guests keep the noise down. In cases of this type, complaint dissatisfaction turns out to be relatively low, despite the inadequate problem solution, if the provider makes it clear that he is seriously trying to eliminate the problem and searching for creative alternative solutions.

The situation is different for Case 3 ("Able but unwilling"). Here, the provider could solve the problem but is not prepared to do so. The

Willingness Matrix of Complaint Reaction

Ability \ Willingness	Yes	No
Yes	Case 1 **Able and willing** (high complaint satisfaction)	Case 3 **Able but unwilling** (high complaint dissatisfaction)
No	Case 2 **Willing but unable** (low complaint dissatisfaction)	Case 4 **Unable and unwilling** (high complaint dissatisfaction)

Adapted (with changes) from: Cottle 1990: 247

Figure 8.3

hotel manager, for example, declines to get actively involved with respect to the noisy group of guests. Insufficient willingness to strive for a problem solution leads directly to higher complaint dissatisfaction. Customers experience particularly negative emotions such as frustration or anger (McColl-Kennedy and Sparks 2003).

These insights make it clear that from the customer's perspective, the actual problem solution ("what" the complaining customer receives) is not judged independently from the way the firm treats the customer in case of a complaint ("how" the customer is treated).

8.3.2 CASE SOLUTION WITH OR WITHOUT AN INDIVIDUAL CASE EXAMINATION

Many firms are only prepared to offer compensation, even of an insignificant kind, after they have subjected the case to a thorough examination. While they are extremely sensitive to the possible compensation costs, they neglect the costs of the extensive case investigation. As a simple arithmetic example shows, this behavior is hardly rational.

For the following example, it is assumed that it costs $100 to satisfy a customer who is complaining, and a careful examination of the facts, as well as the activities associated with that examination, results in costs in the amount of $50 per complaint.

If the individual case examination results in the recognition of 80 out of the 100 complaints received as justified, a cost comparison comes to the following conclusion: Without the examination, reaction costs alone in the amount of $10,000 would have accrued. With an examination of the facts, the reaction costs for 80 cases ($8,000) and the additional examination costs of $5,000 accrue. The "success" of the refusal of 20 percent of the demands as unjustified was purchased with additional costs in the amount of $3,000. There is also the loss of the positive effects of the firm's image and to customer satisfaction that would have occurred if the customers had experienced an unbureaucratic problem solution (Cannie and Caplin 1991; Walther 1994).

Naturally, the consequence of this arithmetic example is not that qualifying examinations should be renounced on principle. Nevertheless, the question must be answered about the compensation amount up to which the firm can forego an individual case examination.

The starting point is the experience that a majority of the expenditures that accrue for problem solutions are allotted to a relatively small share of complaints. Conversely, this means that the majority of complaints take up only a minor share of the total settlement expenditures. It then seems reasonable to restrict the detailed individual case examinations to the few cost-intensive cases.

In order to do this, Blanding (1991) suggests applying the 80-20 Rule to complaint management. He proceeds from the assumption that 80 percent of the amount of money that must be expended for problem solutions is allotted for 20 percent of the complaints. Accordingly, 80 percent of the complaint cases account for only 20 percent of the total expenditure. On the basis of this assumption, he suggests subjecting only those complaints that account for 80 percent of the total expenditure to an individual case examination, or foregoing an extra examination for those complaints that account for 20 percent of the total expenditures. The outcome of this process is an Immediate Reaction Amount, up to which the solution desired by the customer can be offered without further examination. The process includes the following steps (in accordance with Blanding 1991; see also the example in Figure 8.4):

1. Determination of the total amount of money that will be spent on problem solutions in the time period under consideration (Total Reaction Amount).

Example of How to Determine the Immediate Reaction Amount

1. Total reaction amount/year

$ 60,000

2. Noninvestigation share = 20%

$12,000

3. Complaint volume/year

40 Complaints

4. Ordering of the complaints according to their reaction costs and determination of the number of complaints that can be processed before noninvestigation share is reached.

```
20 complaints at $100 each    =   $2,000
10 complaints at $400 each    =   $4,000
 2 complaints at $3,000 each  =   $6,000
32 complaints                 =  $12,000   = noninvestigation share (20%)
```

5. Determination of the immediate reaction amount

= highest amount of reaction costs of a complaint included in the noninvestigation share (20%)
= $3,000

6. Calculation of the share of complaints included in the noninvestigation share (20%) of the total complaint volume

$$\frac{32 \text{ complaints}}{40 \text{ complaints}} = 80\%$$

7. Verification of the 80-20 rule

Confirmed

Adapted from: Blanding 1991

Figure 8.4

2. Calculation of 20 percent of the Total Reaction Amount (Noninvestigation Share).
3. Determination of the complaint volume during the period.
4. Arrangement of the complaints according to the respective reaction costs in increasing order and determination of the number of complaints until the Noninvestigation Share (20 percent of the total reaction costs) is reached.
5. Determination of the Immediate Reaction Amount as the highest amount of reaction costs for one of these complaints. All complaints with reaction costs up to this amount can be resolved without further examination in accordance with the customer's wishes. This only applies, however, if the share of the included complaints accounts for 80 percent of the total number of complaints.
6. Calculation of the share of the included complaints of the total complaint volume.
7. Verification of the 80-20 Rule. One can abide by the Immediate Reaction Amount even when the rule is not completely confirmed; however, the 20% of the total reaction costs should be allotted to at least 50% of the complaint cases.

In the example depicted in Figure 8.4, 80 percent of the complaint cases that cause individual reaction costs of up to $3,000 account for 20 percent of the total reaction costs. The 80-20 Rule thus applies in this example so that complaints up to the amount of the determined Immediate Reaction Amount of $3,000 can be settled without individual case investigation.

This approach is associated with three advantages for the firm: (1) Eighty percent of all complainants can be satisfied immediately. (2) In 80 percent of the cases, the customer-contact personnel can decide the problem solution immediately, which brings about motivational effects. (3) For 80 percent of complaints, no internal processing costs accrue.

Spotlight 6 shows how the Global Service & Parts Division of DaimlerChrysler AG manages an automatic complaint reaction with the aid of a value limit defined in the system.

SPOTLIGHT 6

Automatic Complaint Reaction at DaimlerChrysler AG, Global Service & Parts

Among the fundamental tasks of the Global Service & Parts business division is the worldwide, comprehensive supply of spare parts for all of DaimlerChrysler AG's automotive groups. With about 340,000 original parts and accessories for the entire product range of the Mercedes-Benz brand, the Global Logistics Center in Germersheim serves as the central warehouse. The logistics center looks after approximately 300 customers on the wholesale level, who in turn supply around 5,700 distribution and service bases all over the world. In order to guarantee a uniform, swift and profitable processing of the entire complaint volume in this complex replacement-part organization, database-supported claims management was introduced.

In order to achieve high customer satisfaction and, at the same time, a reduction of the costs of claims processing, special importance is attached to automating the processes and integrating the various levels of the spare parts organization into this automated process.

To that end, workflow-controlled processing procedures were defined for detailed inquiries and claims. With this workflow control, on the one hand, the customer is relieved of the search for the responsible employee; and on the other hand, it is recorded in the system which claims are to be examined with which intensity. Incoming claims are subject to an automatic examination as to their completeness and plausibility. In a parallel step, the value of the complaint is checked against a maximum amount defined in the system. On the basis of this analysis, it is decided whether the system will independently take over the processing of the claim or whether manual examinations must be initiated. With this procedure, an unprofitable search for errors that is associated with unnecessary time spent and unnecessary costs can be prevented. Lesser processing costs and faster processing times are the desired consequences.

An example may clarify this point: A wholesaler in Hong Kong was supplied with one replacement part fewer than what he ordered and charged for it all the same. He files a claim and desires an appropriate credit. It is now reviewed in the system whether the claim lies above or below a fixed value limit. If the value is over the limit, manual examination activities are necessary. If the amount is below the defined value limit, an automated workflow-controlled processing procedure follows. The system recognizes the responsibility of the "accounting department" on the basis of the customer's desire for a "credit" and transfers the claims data electronically via interface and without intermediate steps to this department. As soon as the credit is produced, an automatic acknowledgment to the complaint management system occurs so that the claim is immediately recorded as being resolved. Through this automatic processing, the required processing time is reduced to a minimum. This time gained is associated internally with substantial cost advantages and leads to higher customer satisfaction.

Peter Diehsle
Global Service & Parts
DaimlerChrysler AG

8.3.3 DEALING WITH "UNJUSTIFIED" COMPLAINTS

Many times the question is raised of how one should react to unjustified customer demands. This question requires, however, an explanation of when a complaint should be viewed as unjustified.

8.3.3.1 THE SUBJECTIVE JUSTIFICATION OF CUSTOMER COMPLAINTS

The question of the justification of a complaint should be primarily posed from the customers' perspective. One can proceed from the assumption that the vast majority of complainants are subjectively fully convinced that their concerns are justified. Only a very small percentage of complainants can be assigned to the group of those who complain to the firm with intent to defraud and thus have no reason for complaint from their subjective point of view.

For this reason, it makes sense from the firm's perspective to accept this customer perspective, independent of whether a later investigation reveals that the firm cannot objectively be held responsible for the problem. Regardless of whether the problem can be attributed to a lack of information or a misunderstanding on the part of the customer, annoyance and disappointment are present for the customer in every case and have their causes. To prove to these customers that they are in the wrong only increases their annoyance and dissatisfaction.

The central requirement of complaint reaction is, therefore, never to doubt the justification of the customer's complaint. Nevertheless, this primary acceptance of all complaints does not mean that all of the customer's demands are to be fulfilled. An objective examination of the facts may show a different picture. It may turn out, for example, that the customer has depicted the circumstances incompletely or incorrectly, or that he has either caused the problem or contributed to its cause. In these situations, the subjective justification from the customer's point of view and the objective justification from the firm's point of view fall apart.

From the firm's perspective, it is sensible to ascertain the extent of these "unjustified" complaints because they provide important indications of the necessity of corrective measures. They might show where information deficits exist for the customer or where operating instructions are unclear.

8.3.3.2 REACTIONS TO "UNJUSTIFIED" COMPLAINTS

Accommodating Reaction to "Unjustified Complaints"

As far as the firm's reaction to objectively unjustified complaints is concerned, it is necessary to differentiate. While the subjective reason for the complaint may not be questioned in the answer to the customer, the decision concerning voluntary rebate and goodwill payments depends on various factors. The tendency to fulfill the customer's expectations despite objective reasons for a complaint not existing is thus greater, the more the customer's perspective is understandable, for instance, due to the especially unlucky conditions of the case. An analogous situation exists when the examination costs for a complete clarification of the incident turn out to be higher than the reaction costs. A refusal of the customer's wishes and an insistence on an "objective" point of view would seem to be absurd if a long-lasting, successful, and profitable business relationship were endangered by such actions.

For this reason, there is much to be said for considering the problem of objectively unjustified complaints from an economic perspective. In accordance with Sewell and Brown (1992), the following pragmatic approach is recommended for deciding on voluntary rebate and goodwill payments:

- First, determine the costs that arise from the fulfillment of the unjustified customer demand.
- Cases whose reaction costs are below the individual-case examination costs should be immediately resolved according to the customer's wishes without restrictions or expressions of mistrust of any kind.
- If the reaction costs are more than the examination costs and the obvious nonjustification of the complaint comes out during the examination, a customer-individual treatment depending on the customer's value should occur. If the customer's value is substantially more than the reaction costs, even an unjustified complaint should be solved in accordance with the customer's wishes. Negotiations with the customer about a reduction of his demands are not recommended, since then the settlement will not cause positive effects. Sewell and Brown (1992: 57) express it as follows: "If you want to keep their business, give customers exactly what they ask for—or even more—without any hesitation. If you do anything less, you might as well offer them nothing, because you'll have lost their good will." However, the customer's unjustified demand and the type of the firm's reaction should be recorded in the customer database in order to be able to make a different decision, if need be, should the situation repeat itself.
- If, based on the individual case examination, it turns out that the demand of a less attractive customer is unjustified or that this same customer has already attracted attention for his deceitful behavior, the demands should be refused in a clear but friendly manner. Sewell, a successful car dealer, says laconically: "Sometimes we even give the directions to our 'favorite' competitor" (Sewell and Brown 1992: 59).

Independent of the terms under which rebate and goodwill decisions occur, these decisions must be made very carefully in every case. Rash promises made during the initial contact should be avoided, as these can rarely be taken back. Goodwill and rebate payments are very cost-intensive and are among the largest cost pools in complaint management in many industries—as, for example, in the automobile or tourism industry. A further reason in favor of a cautious approval of monetary demands has to do with word of generously granted goodwill payments getting around quickly so that a lasting influence on the expectations of other complainants follows. If the rebate or goodwill policy is later changed, it can lead to great irritation, since customers with similar or identical problems are not granted a commensurate payment.

Refusal of "Unjustified" Complaints

If neither an objective nor a subjective complaint cause exists, the complaint is to be rejected. However, the judgment of whether the complaint has a subjective complaint cause must be undertaken on the basis of "hard" data, not on the basis of employee assessments. This requires that the firm has clear evidence that the complainant belongs to the small group of grumblers, grousers, and crooks ("customers from hell").

All complaints that have no objective foundation and for which no specific reason to comply with the customer's subjectively based demands exists should also be denied. This is the case when no special problem is discernable and the value of the customer is deemed to be slight. These reasons, however, are only to be applied if the reaction costs are relatively high, such that the absence of an objective complaint cause was proven in an individual case examination.

If the customer's complaint expectations are not fulfilled due to clear-cut and understandable facts, then this decision must be explained to the customer matter-of-factly and without dogmatic instructions.

8.4 COMMUNICATION WITH THE COMPLAINANT DURING COMPLAINT PROCESSING

As soon as the complainants have articulated their complaints, they begin to wait for an answer. The longer this waiting time lasts, the more impatient and dissatisfied they become. Therefore, what matters is to avoid the creation of this type of dissatisfaction by means of communicative measures. The following forms of communications come under consideration: the confirmation of the receipt of the complaint in the case of written complaints, the notification of where the processing stands in intermediate replies, and the communication of the problem solution in a final reply. All intermediate inquiries by the customers must be answered.

8.4.1 FORMS OF COMMUNICATION

8.4.1.1 CONFIRMATION OF RECEIPT

For written complaints that cannot be solved immediately, it is necessary to confirm to the customers that their complaint has been received. It may also be advisable to confirm complaints that have been made verbally by the customers, for example, if the complaint is simply accepted and the customers are promised that it will be forwarded to the responsible department.

In cases for which the processing will take up a longer period of time, the confirmation of receipt should contain the following information in terms of content:

* The thank-you for the complaint
* the date the complaint was received in the firm

- a summary of the customer's problem
- an honest and sincere regret about the inconvenience experienced by the customer
- the measures implemented, and
- an expected settlement deadline or, if this is not possible, a date (day or week) by which the customer will be informed once more about his case.

The customer is thereby given the security of knowing that his complaint has arrived at the appropriate unit and that his problem has been understood properly. He knows, furthermore, that measures to eliminate the problem have been introduced, and he is informed about the duration of the processing. In doing this, the firm signals him that his problem is in the right hands and that one is trying to find a solution.

The firm can forego a confirmation of receipt if the time span expected by the customer with regard to the reaction to complaints will not be exceeded by the expected closure of the complaint process.

Confirmations of receipt can take place in writing or over the telephone. The telephone reaction form often proves to be the better way. The respective employee can record the customer's problem and the expected solution more exactly during the conversation; the employee can also explain to the customer why certain expectations cannot be fulfilled. In addition, the firm can apologize in a personal way, which is desired by many customers.

Limits are, however, placed on telephone reaction forms when the written complaint volume reaches such an extent that the individual complaints can only be confirmed in the form of a standard letter. In using letters such as these, however, the firm must avoid giving the impression that no individual case examination will take place. This can be achieved by making reference to the particular circumstances of the case and providing the name of a contact person for possible follow-up questions. In cases with a high level of urgency, telephone contact should occur even when the complaint volume is high, in order to accelerate the processing and solution procedure.

8.4.1.2 INTERMEDIATE REPLIES

Sending out intermediate replies is always necessary when

- no settlement date can be given to the customer in the confirmation of receipt
- the intermediate deadlines agreed on with the customer in the confirmation of receipt or the settlement deadline cannot be kept
- deviations from the problem solution about which the customer has been notified or from other promises made in the context of the complaint processing crop up, or
- such a long period of time lies between the confirmation of receipt and the final problem solution that the customer could get the impression that his complaint was neglected or has been forgotten.

Of crucial importance for the reestablishment of the complainant's satisfaction is that the firm proves the effort it is putting into a problem solution and creates transparency in the case examination and the current state of the processing. Consents and promises to the customer in the context of the complaint case must also be kept. Should this not be possible for particular reasons, the firm must inform the customer about the respective deviations without delay. For processing procedures of longer duration, temporal standards should be fixed, within which an intermediate reply must be produced and sent. In the context of PC-supported complaint management systems, this process can be largely automated.

In choosing between telephone and written methods of communicating with the customer, the telephone is also preferred in the case of intermediate replies. In this way, the customer is informed in a more individual and detailed way about where things stand. Moreover, the customer has a stronger impression that someone is dealing with his problem and does not want to lose him as a customer.

8.4.1.3 FINAL REPLY

Final replies contain the problem solution developed by the firm and the communication that the complaint case is closed for good. As far as content is concerned, the answer should contain the following points:

- the thank-you for the complaint
- a short, repeated summary of the problem
- the expression of regret for the inconvenience encountered by the customer
- the result of the problem analysis
- the suggested solution
- and—for customer-oriented problem solutions—the request to have confidence in the firm again in the future.

The final reply should occur in writing in order to prevent possible discrepancies with the actual result of the problem solution later on. This must happen independent of whether the firm was able to solve the customer's problem completely, partially, or not at all in accordance with the customer's wishes. In cases that had no solution or an inadequate solution from the customer's point of view, it is further recommended that the reasons for the lack of a solution or partial solution be explained to the customer and that the firm's good intentions be stressed once again.

8.4.1.4 FOLLOW-UP SURVEY

In order to determine whether the complaint reaction actually led to the desired complaint satisfaction of the customer, it is advisable to carry out follow-up surveys, that is, to contact the complainant immediately after the closure of the complaint process. In this way, it can be simultaneously ensured that the complaint process is classified as closed, not only from the perspective of the firm, but also from the complainant's point of view.

In contrast to the performance measurements for complaint satisfaction that will be introduced in Chapter 10.2.1.1, the primary target of follow-up surveys does not consist of deriving average data about the quality of the perceived complaint processing, but rather of making sure that a complaint was actually closed to the individual satisfaction of the customer and that the business relationship was truly stabilized. The survey thus has to take place in an immediate temporal reference to the complaint reaction and has a direct effect on customer retention, since the firm demonstrates genuine interest in the customer relationship.

In the case of dissatisfaction, the customer will take this contact as the occasion to bring up his criticism, address unresolved questions, or point out further demands that exist. He then expects specific answers to these articulations. In this way, follow-up complaints are stimulated by follow-up contacts if needed.

If a survey of all complainants is impossible for capacity reasons, a sample can be defined, and it can be determined in accordance with the sample size that the complainant from every third, fifth, or tenth complaint process will be surveyed. In doing so, the requirement of random selection is fulfilled, since the selection is oriented on the time of receipt in the firm and each complaint case has the same probability of being considered for the survey.

Since the primary point of follow-up measurements is not, however, to obtain representative results, but rather to assure customer retention, it also makes sense to carry out a methodic selection of the complainants to be surveyed subject to customer value or the type of problem. It is also necessary that the surveying employee have immediate access to the complaint case in order to bring about a solution immediately if necessary.

8.4.2 TEMPORAL DESIGN OF THE FORMS OF COMMUNICATION

For the complainants' satisfaction, it is not only important that they are always informed, but that they receive this information within appropriate time limits. Therefore, temporal standards for the sending out of official notices must be fixed.

For the confirmation of receipt and the intermediate reply, the total processing time should be determined and the time when they should be mailed.

A confirmation of receipt is only necessary when the problem cannot be conclusively resolved within a very short time span (e.g., five days). This confirmation should then follow as quickly as possible to the customer (e.g., 48 hours after the arrival of a written complaint at the latest, or up to 24 hours after the receipt of an electronic complaint). Intermediate replies should be produced when the processing drags on for a longer period of time (e.g., more than two weeks). They should be sent out when the length of the processing time can be foreseen (e.g., after eight days). If the case cannot be resolved in the presumed processing time, the customer must be provided an explanation for the delay in another intermediate reply after a short time (e.g., after eight additional days) and at this time be given a definitive deadline for the final clarification of the case. If the customer sends documents that are still needed during the processing of the complaint case, the receipt must be confirmed as soon as possible (e.g., within two days). The final reply with the solution suggested by the firm should be mailed out immediately after the decision about the case solution has been made.

8.4.3 ANSWERS TO CUSTOMER REQUESTS DURING THE COMPLAINT PROCESSING

Active complaint management implies that after the receipt of a complaint, all the activities start from the part of the firm and no further contact is required from the customer.

If the customers deem it necessary to make follow-up requests or if they hand in additional information later, the employee addressed in each case must be in a position to provide them with the name of the responsible department, or they must see to it that the customers are contacted directly.

If the intermediate customer articulation reaches the responsible employees, they must decide whether it is actually a matter of a further inquiry or a follow-up complaint. Frequently the customers are asking about the status of the handling of the case but really would like to express their dissatisfaction with particular aspects of the complaint processing at the same time. This is the case, for example, if they point out that a promised callback did not take place or the promised intermediate reply did not arrive by the deadline they were given. In such cases, the accepting employees should respond to these points and record the follow-up complaint. This complaint can then be considered in the wording of the final reply. Moreover, information exists that can be used for the improvement of the complaint processing procedures.

Complaint Analysis

9

The area of complaint analysis is the first building block of indirect complaint management, whose measures can be carried out without direct customer contact. What is important here is systematically exploiting the information potential that is contained in the critical customer statements. The more precisely the complaint analysis captures the "voice of the customer," the more the firm is in a position to move from problem diagnosis to effective problem prevention. Basically, it can be distinguished between quantitative and qualitative complaint analysis.

9.1 QUANTITATIVE COMPLAINT ANALYSIS

In order to utilize effectively the indications of operational weaknesses and market opportunities that are found in complaints, it is essential that the entire complaint volume be analyzed quantitatively with respect to certain important characteristics. This analysis occurs in the context of quantitative complaint analysis through the use of frequency distributions and cross-tabulations, as well as the aid of the Frequency-Relevance Analysis of Complaints (FRAC).

9.1.1 FREQUENCY DISTRIBUTIONS AND CROSS-TABULATIONS

In the context of quantitative methods of analysis, one must distinguish between univariate and bivariate techniques. Primary among the univariate techniques are absolute and relative frequency distributions, as well as mean values (such as the arithmetic mean). Bivariate methods (such as cross-tabulations) permit the examination of correlations between two variables. These methods will be addressed in greater detail below, using an illustration of a package delivery service's complaint analysis as an example.

Univariate Analysis Techniques

It is imperative to achieve an overview of the quantitative distribution of the complaint volume—to find out how the number of complaints within a criterion (e.g., the type of problem) is distributed across its attributes (e.g., individual problem categories). This is accomplished by means of absolute and relative (percentage) frequency distributions.

In the following example, a package delivery service is interested in knowing how the annual volume of 1,200 total complaints is distributed across five defined problem categories: Loss of the Package, Damage to the Package, Late Delivery, Wrong Delivery, and Unfriendly Treatment of Customers. Figure 9.1 provides a corresponding overview; it shows that complaints about late delivery appear most frequently (absolute: 600; relative: 50 percent).

Absolute and Relative Frequency Distribution of the Complaint Volume Based on Problem Types

Type of problem	Absolute frequency	Relative frequency%
Loss	120	10
Damage	360	30
Late delivery	600	50
Wrong delivery	24	2
Unfriendliness	96	8
Total	**1,200**	**100**

Figure 9.1

The histogram gives a quick overview of the frequency distribution (see Figure 9.2). In this graphic representation, the individual criteria (problem categories) are plotted on the horizontal axis, while the relative complaint frequencies are plotted on the vertical axis. The height of each bar corresponds to the percentage frequency of a problem category.

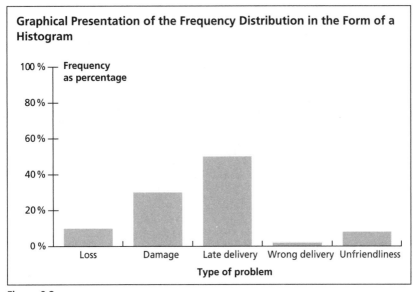

Graphical Presentation of the Frequency Distribution in the Form of a Histogram

Figure 9.2

Frequency Distributions of Complaint-Content Information

Complaint-content information	Questions in the context of frequency analysis	Relevance of analysis result
Complainant		
Internal or external complainant	• How many internal complaints were there in the reporting period? • What is the share of internal complaints in relation to the total number of complaints?	• Internal process monitoring • Cause analysis
Individual complainant (master data)	• How many complainants were there in the reporting period? • How many times did an individual customer complain during this period? • How many customers complained several times? • How is the total number of complaints distributed across different customer groups?	• Complaint management controlling (calculation of articulation rate) • Identification of repeat complainants and of gumblers • Determination of customer group-specific problem perceptions • Development of customer group-specific stimulation measures
Complainant's connection to the complaint case	• To what extent did the person who was directly affected by the problem take the initiative and complain in person? • Which other persons/institutions complained on behalf of the person affected?	• Detection of complaint barriers • Complaint stimulation • Development of sender-specific forms of reaction
Complainant's degree of annoyance	• How often were the customers annoyed and to what extent? • What is the mean value on the annoyance scale?	• Evaluation of the relevance of the problems from the customer's perspective • Basis for the implementation of the FRAC
Complainant's behavioral intentions	• Which behavioral intentions have the complainig customers expressed, and how many times? • What is the number of customers who threaten to switch? • What is the number of customers who engage third-party institutions (media, consumer organizations)?	• Evaluation of the relevance of the problems from the customer's perspective • Clues for identifying jeopardized customer potential • Development of reaction forms and dialogue instruments directed towards third-party institutions
Complaint problem		
Type of problem	• Which problems led to complaints and how often?	• Priorities in the context of the continuous improvement process • Cause analysis
Place where the problem occurred	• How many complaints were there per sales region (sales district, subsidiary) in the report period?	• Monitoring and controlling of decentralized units • Detection of major problem areas specific to each organizational unit • Cause analysis
Date and, if applicable, time the problem occurred	• Are there particular times when more problems occur (time of day, week, month)?	• Cause analysis

Figure 9.3 Part A

Initial or follow-up complaint	• How many first complaints were addressed to the firm during the reporting period? • How many follow-up complaints were addressed to the firm during the reporting period? • What is the share of follow-up complaints in relation to the total number of complaints?	• Configuration of complaint management capacity and processes • Calculation of performance figures in the context of complaint management controlling (follow-up rate) • Monitoring of the degree of goal achievement in complaint stimulation and problem minimization
Case solution desired by the customer	• Which solutions/compensations were expected by the complainants and how often?	• Clues to customer expectations in problem situations • Indications of desired reactions • Indications of adjustments needed in the existing problem solution/compensation policy
Warranty or goodwill case	• In how many complaint cases were warranty claims asserted? • In how many cases did the customer request a goodwill solution? • What are the respective shares of the above cases in relation to the total number of complaints?	• Monitoring of the warranty policy • Monitoring of the goodwill policy • Problem analysis in R&D and manufacturing
Urgency of reaction	• In how many complaint cases did the defined urgency levels have to be activated and how often in each case?	• Identification of serious problems • Monitoring of nonroutine processes
Complaint object		
Product and/or service	• How many times during the reporting period did the customer perceive a product/service as problematic? • Which products/services were most frequently addressed in complaints (in absolute and in relative terms)?	• Cause analysis • Indications of the setting of priorities in improvement measures • Assessment of the potential dangers with respect to product-related sales decreases, image losses, or cross-selling losses
Other aspects of the market offering	• To what extent are other aspects of marketing made the subject of complaints? • What is the share of complaints that are related to pricing (promotional) measures?	• Indications of weaknesses in the strategic and operative marketing planning • Evaluation of the urgency of marketing-related corrective measures
Sociopolitical behavior	• To what extent are sociopolitical topics addressed in complaints? • How are sociopolitical complaints distributed across the specific subject areas?	• Indications of perceived weaknesses of the firm's socio-political engagement • Evaluation of the urgency to make modifications in the basic corporate strategies with social reference

Figure 9.3 Part B

Frequency Distribution of Complaint Handling Information

Complaint-handling information	Questions in the context of frequency distributions	Relevance of the analysis results
Complaint acceptance		
Date of acceptance	• How many complaints reached the firm at different times or in different periods of time?	• Basis of the capacity planning in the area of complaint management (particularly for the complaint center)
Complaint channels	• Which complaint channels were used by dissatisfied customers and how often?	• Monitoring of complaint stimulating measures • Resource planning
Addressee of the complaint	• How many complaints were addressed to which persons/ departments? • How many complaints were directly addressed to the top management?	• Monitoring of complaint stimulating measures
Complaint accepting employee	• Who or which department has accepted how many complaints and in which period?	• Monitoring of the adherence of the principle of complaint ownership • Resource planning • Indications of the targeted use of personnel-oriented measures
Complaint processing		
Complaint owner	• Which employee was involved in which processing procedures and how often?	• Monitoring of the adherence of the principle of complaint ownership
Complaint pro-cessing procedure	• Which processing procedures were initiated and how often?	• Monitoring of the complaint processing procedure
Complaint reaction		
Actually realized solution	• Which problem solutions/ compensations were realized and how often?	• Monitoring of the reaction policy
Promises made to the customer	• Which promises were already made during the acceptance and how often?	• Monitoring of the complaint acceptance • Basis for trainings

Figure 9.4

In principle, univariate frequency analyses, as they are presented here in an example citing problem categories, make sense for all complaint information. Figures 9.3 and 9.4 make this clear for complaint content and complaint handling information and provide indications for which questions can be answered with the respective frequency distribution and for which individual tasks of complaint and retention management the answers provide an informational basis.

Frequency analyses provide an overview of the distribution of the total complaint volume across the important criteria. Based on such an analysis, it can be established, for example, how often a particular problem appeared and to what extent various products are affected by it.

Cross-Tabulation of "Complaint Object" and "Type of Problem"

Type of problem Complaint object	Loss	Damage	Late delivery	Wrong delivery	Unfriendliness	Total
Standard	60 (7.5%)	200 (25%)	450 (56.25%)	8 (1%)	82 (10.25%)	800 (100%)
Express	60 (15%)	160 (40%)	150 (37.5%)	16 (4%)	14 (3.5%)	400 (100%)
Total	120	360	600	24	96	1,200

Figure 9.5

However, whether a systematic correlation exists between problem appearance and complaint object (product) can only be determined with bivariate methods that simultaneously include two criteria—for example, problem category and complaint object—in the analysis.

Bivariate Analysis Techniques

Cross-tabulation should be regarded as the most important bivariate technique. Here the characteristic values of two variables are arranged in a matrix, and the frequency with which each combination occurs is recorded. An example of a cross-tabulation in the context of complaint analysis is reproduced in Figure 9.5.

This cross-tabulation links the criteria "Complaint Object" and "Type of Problem" and provides an answer to the question: "What relationship exists between the complaint object (product/service) and the type of problem occurred?" In the example, it is assumed that the package delivery service offers two types of transport services—"Standard" and "Express"—and differentiates among the five problem categories named.

The absolute and relative frequencies indicate that for the "Standard" product group, it is primarily the problem of "Late Delivery" that crops up (56.25 percent) and for the "Express" product group, there are especially the problem areas of "Damage" (40 percent) and "Late Delivery" (37.5 percent) that appear.

Naturally, it is only appropriate to perform a cross-tabulation if a useful relationship between the complaint criteria can be assumed. It is conceivable, for example, that the type of problem experienced influences the extent of the customer irritation, or that customers who belong to different customer groups also perceive different problems. For this reason, consideration must be given to logical correlations such

Particular Reasonable Relationships between Variables of Complaint Information

	1. Type of problem	2. Place	3. Warranty or goodwill case	4. Urgency of reaction	5. Customer group	6. Extent of annoyance/behavioral intention	7. Product and/or service	8. Complaint channel	9. Addressee of the complaint	10. Actually realized solution
1. Type of problem						●				●
2. Place	●									
3. Warranty or goodwill case										
4. Urgency of reaction										●
5. Customer group	●						●	●	●	
6. Extent of annoyance/ behavioral intention										
7. Product and/or service	●		●							
8. Complaint channel										
9. Addressee of the complaint										●
10. Actually realized solution										

Figure 9.6

as these and then consulted when making the choice of which criteria will be combined. Figure 9.6 contains an overview of especially meaningful relationships among categories of complaint information.

Considerations of the relationships between the variables are directly associated with assumptions about which variable can be used as a predictor of another variable. The variable used as a predictor is designated as the "Predictor Variable," and the variable to be forecast as the "Response Variable." This is taken into account in the corresponding arrangement of the criteria in the matrix: The attributes of the response variable are shown in the columns, whereas the predictor variables are arranged in the rows. The percentage values are always calculated in the direction of the independent variable (row by row). In the example, we assume that whichever problems appear depend on the type of product. Therefore, the variable "Complaint Object" is the predictor variable, and "Type of Problem" is the response variable.

Explanation of Important Cross-Tabulations

Considered variables	Relationship	Relevance of the relationship
Type of problem and degree of annoyance/ behavioral intention	The customer's degree of annoyance and his/her behavioral intention depend on the problem type.	• Problem orientation from the customer's perspective • Access to problems that induce the customer to switch
Type of problem and actually realized solution	The actually realized solution depends on the problem type.	• Indication of consistency and appropriateness of complaint solutions
Place of problem occurrence and type of problem	Different problems occur more often at certain places (subsidiaries, branch offices).	• Indications of subsidiary-specific problem focus
Urgency of reaction and actually realized solution	The actually realized solution depends on the reaction urgency of the complaint, above all on the customer's threat potential.	• Indication of the compliance with guidelines for the treatment of special cases
Customer group and type of problem	The articulated problem types depend on the complainant's affiliation to a certain customer group.	• Segment-specific problem identification • Segment-specific urgency to eliminate problems
Customer group and product/ service	Members of different customer groups complain about problems regarding different products/ services.	• Segment-specific identification of problem afflicted products/ services
Customer group and complaint channel	Members of different customer groups use different complaint channels.	• Segment-specific stimulation measures
Customer group and addressee of the complaint	The addressing of a complaint depends on the complainant's affiliation to a customer group.	• Segment-specific stimulation and channeling
Product/service and type of problem	The occurrence of problems depends on the particular complaint object (product/service).	• Indications of product- and service-related causes of the articulated problems • Setting of priorities in the context of improvement measures
Product/service and warranty or goodwill case	The occurrence of warranty or goodwill cases depends on the particular complaint object (product/service).	• Setting of priorities in the context of improvement measures in order to reduce warranty costs and goodwill costs
Addressee of the complaint and actually realized solution	The actually realized solution depends on the addressee of the complaint.	• Indication of the consistency of the complaint reaction

Figure 9.7

In Figure 9.7, cross-tabulations with important conclusions for complaint management are characterized. In the figure, the observed variables are always given in the order of the predictor variable followed by the response variable.

The next step is to pose the question of how unambiguous the results of the cross-tabulation are. This occurs in the context of a contingency analysis, which helps clarify whether the variables are independent of one another and how strong the association between the predictor and the response variable is.

The Temporal Dimensions of Quantitative Complaint Analyses

In addition to the content dimension, the temporal dimension of the complaint analysis must also be considered. In doing so, one must differentiate between a time-period analysis and a time-series analysis.

In time-period analyses, the facts to be examined are considered for a specific time period, for example, a year. From this analysis, one obtains a status report about the time period under consideration. The package delivery firm in question is, for instance, interested in knowing how often the five problem categories have given the customer reason to complain during the current business year. The corresponding frequency distribution is then specifically created for the time period of this year. Depending upon the degree of time detail desired, other relevant time periods (a day, a week, a month, or a quarter) can be selected.

If frequency distributions and cross-tabulations are performed for different points in time (e.g., days or weeks) that follow one another chronologically within a certain time period, one can speak of time-series analyses. They make clear the temporal development of the analyzed contents over the time period under consideration and are especially significant in analyses of the effectiveness of measures related to complaint management and quality management. If the subject package delivery firm has, for example, resorted to certain measures to resolve the problem of "Late Delivery," an idea of the effectiveness of these measures can be gained from the development of complaints related to the problem (see Figure 9.8).

If time periods and time series from different periods are contrasted with each other in the complaint analyses shown here, one can speak of period comparisons. The results for a particular time period or time series are compared with the results of a corresponding time period or time series. Again, the goal of this comparison is to track certain developments, although it is not the chronological progression that is the focus, but rather the comparison of the results from corresponding points in time from different periods. It may be of interest to know how the effects of problem-prevention measures develop from year to year (see Figure 9.8).

9.1.2 ANALYSES FOR THE PRIORITIZATION OF PROBLEMS

What is important in the next step of the analysis is to prioritize the problems articulated in the complaints from the customer's point of view and consequently to make the "voice of the customer" the maxim for the

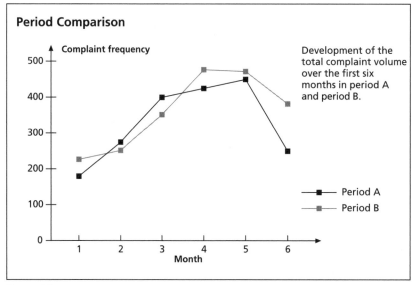

Period Comparison

Development of the total complaint volume over the first six months in period A and period B.

Figure 9.8

continual improvement process. This prioritization is not based exclusively on the frequency with which a certain problem is made the object of a complaint, but also on the subjective importance that the customer attaches to a problem. An important instrument of analysis here is the Frequency-Relevance Analysis of Complaints (FRAC). The result of this analysis is quantified monetarily in the context of the Problem-Related Market Loss Analysis.

9.1.2.1 FREQUENCY-RELEVANCE ANALYSIS OF COMPLAINTS

The Frequency-Relevance Analysis of Complaints (FRAC) is based on the fundamental consideration that the more frequently a problem occurs and the more annoying or significant the customer finds its occurrence, the more urgently the problem requires the attention of management. Two types of information are necessary in each case with respect to the problems experienced by customers: Data on the frequency of the problem occurrence are required and information is also necessary on how significant the customers consider this problem to be (relevance).

Determination of the Frequency and Relevance of Customer Problems

Frequency analysis provides unambiguous and objective values concerning the frequency with which customers articulate a particular problem. The relevance of the problem from the customer's point of view, in contrast, is expressed by the value on a relevance scale. The scales that are shown in Chapter 6.2.2.1.1 for recording complaint information provide examples. These are scales that record the degree of irritation and the consequences for action that result from this irritation.

In the complaint situation, however, customers cannot be directly requested to indicate the extent of their irritation on a scale. This is only possible in the case of Internet complaints if the complaint mask provides an appropriate field. Consequently, an external evaluation of the problem relevance by employees in complaint contact must take place. These evaluations must follow an appropriate classification based on the complainant's wording and pattern of behavior. Since there are no fully unambiguous criteria for this, and the evaluations by various employees can also turn out differently, values derived in this way are to be interpreted with a certain degree of caution.

An alternative to this external evaluation is to survey the customers immediately after closing the complaint process in the context of follow-up interviews to determine the extent of the customers' irritation and the steps they have taken or consider taking. A corresponding scale for the measurement of the perceived relevance is to be integrated in the survey instrument. These results also involve some distortion, since a certain period of time has already elapsed and additional complaint experiences now exist. However, the degree of the irritation is assessed by the customers themselves, not by the employees. By comparing the subsequent customer information with the direct employee estimates, the extent of agreement can be determined, which provides an initial indication of the accuracy of the employees' evaluation.

The FRAC Diagram

If the data on frequency and perceived relevance exist for all problem categories, the FRAC is feasible.

In Figure 9.9, the methodological approach will be demonstrated in an example from a car dealership's complaint volume.

By multiplying the frequency and the average relevance, the problem-related relevance values can be obtained. By subsequently dividing the problem-related relevance values by the total sum of all relevance values, the respective Problem-Value Indices (PVI) are obtained. They express the percentage share of each problem with regard to the total customer dissatisfaction articulated in complaints.

In order to visualize the urgency of troubleshooting measures, it now makes sense to depict the PVI graphically in the form of a Pareto diagram (see Figure 9.10). On the abscissa, the problems—arranged in descending order according to their PVIs—are represented as bars, and their cumulative sums are subsequently drawn in as a line plot. In the example, the first four problem categories account for about 80 percent of the total problems.

It is obvious that problems with the greatest PVI also have the highest priority and thus take precedence in being systematically analyzed and solved.

Calculation of Problem-Value Indices (PVI)

Customer problem	Frequency	Ø Relevance	Relevance value	PVI*	Rank
Work not carried out first time	16	4.2	67.2	7.38	⑥
Long waiting periods at reception	15	1.8	27.0	2.97	⑦
Car returned in dirty state	32	3.0	96.0	10.55	⑤
Car not ready at promised time	51	2.1	107.1	11.77	④
Bill unclear	52	3.2	166.4	18.28	②
Unfriendly service	63	2.4	151.2	16.61	③
Work not agreed on carried out	72	4.1	295.2	32.44	①
Total	301	—	910.10	100.00	—

$$* \text{ Problem Value Index (PVI)} = \frac{\text{Relevance value} \times 100}{\text{Sum of relevance values}}$$

Figure 9.9

Pareto Diagram of the Problem-Value Indices (FRAC Diagram)

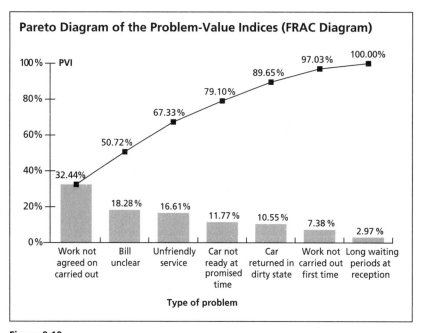

Figure 9.10

The FRAC Matrix

A different form of prioritization of customer problems on the basis of the frequency and relevance values can take place with the help of a two-dimensional diagram that shows the complaint frequency (in percent) on the horizontal axis and the average relevance per problem on the vertical axis. Each problem can then be exactly placed in the diagram according to the (percentage) frequency of its occurrence and the perceived average relevance. By plotting dividing lines, one can obtain a FRAC matrix in which the problems are assigned to one of four fields according to their respective frequency-relevance combination (see Figure 9.11).

Naturally, the problems found in the upper right quadrant ("Work not agreed on carried out" and "Bill unclear") take first priority. After that, it has to be asked whether the problems that are perceived as having low relevance by many customers (lower right quadrant) should be solved first or whether one should primarily eliminate those problems that actually appear less often, but are rated as more relevant (upper left quadrant). There is no general recommendation for making this decision, but there is a lot to be said for first addressing the problem with the greater relevance. This is especially necessary if one comes to the conclusion that this problem will increasingly appear in the future or that customers who are extremely irritated will threaten to take serious sanctions. If, however, one deems the negative effects of the problems that are located in the upper left or the lower right quadrant to be equally serious, then the decision about which should be addressed first should be made according to what is the quickest, easiest, and most cost-effective solution. The problems shown in the lower left quadrant that

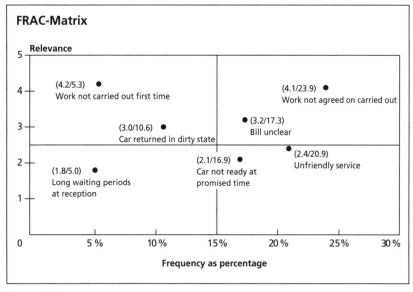

Figure 9.11

have low relevance and occur with low relative frequency have, of course, the lowest priority.

The FRAC in a Time Series

With respect to the analysis over several periods, there are two possibilities: FRAC with a variable problem set and FRAC with a constant problem set.

(1) The FRAC has a dynamic character because the problems recorded vary according to their respective appearance and their perceived importance (FRAC with a variable problem set). This version takes into consideration that new problems may occur or that customers may assess problems differently over time.

(2) In contrast to the above version, it may be advisable for purposes of analyzing the effectiveness of certain measures to carry out a FRAC with a constant problem set. The PVI is calculated at regular intervals for a fixed number of relevant problems, restricting the analysis to the main problems. From this time-period comparison of the PVIs, one obtains an instrument of control over whether the measures that are introduced to eliminate a particular problem have in fact led to the desired result. These problems would have to fall into the lower rankings of the "Top 5" or "Top 10" problem lists, taking into account the expenses for the elimination of the problem's cause(s). One must verify at regular intervals, however, whether the constant problem set still records the key problem categories and make an appropriate adjustment if necessary.

9.1.2.2 PROBLEM-RELATED MARKET LOSS ANALYSIS

An especially meaningful ranking of problems is provided when it is possible to estimate the economic losses that result from the respective problems.

Monetary Valuation on the Basis of the FRAC

A market loss due to dissatisfaction is generated when customers switch because of the perceived problem relevance. In the context of the FRAC, those customers must be regarded as being in danger of switching who indicate scale values of 4 or 5 on the relevance scale. Therefore, the first step is to determine the number of customers with such serious problem ratings. If it is not only the problems experienced and the relevance estimates of the complainants that are recorded in the customer database, but also the complainants' annual sales volume and annual profit contribution, the market losses caused by the individual problems can be calculated immediately. This calculation is made by multiplying for each problem the number of customers who rate the problem as serious by the customers' economic values (see Figure 9.12).

If the customer-individual sales or profits are not available, average values can be used for the calculation of the market loss. Such a calculation provides problem-oriented estimated values for the monetary consequences of the problems that lead to customer complaints.

Problem-Oriented Market Loss Analysis

Type of problem	Switch/terminate	Call-in of third-party institutions	Call-in of media	Employ a lawyer	Total	Rank according to Problem-Value Index	Ø individual sales volume of all customers affected	Problem-oriented market loss	Rank according to the monetary valued Problem-Value Index
Bill unclear	14	2	2	1	19	②	$ 7,200	$ 136,800	①
Work not carried out first time	6	2	1	1	10	⑥	$ 9,600	$ 96,000	②
Work not agreed on carried out	10	4	1	5	20	①	$ 4,500	$ 90,000	③
Unfriendly service	9	3		4	16	③	$ 5,400	$ 86,400	④
Car not ready at promised time	8		3	3	14	④	$ 4,300	$ 60,200	⑤
Car returned in dirty state	6	4	1		11	⑤	$ 3,800	$ 41,800	⑥
Long waiting periods at reception	4				4	⑦	$ 6,700	$ 26,800	⑦

Figure 9.12

If average values for customer sales volume and profit contribution are used in the context of monetary weighting, there will be no change in the ranking of the individual problems. If, on the contrary, one can access customer-individual values, it is conceivable that the original ranking could change. This is always the case when customer groups with different quality ratings with respect to sales volume and profit contribution also differ in being confronted with different problems or reacting to varying degrees of switching when particular problems occur.

Monetary Valuation of Problems Based on Customer Surveys

Adamson (1993), as well as Klein and Sasser (1994), suggest a different version of the problem-related calculation of market losses. According to this method, a representative group of current and former customers are questioned in an independent survey whether the particular problems occurred and what influence these problems have on repurchase behavior or repurchase intentions. For every problem in the analysis, it is determined what percent of those surveyed definitely will not purchase or definitely did not purchase the product due to the occurrence of the problem. On this basis, the number of customers the firm may lose or has already lost as a consequence of the occurrence of the respective

Problem-Oriented Calculation of Market Losses Considering an Airline as an Example

Type of problem \ Monetary valuation/market loss	Number of complainants within the segment	Number of complainants definitely switching airlines due to the problem	**Lost customers**	Market loss = lost customers × Ø customer contribution to the margin ($400)	**Rank**
Overbooking	360	35%	**126**	$ 50,400	①
Unfriendly ground personnel	720	15%	**108**	$ 43,200	②
Cancellation of flights	435	20%	**87**	$ 34,800	③
Lack of seat comfort	720	9%	**65**	$ 26,000	④
Baggage loss	180	25%	**45**	$ 18,000	⑤
Delay	645	6%	**39**	$ 15,600	⑥
Lack of catering on board	540	5%	**27**	$ 10,800	⑦
Total	**3,600**	—	**497**	**$ 198,800**	—

Ø Customer contribution to the margin: $400

Adapted (with changes) from: Adamson 1993: 443; Klein and Sasser 1994: 15

Figure 9.13

problem can be calculated. If one then multiplies the number of the potential or actual lost customers per problem by the average customer profit contribution, one can also make a rough calculation of the market losses caused by the respective problems. The extent of the market losses then determines the ranking on the priority list. Figure 9.13 shows a fictitious example of a problem-related calculation of market losses for an airline.

The methods depicted represent not only instruments of analysis, but also controlling instruments for the process of improvement. PVIs from the Frequency-Relevance Analysis and problem-related market-loss values provide an important orientation for the decision regarding the priority of measures taken to improve products and processes. In addition, they are key factors for the verification of the success of corrective measures. In a comparison of time periods, reduced PVIs and market-loss values provide important indications that quality-improvement measures have actually led to improvements that are clearly perceived by customers.

9.2 QUALITATIVE COMPLAINT ANALYSIS

The results of the quantitative complaint analysis must be more broadly interpreted in the next step, since they in fact reveal organizational weaknesses but cannot provide clear indications of the actual causes of the deficiencies. A qualitative complaint analysis is thus required, whose purpose is to analyze the diagnosed problems with regard to their exact causes by using special instruments and then to derive measures for improvement.

The focus of qualitative complaint analysis is the detailed investigation of the individual case and a systematic cause-and-effect analysis. At the start of each causal analysis, it is necessary to undertake an exact definition of the problem. For this purpose, the individual cases within a problem category should be investigated in detail. In doing so, it usually turns out that indications of possible problem causes can be found in the detailed description of the problem's circumstances. In order, however, to avoid rash conclusions and uncover further causes and their interdependencies, the analysis must be carried out in a systematic manner. The Cause-and-Effect Diagram (Ishikawa or Fishbone Diagram) is a graphic tool that is particularly well suited to this purpose.

In a cause-and-effect analysis, we are concerned with a process by which all the possible influencing variables (Causes) are determined for each clearly defined problem (Effect). These influencing variables and their relationships to one another are described in a structured manner in the Cause-and-Effect Diagram, and the goal of this process is to identify the causes that are actually responsible for the occurrence of the problem by tracing the chain of events back to its origin.

The construction of Cause-and-Effect Diagrams usually involves six steps:

1. Problem Formulation (Effect): Based on the problem focuses shown in the complaint analysis, a specific problem is selected and defined. This problem is recorded on the right side of a chart in the "effect box," and a long horizontal arrow ("spine") is drawn from the left to the problem on the right.

2. Identification of the Main Causes (Cause): The Cause-and-Effect Diagram receives its structure from the identification of global causal dimensions. In order to uncover all the potential key influencing factors, it is advisable to fall back on generally accepted determinants in the first step of the analysis such as the "3 M and P": method, material, machinery, and people. The main causes identified are written in boxes above or below the spine, and the boxes are connected to the spine.

3. Identification of Detailed Causes for the Global Causal Dimensions: As a next step, all the possible detailed causes for each causal dimension are compiled during a brainstorming process. They appear in the diagram as branches within the "bones." Each cause

itself can again be described more exactly in the form of "smaller bones." At this point, it is important to consider only the causes of errors, not possible solutions.

4. Identification of the Most Likely Detailed Causes: The detailed causes identified must be analyzed and evaluated to determine which are probably most responsible for the occurrence of the problem. These causes are then visually highlighted in the diagram.

5. Verification of the Detailed Causes Identified: The causes identified are now subjected to a detailed examination in the order of their probable influence. This process continues until a consensus is reached within the improvement team about the key individual causes.

6. Derivation and Introduction of the Problem Solution(s): On the basis of this analysis, action plans are developed for how the problem can be eliminated in the long term. In developing these plans, both the advantages and the possible disadvantages associated with each potential problem solution should be brought out so that a balanced decision can be made.

Before the measure on which the team has decided is implemented, it must be discussed by all the departments and people affected in the firm and modified if necessary. If a consensus is reached in the course of this feedback process, indicating that all those in charge support the suggested measures, then the suggested solution is implemented. After the implementation of the measures for improvement, the firm must verify whether it was in fact able to minimize the occurrence of the problem or that new and different problems were not created by the implementation of the problem solution. If the complaint volume for a certain problem that had to be eliminated was very high before the initiation of the continuous improvement process, the measures introduced must be reflected in a lower complaint volume for the observed problem in the short term.

In Spotlight 7 below, the strategy of the Cause-and-Effect Analysis will be made clear by means of an example case.

SPOTLIGHT 7

The results of a firm's complaint analysis showed that many customers complained about not being able to reach the firm by telephone. The phone often rang more than ten times before an employee answered. At times, it seemed that the firm was completely unreachable.

Since neither technical errors nor low personnel capacity could account for the cause at first glance, an improvement team was given the task of uncovering the actual cause.

The problem of "Phone Not Answered" was first defined even more narrowly. A reaction was rated as "delayed" when callers

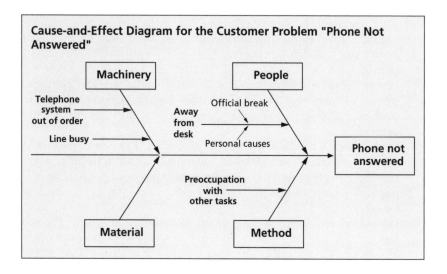

Cause-and-Effect Diagram for the Customer Problem "Phone Not Answered"

heard more than three rings before they were greeted. The "3 M and P" (method, material, machinery, and people) were initially entered on the diagram as the main causes.

To specify the causes further, a brainstorming session was held, which led to the identification of a series of individual causes (see the following illustration of a cause-and-effect diagram). In the discussion about the reasons for the excessively long waiting times, the team rated the factors "Away from Desk" and "Preoccupation with Other Tasks" as especially likely. The firm did not have a main switchboard. Instead, the receptionist took the incoming calls.

In order to verify whether these reasons were in fact responsible, the reception area and the telephone reaction behavior was carefully observed for five days. It turned out that the receptionist was not at her desk for an average of 65 minutes per day. She left her desk for breaks and when she accompanied important guests to the CEO of the firm. During this time, the firm received an average of twelve calls that were not answered. In addition to this problem, the receptionist took about eight calls per day only after the phone had rung numerous times because she was busy with other activities (receiving mail, greeting customers, providing information). The results of the observation confirmed the presumed problem causes and provided the basis for the development of the following specific suggestions for improvement:

- A second employee, who primarily carries out paperwork, is made responsible for accepting telephone calls and trained for this task.

- During the receptionist's official break times, this employee completely takes over the reception desk and the telephone.

- If the receptionist has to leave her desk briefly for other reasons, she switches over the telephone system. The colleague is automatically informed by the system about this switchover.

- The receptionist no longer accompanies important customers to the CEO, but instead informs the secretary to pick up the guests in the reception area.

- If the employee at the reception desk is so busy with other tasks that she cannot attend to the telephone immediately, she transfers the call to the colleague by simply pressing a button.

When the firm attempted to implement these suggestions, personnel (training), technical (telephone system) and organizational (workplace of the former typist) issues had to be solved, which required the cooperation of a number of affected employees.

The recommendations of the team were finalized by management and subsequently implemented. In order to be able to judge properly the effectiveness of the measures introduced, a comparative observation was carried out and the number of related complaints was used as a comparison.

10
Complaint-Management Controlling

Complaint management is a complex area of activity that must be controlled in a planned fashion with respect to corporate goals. It therefore requires systematic controlling that puts complaint managers in a position to set specific goals and constantly monitor the extent to which those goals have been reached and—if necessary—develop corrective actions.

One must differentiate between evidence controlling, task controlling, and cost-benefit controlling in the context of complaint management controlling:

- The central issue in evidence controlling is the study of the extent to which customer dissatisfaction is expressed in complaints and the degree to which the complaints registered in the firm reflect the complaints actually articulated by customers.

- The focus of task controlling is the specification and monitoring of quality and productivity indicators and standards for all complaint management activities. In the context of objective task controlling, compliance with performance standards in all the task areas of complaint management is monitored through objective measurement categories. In the course of subjective task controlling, the satisfaction of the complainant with the direct complaint management process (complaint satisfaction) is documented.

- In cost-benefit controlling, the costs arising from complaint management are systematically processed, and the benefit components of complaint management are operationalized and monetarily quantified. On this basis, the profit of complaint management, as well as the "Return on Complaint Management (RoC)," can be calculated.

10.1 EVIDENCE CONTROLLING

The fundamental task of evidence controlling is the determination of the extent to which complaint management is in a position to make the degree of dissatisfaction of the firm's customers evident to management. Two main starting points must be differentiated. It is important to identify the unvoiced complaints of dissatisfied customers. It is also necessary to determine the extent of those complaints that are articulated, but not registered in the firm, so-called hidden complaints.

10.1.1 ARTICULATION RATE, COMPLAINT EVIDENCE RATE, AND FOLLOW-UP COMPLAINT EVIDENCE RATE

Before the key figures of the evidence controlling are presented, it is first necessary to address briefly a figure that firms frequently use as an indicator when estimating the relevance of the complaint volume, but whose use is extraordinarily problematic—the complaint rate.

The Problematic Complaint Rate

The complaint rate (CR) represents the share of all customers who complain to the firm in relation to the total customer base. The CR is expressed as the quotient of the total number of complainants and the total number of customers. If the firm in question receives 5,000 complaints, then the complaint quote with a customer base of 100,000 amounts to 5 percent. This figure is calculated by many firms and, when it turns out to be low, is interpreted as proof of high customer satisfaction. This conclusion is, however, incorrect, since only a fraction of customer dissatisfaction is expressed in complaints. The meaningfulness of this relative figure, therefore, is slight. If it is calculated regularly all the same, the firm should strive to minimize it by reducing customer dissatisfaction.

Articulation Rate: Determination of the Extent and Share of Nonarticulated Complaints

By no means do all dissatisfied customers complain, so only the tip of the dissatisfaction iceberg is visible in complaints. The first goal of evidence controlling is to make the size and structure of the dissatisfaction iceberg transparent. Evidence controlling provides information about how the complaint volume registered in the firm should be analyzed and what importance should be placed on complaint stimulation.

Of central importance is the total articulation rate (TAR), which expresses the ratio of the number of complainants to the number of all dissatisfied customers who have a reason to complain. The greater the articulation rate, the more the firm has succeeded in inducing disappointed or nonconvinced customers to complain. The firm should strive to maximize this rate, that is, to convert all "unexpressed" complaints into articulated complaints if possible.

Figure 10.1 shows the dissatisfaction iceberg. The part that is visible indicates the percentage of dissatisfied customers who complain; the part that is "underwater" shows the percentage of dissatisfied customers who do not complain.

A portion of the articulated complaints remains hidden to the directors of complaint management. These are complaints that are not directly submitted to the complaint department and usually are not documented either so that their existence is not obvious. This applies primarily to all complaints that are expressed to customer-contact personnel. The associates accepting the complaints are often unprepared for complaint situations or are afraid of negative consequences and thus record

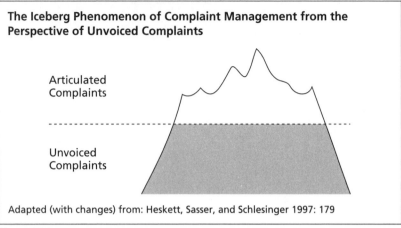

Figure 10.1

only a fraction of the complaints. Studies show that, depending upon the industry and the extent of the problem, only about 10 to 60 percent of the customer complaints that are articulated in decentralized customer-contact locations are registered and are therefore known to the central customer care department (Goodman, O'Brien, and Segal 2000).

If, in addition to the nonarticulated complaints, one also considers the "hidden" complaints that are submitted to decentralized locations but not registered, estimates seem realistic that the main department responsible for complaints is only informed of about 1 to 5 percent of customer problems. Figure 10.2 makes this clear by showing that the part of the iceberg that is visible to management shrinks considerably when one takes the hidden complaints into consideration. At the same time, it becomes clear that a larger part of the iceberg can be made visible not only by way of complaint stimulation measures, but also by way of internal measures for the improvement of complaint acceptance and transfer.

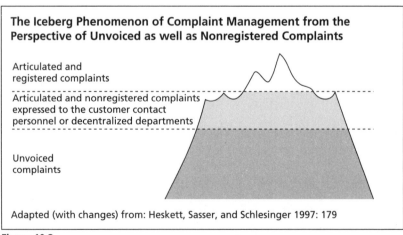

Figure 10.2

The difference between registered and nonregistered complaints makes it possible to calculate the registered articulation rate (RAR) in addition to the total articulation rate, by relating the number of complaints actually registered to the absolute number of dissatisfied customers. As a rule, this quotient is much lower than the quotient of the total articulation rate. The share of the complaints that are hidden in the firm is then reflected in the difference between the two articulation rates.

A high share of hidden complaints also implies that inexact knowledge exists in management as to the reactions of the decentralized units and the level of complaint satisfaction that is reached. A small part of the dissatisfaction that still exists becomes clear when dissatisfied complainants themselves approach the next higher level of authority in each case. Since only relatively few complainants take this route, however, these follow-up complaints also represent merely a tip of the complaint dissatisfaction iceberg, which furthermore becomes smaller and smaller, the more hierarchical levels are added. Figure 10.3 gives an example and shows that it is quite possible that of 500 dissatisfied customers, in the end only one complaint (0.2%) is visible to the central complaint unit or to top management.

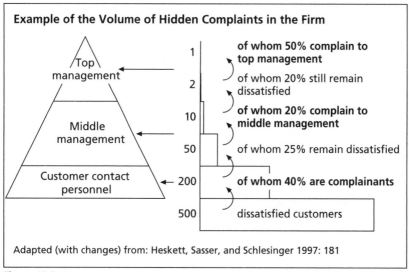

Example of the Volume of Hidden Complaints in the Firm

Adapted (with changes) from: Heskett, Sasser, and Schlesinger 1997: 181

Figure 10.3

Evidence Rates: Determination of the Extent and Share of Hidden Complaints

Since the danger exists that the directors of complaint management and top management will have a false perception of the extent and type of dissatisfaction despite complaint analysis, the second goal of evidence controlling is to reveal the extent and share of hidden complaints. The complaint evidence rate and the follow-up complaint evidence rate aid in achieving this goal.

The complaint evidence rate is the result of comparing the number of complaints recorded in the firm and the collective number of articulated complaints. This rate indicates what percentage of the complaints articulated to any given department are also documented and available to the directors of complaint management for purposes of analysis and information utilization.

The follow-up complaint evidence rate is the relationship between the number of follow-up complaints documented in the firm and the collective number of follow-up complaints articulated to the firm. It expresses the extent to which the directors of complaint management are informed about the volume of those complaints that are due to complainants' dissatisfaction with the handling of their initial complaints.

The question of whether these rates should be maximized is answered differently for the complaint evidence rate and to the follow-up complaint evidence rate.

As far as the hidden complaints are concerned, inducing customer-contact employees to record thoroughly every critical statement that occurs during customer contact is not always financially justifiable, nor can such an approach always be implemented. This applies especially in the case of smaller concerns that can be immediately solved to the customer's satisfaction. The firm should, therefore, only strive to maximize the complaint evidence rate if it can be demonstrated that the financial benefit of completely documenting all the critical statements exceeds the costs of doing so. Otherwise, firm-specific minimum standards should be established. The value of the calculated complaint evidence rates comes from the firm obtaining a realistic idea of the actual complaint volume. On this basis, decisions about priorities for corrective measures and measures for the complaint-specific training of customer-contact employees can be made.

In terms of the follow-up complaint evidence rate, the situation must be assessed differently. When dissatisfied complainants have to complain a second time, one can always assume that they are highly dissatisfied and in danger of switching. In addition to this, the firm incurs relatively high processing costs. For these reasons, the firm should obtain as precise a view as possible of these incidents, which means that it should strive to maximize the follow-up complaint evidence rate.

Figure 10.4 shows an overview of the evidence controlling rates.

10.1.2 INFORMATIONAL BASES FOR THE DETERMINATION OF THE CONTROLLING VARIABLES OF EVIDENCE CONTROLLING

The data for the calculation of articulation and evidence rates can be taken from complaint analysis and determined through customer surveys. An independent survey is not necessary in this case; rather, one can simply supplement regular customer or complaint satisfaction surveys with questions that refer to complaint behavior.

Control Parameters of Evidence Controlling	
Total Articulation Rate	$\dfrac{\text{Number of complainants}}{\text{Number of dissatisfied customers}}$
Registered Articulation Rate	$\dfrac{\text{Number of registered complainants}}{\text{Number of dissatisfied customers}}$
Complaint Evidence Rate	$\dfrac{\text{Number of registered complaints}}{\text{Number of articulated complaints}}$
Follow-up Complaint Evidence Rate	$\dfrac{\text{Number of registered follow-up complaints}}{\text{Number of articulated follow-up complaints}}$

Figure 10.4

The calculation of the total articulation rate takes into account the number of all customers who complain in the numerator and the number of customers who are disappointed in the firm's performance and have reason to complain in the denominator. In order to determine these two values, customers are asked in the course of customer satisfaction surveys whether they were confronted with a problem that constitutes cause for a complaint. The number of customers who answer yes becomes the value in the denominator. These customers are further requested to provide an answer to the question of whether they have also in fact made a complaint. Customers who once again answer yes reflect the total number of complainants and thus the corresponding variable in the numerator. In determining the registered articulation rate, the denominator is the same as it is for the total articulation rate. The value of the numerator with the number of registered complainants can be taken from the complaint analysis.

The numerators of the complaint evidence rate and of the follow-up complaint evidence rate should likewise be drawn from the complaint analysis, which also reveals the number of follow-up complaints next to the number of registered complaints. The data for the respective denominators should again be collected in the context of the satisfaction survey, in which customers are requested to indicate whether they have complained or had cause to make a follow-up complaint and, if yes, how often and to which person or department. In order to determine the denominator of the follow-up complaint evidence ratio, a similar question can also be integrated into the complaint satisfaction measurements.

Customers who disclose that they have not complained despite being dissatisfied can also be requested to provide reasons for their renunciation of a complaint. The corresponding answers provide important indications of the complaint barriers that are perceived by customers. This information is a significant input for complaint stimulation, since it provides starting points for how management measures can be used to improve the cost-benefit ratio of filing a complaint from the customers' perspective.

Excerpt from a Customer Satisfaction Questionnaire Relating to Complaint Behavior as a Basis for the Calculation of Evidence Controlling Rates

How satisfied are you overall with the products/services offered?

☐   ☐   ☐   ☐   ☐

completely   very   satisfied   less   dissatisfied
satisfied   satisfied   satisfied

Did you experience a problem that gives reason to complain?

☐ Yes   Explain: _____

☐ No

If so: Did you complain?

☐ Yes   To whom did you complain? (If you complained repeatedly or
          to different departments about this problem, please specify!)

          _____

          _____

☐ No   What were the reasons for waiving a complaint?
        ☐ Correct address unknown
        ☐ Correct phone number unknown
        ☐ Too circumstancial
        ☐ Lack of employee's competence
        ☐ Does not lead to a result, anyway
        ☐ Not worthwhile
        ☐ Problem difficult to explain
        ☐ Other _____

Figure 10.5

Figure 10.5 shows an example of the questions that must be posed as part of a general satisfaction survey so that evidence controlling can then provide the information shown.

10.2 TASK CONTROLLING

In the context of task controlling, the quality of complaint management task fulfillment is to be monitored by using meaningful standards. In order to establish these standards, three activities must be carried out:

- selection of quality dimensions
- determination of quality indicators, and
- determination of target figures.

The first step of the planning is to determine quality dimensions for the various tasks on the basis of complaint-management goals. For example, timeliness, keeping of promises, and on-time execution represent quality dimensions of the "complaint processing" task module. Figure 10.6 provides an overview of the quality dimensions of all the tasks in the complaint-management process.

While these quality dimensions can, for the most part, be easily described in general terminology, the next step in the process is to tackle the difficult task of finding quality indicators for these quality dimen-

Quality Dimensions of Complaint Management

Task	Quality Dimensions
Complaint stimulation	• Complaint volume of dissatisfied customers • Correct addressing of customer complaints • Use of existing complaint channels • Easy accessibility
Complaint acceptance	• Customer-oriented design of the initial contact • Prompt forwarding of complaint cases • Correct forwarding of complaint cases • Complete registration of complaint information • Correct registration of complaint information
Complaint processing	• Promptness of complaint processing • Adherance to commitments • Processing on time • Active approach to the customer • Individual treatment of the complaint
Complaint reaction	• Complete solution • Fair solution
Complaint analysis	• User-oriented accomplishment of quantitative analysis • Precision of cause analysis
Complaint reporting	• User-oriented provision of information • On-time provision of information • Adherence to scheduled reporting dates
Complaint information utilization	• Use of complaint information for quality improvements • Use of complaint information for the development of new products/services

Figure 10.6

sions. Here we can distinguish between subjective and objective indicators. In the case of the subjective quality indicators, the satisfaction of the complainant is chosen as the benchmark, for instance, satisfaction with the promptness of the complaint processing. In the case of the objective quality indicators, the quality dimensions are specified independent of the opinion of the affected person (e.g., the time frame for complaint processing).

If the quality indicators have been defined, the desired targets must be determined, and target values must be fixed on a measurement scale. An average satisfaction level of 90 percent or a time frame of ten days for complaint processing could thus be established as target values for the promptness of the complaint processing.

Combining quality indicators with desired targets results in standards that are the target figures upon which planning and monitoring are based. The performance expectations of management are reflected in the standards. They are, therefore, task specifications and benchmarks at the same time, based on which the employees can evaluate themselves and management can evaluate the performance of the employees and of the firm (Berry, Zeithaml, and Parasuraman 1990). In establishing the objective standards, one must keep in mind that they are based on the expectations of the customers, which ensures that the processes are consistently directed toward the complaint satisfaction being targeted. Furthermore, all standards must be realistic in order to avoid discouraging the employees. Therefore and to assure the acceptance of the standards, it is necessary that employees be involved in the determination of the standards.

The focus of subjective and objective task controlling is the monitoring of the standards. A discrepancy between the actual values of a current measurement and the target values of the standards must lead to a verification of the causes and to the introduction of corrective measures.

10.2.1 SUBJECTIVE TASK CONTROLLING

Within the framework of subjective task controlling, the firm determines how the quality of task fulfillment in the context of complaint management is assessed by the people concerned. For the tasks of the direct complaint-management processes, the people concerned are the complainants; for the tasks of the indirect complaint-management process, the people concerned are the internal customers of complaint management.

10.2.1.1 MEASUREMENT OF COMPLAINT SATISFACTION

A fundamental criterion for the successful execution of complaint-management tasks is the satisfaction of the complainant. Customers associate their complaint articulation with certain expectations pertaining to the accessibility of the firm, the processing of the case, and the resolution of the problem. They then take this complaint expectation as a benchmark that they use to compare their actual experience with the corporate reaction. Depending on whether their expectations were fulfilled or exceeded, or were not fulfilled, they experience complaint satisfaction or complaint dissatisfaction. The extent of this feeling of satisfaction or dissatisfaction has an extraordinarily large influence on the attitude as well as on the communication and purchase behavior of the complainant. Satisfied customers thus develop an especially positive attitude toward the firm, talk about their good experiences within their social sphere and are characterized by particularly high loyalty. What is important, therefore, is to determine complaint satisfaction regularly for purposes of performance measurement and to identify the strengths and weaknesses of complaint management that are perceived by customers.

Complaint-satisfaction measurement involves decisions about the content of the questionnaire, the date of the survey, the choice of respondents, and the use of the survey results for the derivation and monitoring of standards.

Design of the Contents of the Survey

With respect to the contents of the survey, the firm can fall back on insights of complaint satisfaction research into the fundamental dimen-

sions and attributes of complaint satisfaction. According to this research, customers primarily evaluate corporate complaint management on the basis of the following four central quality dimensions:
- Accessibility
- Quality of Interaction
 –Friendliness/Politeness
 –Empathy/Understanding
 –Effort/Helpfulness
 –Activity/Initiative
 –Reliability
- Promptness of Reaction
- Adequacy/Fairness of the Solution.

Satisfaction values are to be defined as subjective quality indicators for these quality indicators of complaint management (see Figure 10.7).

Complaint-Satisfaction Values as Subjective Quality Indicators of Complaint Management

Task	Quality dimensions	Subjective quality indicators (Complaint satisfaction)
Complaint stimulation	• Easy accessibility	• Satisfaction with accessibility
Complaint acceptance	• Customer-oriented design of the initial contact	• Satisfaction with friendliness/ politeness • Satisfaction with understanding • Satisfaction with helpfulness/ empathy
Complaint processing	• Promptness of complaint processing	• Satisfaction with promptness of processing
	• Adherence to commitments	• Satisfaction with reliability
	• Active approach to the customers	• Satisfaction with the activity/ initiative regarding the approach
	• Individual treatment of the complaint	• Satisfaction with the individual treatment of the complaint
Complaint reaction	• Complete solution	• Satisfaction with the completeness of the solution
	• Fair solution	• Satisfaction with the fairness of the solution
	• Solution as a whole	• Satisfaction with the overall solution

Figure 10.7

The determination of complaint satisfaction occurs by using a standardized questionnaire that is either mailed within the context of a written survey or that forms the basis for a telephone interview. Figure 10.8 shows a corresponding questionnaire used to determine complaint satisfaction.
- The customer is initially (in Question 1) asked about the problem that gave rise to the complaint.

- In Questions 2 through 4, the customers are asked to describe and to assess the process of complaint articulation. After the factual questions of the chosen complaint method and the addressee, the complainants have the opportunity to make statements about the firm's accessibility and to describe access problems more clearly.

Complaint Satisfaction Questionnaire

1. **In the past months, you were annoyed with our firm and you complained. What was the exact reason for the complaint?**
   ☐ Problem A   ☐ Problem B   ☐ Problem C   ☐ Problem D   ☐ _____

2. **Through which channel did you articulate your complaint?**
   ☐ in writing ☐ in person ☐ by phone ☐ by fax ☐ by e-mail ☐ _____

3. **To which person/department did you address your complaint?**
   _____

4. **Was it easy for you to complain to us?**

   ☐   ☐   ☐   ☐   ☐
   very easy   rather easy neither easy   rather difficult very difficult
                             nor difficult

   If difficulties arose, what were they about?
   _____

5. **Which solution did you want to achieve by articulating your complaint?**
   _____
   _____

6. **Which solution was offered to you?**
   _____
   _____
   _____

7. **How satisfied were you with the solution?**

   ☐   ☐   ☐   ☐   ☐
   completely satisfied very satisfied satisfied   less satisfied dissatisfied

8. **How do you rate our reaction to your complaint (concerning the acceptance, inquiry calls, our reply) relating to**

	completely satisfied	very satisfied	satisfied	less satisfied	dissatisfied
Professional competence	☐	☐	☐	☐	☐
Friendliness	☐	☐	☐	☐	☐
Understanding of your situation	☐	☐	☐	☐	☐
Individual treatment of your case	☐	☐	☐	☐	☐
Helpfulness	☐	☐	☐	☐	☐
Active approach to you	☐	☐	☐	☐	☐
Adherence to commitments	☐	☐	☐	☐	☐

9. **How long did it take until the case was closed (from filing the complaint to final answer)?**
   _____

Figure 10.8 Part A

- The perceived thoroughness and fairness of the solution, as well as the overall satisfaction with the solution, is verified in Questions 5 through 7. The respondents are also requested to specify both their expectations and the actual solution and to provide the degree of their satisfaction based on a comparison of these two items.

10. **How satisfied were you with the promptness of the overall complaint processing?**

☐	☐	☐	☐	☐
completely satisfied	very satisfied	satisfied	less satisfied	dissatisfied

11. **You will probably not rate all aspects of our complaint processing equally. Therefore, in the following table, we list four aspects and ask you to rate these aspects. Twenty points are at your disposal. Please distribute them among the specific aspects so that the most important aspect receives most of the points, the second most important aspect gets fewer points than the most important aspect, and so on.**
    - Accessibility of our firm (reachability of the responsible department and availability of the complaint address) .... _____
    - Type of reaction (friendliness, empathy, helpfulness, individuality, reliability) .... _____
    - Adequacy of the solution (completeness of the solution, fairness of the compensation) .... _____
    - Promptness (quick answer, short handling time) .... _____

    Total   20

12. **If you consider your overall experience with this complaint, how satisfied are you with the handling of your complaint case?**

☐	☐	☐	☐	☐
completely satisfied	very satisfied	satisfied	less satisfied	dissatisfied

13. **What could we have done better regarding the handling of your complaint?**

_____

_____

_____

14. **How is/was your opinion about us**

	very good				very bad
• before the problem occurrence?	☐	☐	☐	☐	☐
• after the problem occurrence?	☐	☐	☐	☐	☐
• today after the finalization of the complaint case?	☐	☐	☐	☐	☐

15. **Did you talk about your complaint experience to other people (friends, relatives, colleagues)?**

    ☐ Yes ☐ No If Yes, to how many people?
    - In the circle of family and relatives: .. Approx. _____ People
    - In the circle of colleagues: .... Approx. _____ People
    - In the circle of friends/acquaintances: Approx. _____ People
    - In the circle of club colleagues: ...... Approx. _____ People

16. **Did you recommend to other people (friends, relatives, colleagues) to buy products/services of our firm due to your complaint experience?**

    ☐ Yes ☐ No If Yes, to how many people?
    - In the circle of family and relatives: .. Approx. _____ People
    - In the circle of colleagues: .... Approx. _____ People
    - In the circle of friends/acquaintances: Approx. _____ People
    - In the circle of club colleagues: ...... Approx. _____ People

Figure 10.8 Part B

17. Did you discourage other people from buying products/services of our firm due to your complaint experience?

☐ Yes   ☐ No   If Yes, to how many people?

- In the circle of family and relatives: .. Approx. _____ People
- In the circle of colleagues: .... Approx. _____ People
- In the circle of friends/acquaintances: Approx. _____ People
- In the circle of club colleagues: ...... Approx. _____ People

18. Did you purchase a product or a service from our firm or did you continue the business relationship since the day you articulated your complaint?

☐ Yes   ☐ No

18.1 If Yes, which impact did the complaint experience for the continuance of the business relationship have?

☐ Crucially or great impact
☐ Low or no impact

18.2 If No, will you buy products/services from our firm, or will you continue the business relationship in the future?

☐ Yes   ☐ No

Which impact did the complaint experience for your decision have?

☐ Crucially or great impact
☐ Low or no impact

Figure 10.8 Part C

Question 8 registers the assessment of the interactions during acceptance and interim communications with respect to competence, friendliness, understanding, effort, activity, and reliability.

- The promptness of the processing is taken into consideration with one factual question regarding the duration of the processing and another regarding the assessment of this time period (Questions 9 and 10).
- In Question 11, the customers are given the task of weighting the four key dimensions by distributing a certain number of points according to the perceived importance of the dimensions.
- Global satisfaction with the entire complaint handling process is then surveyed (Question 12). In this way, the influence of the various dimensions on the global judgment can be calculated in the context of a regression analysis, and the actual weighting can be compared with that provided by the customer. Customers are also provided the opportunity to make specific suggestions that point to shortcomings they might have experienced or opportunities for improvement they might have seen (Question 13).
- In the concluding block of questions, the effects of the complaint experience on the attitudes and behavior of the customer are surveyed. First, an attempt is made to reconstruct the change in the customer's attitude toward the product and the firm during the entire process, that is, from before the problem occurred to after it occurred and up until the moment after the complaint case was conclusively terminated (Question 14). Subsequently, the customers' communica-

tion behavior is documented in terms of how they related the complaint experience and any specific recommendations for or against the product or firm (Questions 15 through 17). Finally, Question 18 helps to determine whether the complainant has maintained the business relationship since the time the complaint was made and how important complaint handling was.

This questionnaire must, of course, be modified for specific purposes. Changes arise based on the product's purchase frequency and relevant specific analysis goals. In addition, it makes sense to acquire sociodemographic data (age, gender, customer group, etc.)

Survey Intervals

There is a great deal to be said for carrying out the complaint satisfaction survey at fixed intervals. In small and medium-sized businesses with a low complaint volume, an annual survey may suffice. In large firms with a high complaint volume, a continual survey at monthly intervals would appear to be wise. The period of time that elapses before the final complaint reaction is always short and of approximately the same duration, so the customers' immediate impressions are measured in a uniform way. The firm constantly has current data at its disposal, which also puts it in a position to react quickly to arising problems.

Satisfaction Standards

The results of the complaint satisfaction survey serve as the basis for the formulation of subjective quality standards for the tasks of the direct complaint-management process.

In the following section, we will proceed on the assumption that, as in the questionnaire in Figure 10.8, complaint satisfaction is measured on a five-point scale that ranges from "fully satisfied" to "dissatisfied."

For the analysis of the results, the values of this scale are assigned to three groups. Customers who marked the response category "fully satisfied" make up the first group of convinced complainants. The satisfied complainants are those customers who marked the response category "very satisfied" or "satisfied." All the customers who answered "less satisfied" or "dissatisfied" belong to the group of disappointed complainants.

The reason for forming two satisfaction groups lies in a shortcoming of the traditional approaches taken by many firms, which add the values for "fully satisfied," "very satisfied" and "satisfied" and in this way frequently calculate success rates of over 80 percent. Improvements in complaint management then seem neither necessary nor sensible to them in view of this high value. Often, however, this turns out to be a false conclusion. The complainants who are "very satisfied" or "satisfied" but not fully convinced prove to be less loyal than convinced complainants. For this reason, it is important to reach the greatest possible percentage of convinced complainants, and this figure thus becomes the key criterion for the derivation of standards.

Once the current status is known, standards must be established as targets. To accomplish this, target specifications must be defined for the respective subjective quality indicators. This definition occurs primarily in the form of minimum percentages of convinced complainants for whom the highest probability of loyalty exists. At the same time, however, standards for the maximum percentages of disappointed complainants should be formulated.

Figure 10.9 shows an example of this use of complaint satisfaction values as subjective quality standards. Minimum standards for "Convinced Complainants" and maximum standards for "Disappointed Complainants" are established for global complaint satisfaction and the various individual characteristics. Because different targets created for individual characteristics can be traced back to the current status indicates a different level in each case and is of differing importance for global complaint satisfaction. The goals may also be achievable to different degrees. This is the case, for example, when the requirements for rapid processing of complaints are already established, but measures for improving customer contact, such as the establishment of a hotline, are not planned until a later date. The standard values in our example for the indicators "Satisfaction with the Activity/Initiative in Making Contact" are lower than for the indicator "Satisfaction with the Promptness of Complaint Processing."

Since the fundamental goal of complaint management is to achieve customer loyalty through complaint satisfaction, it also makes sense to establish standards for the loyalty figures surveyed, such as further recommendation behavior and willingness to repurchase.

Once the results of the complaint satisfaction survey are available, a multiple regression analysis can be performed to determine how the complaint satisfaction of the customers affects their global complaint satisfaction. The firm then obtains statements about which characteristics significantly influence global complaint satisfaction and how great this relative influence is. The results may be presented in a column graph, for instance, so that both the satisfaction values reached and their impor-

Satisfaction Values as Subjective Quality Standards

Subjective quality indicators	Minimum-standard "convinced complainants"	Maximum-standard "disappointed complainants"
Overall complaint satisfaction	65 %	15%
Satisfaction with the promptness of complaint processing	90 %	5%
Satisfaction with reliability	80 %	8%
Satisfaction with the active approach to the customer	60 %	5%
Satisfaction with the individual treatment of the case	65 %	15%
Satisfaction with the solution	85 %	5%

Figure 10.9

tance for the quality characteristics in question are immediately apparent. On the basis of such results, standards can then be formulated that target an improvement in the satisfaction values, whereby special importance is given to those quality characteristics in particular that were proven to have a significant influence on global complaint satisfaction.

By comparing the actual value reached in a current complaint satisfaction survey with the defined target values, the firm can analyze the extent to which the standards were met. The results can then be presented in the form of degrees of fulfillment (performance indices). If performance standards are not met, thorough causal analyses must be performed in order to introduce appropriate improvements in task fulfillment. Such measures may refer, among other things, to

- a more efficient flow of processing procedures, from the customer's perspective
- sociopsychological training and recommendations for dealing directly with dissatisfied customers
- time standards for communication with dissatisfied customers during the processing of their cases, or
- the fundamental revision of the problem solution or compensation policy.

By comparing the values over time, one can follow developments and thus obtain insights about the effectiveness of the measures introduced.

10.2.1.2 MEASURING THE SATISFACTION OF THE INTERNAL CUSTOMERS OF COMPLAINT MANAGEMENT

The quality of task fulfillment in the indirect complaint-management process is relevant not for the complainant, but rather for internal target groups such as top management, quality management, or marketing. For this reason, these internal customers of complaint management are likewise to be surveyed with respect to their satisfaction. Figure 10.10 repeats the relevant quality dimensions for complaint analysis, complaint reporting, and complaint information utilization and exemplarily labels the satisfaction ratings of internal customers as subjective quality indicators.

When measuring the satisfaction of internal customers, the same problems arise as in the case of complaint satisfaction measurement. As far as content is concerned, the relevant dimensions and attributes of quality are to be determined from complaint analysis and complaint reporting. The attributes named in Figure 10.10 can serve as a starting point. For the firm-specific development of the questionnaire, however, it is recommended that extensive discussions be held with the internal customers in order to make sure that all the quality attributes that are relevant to them are in fact documented. As far as time is concerned, there is a great deal to be said for measuring performance on a yearly basis. At this interval, the assessment takes place on a sufficiently large experience basis. Also, the burden placed on the internal customers by the survey is limited to a reasonable level. Regarding the selection of

The Satisfaction of Internal Customers as a Subjective Quality Indicator of Complaint Management

Task	Quality dimensions	Subjective quality indicators (internal target groups)
Complaint analysis	• User-oriented accomplishment of quantitative analyses	• Satisfaction of internal customers with the quantitative analyses
	• Precision of cause analysis	• Satisfaction of internal customers with the precision of the provided data regarding the cause analysis
Complaint reporting	• User-oriented provision of information	• Satisfaction of internal customers with the benefit from the provided information
	• On-time provision of information	• Satisfaction of internal customers with the time availability of the provided information
Complaint information utilization	• Use of complaint information for quality improvements	• Satisfaction of internal customers with the utilization potential of complaint information for quality improvements
	• Use of complaint information for the development of new products/services	• Satisfaction of internal customers with the utilization potential of complaint information for the development of new products/ services

Figure 10.10

respondents, it is usually possible to include all internal customers in the study. This would also appear to be desirable because these customers often belong to different internal target groups that have different information needs and expectations.

10.2.2 OBJECTIVE TASK CONTROLLING

In objective task controlling, objective standards that can be verified independent of the judgments of external and internal customers are to be established for all complaint-management tasks. We can roughly differentiate between objective quality standards and objective productivity standards. Quality standards represent target figures in which expectations related to the quality dimensions and attributes relevant from the customers' point of view are determined. Productivity standards refer to output-input ratios that measure the efficiency of the performance.

10.2.2.1 OBJECTIVE QUALITY STANDARDS

One of the comprehensive concepts of task controlling is to find objective quality indicators for as many complaint-management tasks as possible and to establish standards for these indicators.

Complaint Stimulation

The goal of complaint stimulation is that the largest possible share of customer dissatisfaction be expressed in complaints. This goal is to be

achieved by establishing and actively communicating a complaint channel that is easily accessible (e.g., a central complaint center as
addressee).

In order to verify accessibility, a series of objective indicators is to be
used. In this way, the quality of telephone access can be measured by the
offered call answered rate (OCAR) and the immediate phone acceptance rate (service level). The former performance figure relates the
number of telephone calls accepted to the total number of calls
attempted by customers; the immediate telephone acceptance indicates
the number of telephone calls compared to the total number of all
attempted calls that were accepted within the defined target specifications (e.g., three rings). The immediate telephone acceptance rate is
often defined as a service level in call centers, for example, as an 80:20
ratio, which indicates that 80 percent of the calls should be taken within
20 seconds.

In order to verify the extent to which customer complaints were
addressed to the right corporate department and were received by the
desired complaint channel, two other performance figures may be used.
If, for example, the firm is striving to have as many complaints as possible addressed directly to the central complaint center, then the
addressee rate (ADR) (Complaint Center) indicates the percentage of
complaints that were addressed by complainants in the desired manner.
In a similar fashion, complaint stimulating activities can be designed in
such a way that dissatisfied customers use the written complaint channel
less and instead submit their concern by telephone to the employees of
a newly established Customer Care Center. The complaint channel rate
(CCR) (Telephone) can be regarded as a quality indicator because it
again provides the percentage of the total complaint volume represented by those complaints that were received through the complaint
channel preferred by the firm.

For these objective quality indicators, defined target specifications
that establish the desired degree of achievement and thus constitute the
basis for the monitoring of task fulfillment in the area of complaint stimulation must now be defined (for an example, see Figure 10.11).

Objective Quality Standards for Complaint Stimulation

Offered call answered rate (OCAR):
"At least 90 percent of all calls should be answered."

Service level (SL):
"Eighty percent of all complaints should be answered within 20 seconds."

Addressee rate (ADR) (Complaint Center) :
"Eighty percent of all complaints should arrive at the complaint center
directly."

Complaint channel rate (CCR) (Telephone):
"At least 75 percent of all complaints should arrive by telephone."

Figure 10.11

Complaint Acceptance

The objective quality of complaint acceptance can be seen in the proper and efficient transfer of complaint cases, as well as in the complete and accurate documentation of complaint information.

The speedy transfer of complaints can be verified with the aid of the on-time transfer rate (OTR), which records the share of the total number of transferred complaints represented by complaints that are transferred within defined processing times. It may be helpful to define various on-time transfer rates, depending on the department that received the complaint (e.g., firm management, branch), since communication channels vary in terms of how time-intensive they are. The accurate transfer rate (ATR) measures the accuracy of the transfer by providing the share of the total number of transferred complaints represented by the complaints directly received by the department responsible in each case.

In addition, what is important in the context of complaint acceptance is that the information is completely and accurately taken down so that as little work as possible is repeated during the remainder of the process. The extent to which the respective goals are achieved can be expressed by the information completeness rate (ICR) and the information accuracy rate (IAR). They should particularly be used when the number of complaints in which the information is not completely or accurately documented initially can be quickly determined on the basis of software-supported documentation of complaint processes.

Figure 10.12 summarizes the objective performance standards for complaint acceptance.

Objective Quality Standards for Complaint Acceptance

On-time transfer rate (OTR) (Top management):
"Ninety percent of all complaints addressed to top management have to be available in the responsible department after three work days at the latest."

Accurate transfer rate (ATR):
"Ninety percent of all complaints should reach the responsible department by the first forwarding."

Information completeness rate (ICR):
"In 85 percent of all cases, the complaint information should be registered completely."

Information accuracy rate (IAR):
"In 90 percent of all cases, the complaint information should be registered flawlessly."

Figure 10.12

Complaint Processing

The primary objective of complaint processing is to process the incoming complaints quickly and on schedule.

The promptness of complaint processing is primarily measured by the indicator of the total duration of the process from the receipt of the complaint until the final decision. This total duration is shortest when, in the case of complaints lodged in person or over the telephone, the firm is successful in conclusively solving customers' problems to their satisfaction during the initial contact. The share of the total number of complaints represented by these cases is designated the first-time fix rate (FFR). A low FFR can be an indication that the customer contact personnel either do not have the necessary professional background or do not have sufficient decision-making authority.

Standards with respect to the total process duration of all complaint cases can only be established on the basis of a detailed time-related analysis of the various complaint processing procedures. Since these processing procedures have different requirements with regard to time, it makes sense to define different time standards in each case. If the results of a lengthy test phase show that almost all complaints were solved within a specified time frame (e.g., in ten days), it is possible to make this period a standard that applies to all the procedures and potentially to communicate it to customers as a time-related service guarantee ("We'll solve your problems within ten days").

In order to be able to comply with the total processing duration, it is advisable to establish time standards for important internal subprocesses. This applies primarily to maximal idle times and transfer times. The maximum amount of time that incidents can remain unprocessed (idle time) or how much time can be spent for an internal transfer (transfer time) is to be fixed as a time-period variable (days, hours). Other quality standards should be formulated for complaint cases in which reminders have been made or that are in the escalation process. It is necessary to use the Reminder Rate (RR) and the Escalation Rate (ER) to determine the maximum percentage of complaint cases that should even reach the reminder or escalation process. It also makes sense to formulate standards that pertain to the number of complaints per escalation level, the Escalation Level Rate (ELR), in order to verify how the controlling effects of the escalation process are working.

Figure 10.13 contains an overview of the essential objective performance standards for complaint processing and reaction.

Complaint Reaction

The central goal of the complaint-reaction task module is to process customer complaints actively, reliably, and giving due consideration to the individual circumstances of the case, and to offer the customers complete and fair solutions to their problems.

Active contact applies to the external communication with the dissatisfied customer by means of receipt confirmations, intermediate replies, and final replies. The firm must determine the maximum number of days that can elapse before the receipt of a complaint is confirmed or by what date intermediate replies and the final reply must be mailed.

When customers make a follow-up complaint about the complaint processing or the solution offered to them, an objective indication exists

---

Objective Quality Standards for Complaint Processing and Reaction

First-time fix rate (FFR):
"Eighty-five percent of all complaints that are articulated verbally or by telephone should be solved and completed to the customer's satisfaction within the initial contact so that no following steps need to be initiated."

Total process duration:
"Ninety percent of all complaints of complaint process A should be completed within 14 working days, and 90 percent of all complaints of complaint process B should be completed within 20 working days."

Total handling time:
"Ninety-five percent of all complaints should be completed within ten working days."

Idle time:
"In 95 percent of all cases, the maximum idle time should not exceed one day."

Transfer time:
"In 95 percent of all cases, the maximum transfer time to the next processing level should not exceed one day."

Reminder rate (RR):
"Reminders should be required for no more than 5 percent of all complaint cases."

Escalation rate (ER):
"The escalation process should be initiated for no more than 2 percent of all complaint cases."

Escalation level rate (ELR-4):
"No more than 5 percent of all escalated complaint cases should reach escalation level 4."

Escalation level rate (ELR-3):
"No more than 20 percent of all escalated complaint cases should reach escalation level 3."

Escalation level rate (ELR-2):
"No more than 30 percent of all escalated complaint cases should reach escalation level 2."

Follow-up complaint rate (FCR):
"Of all complaint cases, no more than 5 percent should be follow-up complaints."

Figure 10.13

that the firm has fallen short of achieving the goal of complaint reaction, which is to reestablish customer satisfaction. Therefore, the follow-up complaint rate (FCR), which expresses the share of total complaints represented by follow-up complaints, must be noted and minimized. The higher the follow-up complaint rate is, the higher is the number of customers whose dissatisfaction increases during the process. Figure 10.13 shows the formulation of a standard for the FCR.

Complaint Reporting and Complaint Information Utilization

We will refrain from providing performance target figures for complaint-management controlling and complaint analysis as far as objective task controlling in the context of the indirect complaint-management process is concerned. The verification of the goal orientation of complaint-management controlling should take place more in the context of a process audit and less on the basis of performance figures. The controlling of the complaint analysis is done by means of evaluating the complaint reporting as well as the complaint information utilization, because this is where the quality of the recorded and analyzed complaint information is reflected.

In the context of complaint reporting, it is imperative to supply internal customers with information in a way that is user-friendly and timely, and to observe established reporting deadlines. Particularly with deadlines, it is possible to find an objective quality indicator. If deadline targets are established for regular reporting (e.g., weekly, monthly, yearly reports), the extent to which these activity standards are being observed can be determined with the aid of the on-time report rate (ORR), which is the quotient of the number of timely reports and the total number of reports.

The usage rate (UR), which indicates the share of information used by addressees for quality improvement measures or in the development of new products, can be used as an objective indicator of the target-group orientation of complaint analysis. Determining this rate causes a number of difficulties, because a clear-cut classification of informational units and definition of "usage" can rarely be made successfully. Restricting the information to only what is needed for institutionalized planning considerations (e.g., in quality circles or improvement teams) provides a starting point for the determination of the usage aspect. It makes more sense in this case to record only the absolute quantity of information used in this way and not to express it as a fraction of a larger amount of information.

Figure 10.14 shows an example of standards that apply to complaint reporting and to complaint information utilization.

In Figure 10.15, the objective performance indicators that are most important for the quality dimensions of complaint management are presented.

With respect to all the objective standards defined, regular analyses are to be carried out—similar to subjective task controlling—and the actual values determined are to be compared to the target values of the standards. In this way, standard-specific discrepancies or degrees of goal achievement can be determined (Figure 10.16).

Objective Quality Standards for Complaint Reporting and Complaint Information Utilization

On-time report rate (ORR):
"At least 95 percent of all reports have to be completed on schedule."

Usage rate (UR):
"At least 10 percent of the forwarded information should be used for precise planning measures."

Figure 10.14

Objective Quality Indicators of Complaint Management

Task	Quality dimensions	Objective quality indicators
Complaint stimulation	Easy accessibility	Offered calls answered rate (OCAR) $= \dfrac{\text{Number of calls answered}}{\text{Number of calls offered}}$
		Service level (SL) $= \dfrac{\text{Number of calls answered immediately}}{\text{Number of calls offered}}$
	Correct addressing of customer complaints	Addressee rate (AR) (Complaint center) $= \dfrac{\text{Number of complaints arrived at the complaint center}}{\text{Total number of complaints}}$
	Utilization of existing complaint channels	Complaint channel rate (CCR) (telephone) $= \dfrac{\text{Number of complaints by phone}}{\text{Total number of complaints}}$
Complaint acceptance	Prompt transfer of complaint cases	On-time transfer rate (OTR) $= \dfrac{\text{Number of complaints transferred within defined cycle times}}{\text{Total number of transferred complaints}}$
	Correct transfer of complaint cases	Accurate transfer rate (ATR) $= \dfrac{\text{Number of complaints arrived at the responsible department by the first forwarding}}{\text{Total number of transferred complaints}}$
	Complete documentation of complaint information	Information completeness rate (ICR) $= \dfrac{\text{Number of complaints with completely recorded information}}{\text{Total number of registered complaints}}$
	Correct documentation of complaint information	Information accuracy rate (IAR) $= \dfrac{\text{Number of complaints with correctly recorded information}}{\text{Total number of registered complaints}}$
Complaint processing	Promptness of complaint processing	First-time fix rate (FFR) $= \dfrac{\text{Number of problems solved and closed within the first contact}}{\text{Total number of registered complaints}}$
		Duration of particular complaint processes in days. Total process time in days.
	On-time processing	Idle time
		Transfer time
		Reminder rate (RR) $= \dfrac{\text{Number of complaints within the reminder process}}{\text{Total number of complaints}}$
		Escalation rate (ER) $= \dfrac{\text{Number of complaints within the escalation process}}{\text{Total number of complaints}}$
Complaint reaction	Active approach to the customer	Deadlines for the shipping of external communication (receipt confirmation, intermediate replies, final answer)
	Complete solution / Fair solution	Follow-up complaint rate (FCR) $= \dfrac{\text{Number of follow-up complaints}}{\text{Total number of complaints}}$
Complaint reporting	On-time provision of information	On-time report rate (ORR) $= \dfrac{\text{Number of reports on time}}{\text{Total number of reports}}$
Complaint information utilization	Usage of complaint information for quality improvements and for the development of new products/services	Usage rate (UR) $= \dfrac{\text{Used information}}{\text{Total number of information}}$

Figure 10.15

Discrepancy Calculation Considering Complaint Stimulation as an Example				
Quality indicator	Target value	Actual value	Discrepancy	Realization degree (=actual/target)
Addressee rate	80%	95%	+15%	119%
Complaint channel rate	75%	60%	−15%	80%
Offered calls answered rate	90%	85%	−5%	94%
First-time fix rate	80%	55%	−25%	69%

Figure 10.16

10.2.2.2 OBJECTIVE PRODUCTIVITY STANDARDS

Productivity is a measurement that relates the quantitative output of production to the quantity of the input factors (e.g., the number of employees) utilized. Such a measurement makes it possible to assess the productivity of the input factors and thus the efficiency of the production process. As applied to complaint management, the measurement of productivity therefore serves to measure the efficiency of the production factors used in this process. The essential basis of this measurement is the definition of appropriate output and input parameters.

The key output parameter for performance in the context of the direct complaint-management process is the number of complaints, by which a task-specific differentiation is to be made. For complaint stimulation, the number of additional complaint articulations stimulated is the relevant figure. For complaint acceptance, it is the number of articulations received or registered, and for complaint processing, it is the number of processed complaints. For complaint analysis and complaint reporting as tasks of the indirect complaint-management process, the number of analyses performed and reports produced is to be used.

Since the results of complaint management can only be generated using various input factors (employee, telephone system, software system), there is a possibility of relating the output generated to various input factors. It would, however, seem to be sensible to concentrate on the employee input factor, because it is usually the greatest cost factor. Accordingly, in the following section, only the labor productivity will be considered, in which the output is compared to the labor input. To that end, the quantity of labor employed can be selected as the input. A typical productivity ratio would then be the number of complaints processed per employee.

Productivity ratios such as these make statements about the efficiency of task fulfillment achieved by the employees in complaint management. They can also be defined as standards in terms of target figures, such as, for instance, determining the number of telephone calls accepted per hour. Figure 10.17 provides several examples of possible productivity ratios and standards for complaint acceptance and complaint processing.

Productivity ratios make no statements about the quality of the output. High productivity with regard to the acceptance and processing of complaints may be associated with a high number of failures and intense customer dissatisfaction. Empirical studies in the service sector also confirm a significant negative relationship between productivity and customer satisfaction (Anderson, Fornell, and Rust 1997). It has repeatedly been demonstrated that in cases in which they experience a conflict between quality and quantity goals, employees tend to focus more on the productivity targets because these targets are more easily controlled for and in many cases are the basis of their performance assessments (Singh 2000). For this reason, productivity ratios should never be used alone, but only in connection with subjective and objective quality standards. It is also necessary that management set clear priorities with respect to the weighting of quality and productivity goals.

10.2.3 THE LINKING OF QUALITY AND PRODUCTIVITY STANDARDS IN A COMPLAINT MANAGEMENT INDEX (CMI)

In order to be able to give equal consideration to the subjective and the objective standards, the development of a Complaint Management

---

Productivity Ratios Regarding Complaint Acceptance and Complaint Processing

Task	Productivity dimension	Productivity indicator	Productivity standards
Complaint acceptance	• Number of complaints accepted	Number of accepted complaint calls / Number of employees	• At least 70 accepted complaints per employee and day
		Number of accepted complaint calls / Number of working hours	• At least nine accepted complaints per employee and hour
Complaint processing	• Number of complaints processed	Number of written complaints processed / Number of employees	• At least 20 written complaints processed per employee and day
		Number of written complaints processed / Number of working hours	• At least three written complaints processed per employee and hour

Figure 10.17

Index (CMI) is recommended. Its development consists of five steps that are introduced in an example below:

(1) Selection of the relevant assessment dimensions and attributes. The first step is to select the relevant assessment dimensions and attributes. In our example, attributes for all the relevant quality dimensions are recorded, while the labor productivity of complaint acceptance and processing is considered in terms of productivity (see Columns 1 and 3 in Figure 10.18).

(2) Weighting of the assessment dimensions and attributes. Subsequently, management must weight the dimensions and attributes. The significance assigned to quality in relation to productivity is expressed in this weighting. A weighting of the individual quality and productivity attributes also takes place. Pragmatically speaking, the approach taken is to distribute a point total of 1.0 across the dimensions and attributes (see Column 2 in Figure 10.18).

(3) Establishment of standards. A standard must now be defined for each attribute, as was described in previous chapters. Subjective and objective quality indicators must be selected for the quality attributes, and the target level must be established as a quality standard in each case. A similar principle applies to the productivity attributes (see Columns 4 and 5 in Figure 10.18).

(4) Verification of the fulfillment of standards. In the context of a periodic verification, the firm must now investigate whether the required target standard was actually reached. If this is the case, it is expressed by assigning a value of 1. If the standard was missed, this attribute is assigned a value of 0. The reason for using a 0/1 variable such as this is because only those attributes should go into the index for which the quality and productivity goals were achieved (see Column 6 in Figure 10.18).

(5) Calculation of the Complaint Management Index. The last step is to multiply the respective attribute weights (Column 2) by the value of the 0/1 variable (Column 6) and add up the respective results (Column 7). In the example presented, the firm would obtain a value of 0.64 for the Complaint Management Index (maximum value = 1.00).

The process presented here is characterized by simplicity, transparency, flexibility and feasibility. It requires very little methodical effort and can easily be adjusted to the specific situation in every firm. Each firm must decide individually which assessment attributes should be recorded and how they should be weighted. During this process, it is made transparent at the same time, where the firm's priorities lie with respect to quality and productivity and what significance is given to particular attributes. The system is also very flexible, since the recording of new attributes and new weightings make it possible for the firm to react immediately when action is required.

The Complaint Management Index can be regarded as the key aggregate measurement of task controlling. It makes clear at a glance the extent to which the defined quality and productivity goals have been

Complaint Management Index (Example Calculation)

1 Assessment dimensions	2 Weight	Partial weight	3 Assessment items	4 Key figure	5 Standard	6 Standard fulfilled (yes = 1 no = 0)	7 Score (6 × 2)
Accessibility	0.05	0.02	Easy accessibility	Articulation rate	> 30%	1	0.02
		0.03		Satisfaction with the accessibility	> 80%	1	0.03
Availability	0.10	0.05	Easy availability	Offered calls answered rate	> 80%	0	0.00
		0.05		Service level	> 80:20	0	0.00
Interaction quality	0.300	0.08	Friendliness	Satisfaction with the friendliness	> 70%	1	0.08
		0.07	Empathy	Satisfaction with the empathy	> 70%	1	0.07
		0.08	Helpfulness	Satisfaction with the helpfulness	> 80%	0	0.00
		0.07	Reliability	Satisfaction with the reliability	> 80%	1	0.07
Promptness of reaction	0.10	0.03	Promptness of complaint processing	First-time fix rate	> 70%	1	0.03
		0.03		Duration of the handling process	< 3 days	0	0.00

Figure 10.18 Part A

reached. A more exact analysis of the calculation then reveals very quickly which measures will be necessary for goal fulfillment in the future or whether a revision of the goals is advisable.

Complaint Management Index (Example calculation) continued

1	2		3	4	5	6	7
Promptness of reaction	0.10	0.04	Promptness of complaint processing	Satisfaction with the promptness of complaint processing	> 90%	1	0.04
Problem solution	0.10	0.05	Fairness of solution	Satisfaction with the solution	> 80 %	1	0.05
		0.05	Completeness of solution	Follow-up complaint rate	< 5 %	0	0.00
Quality of complaint processing	0.05	0.05	Prompt transfer of complaint cases	On-time transfer rate	> 90 %	1	0.05
Quality of complaint analysis	0.05	0.02	Usage-oriented information provision	Usage rate	> 10%	1	0.02
		0.03		Internal customers' satisfaction with the quality of complaint analysis	> 70%	1	0.03
Quality of complaint reporting	0.05		On-time information provision	On-time report rate	> 95 %	0	0.00
Customer loyalty	0.10		Willingness to buy	Willingness to buy	> 40 %	1	0.10
Productivity of complaint acceptance	0.05		Accepted complaints	Number of answered complaint calls per day / number of employees	> 70	0	0.00
Productivity of complaint processing	0.05		Handled complaints	Number of written complaints processed / number of employees	> 40	1	0.05
Total	1.00	1.00					

CMI = 0, 64

Figure 10.18 Part B

10.3 COST-BENEFIT CONTROLLING

Another of the main tasks of complaint management controlling is to assess the profitability of complaint management and its contribution to the success of the firm.

Profitability is a measurement category that indicates whether the revenues exceed costs. The extent of the profitability targeted is expressed in the performance goals, which primarily include profit and rate of return.

In order to be able to assess the extent to which the complaint management process is designed in a cost-effective manner, it is first necessary to evaluate in monetary terms the resources that were employed and the results that were achieved. The monetary evaluation of the resources employed, (e.g., the personnel and physical resources) is expressed through the costs that arose from the implementation of those resources. The monetary evaluation of the results achieved is expressed through the sales and profit contributions that were secured or additionally brought about through complaint management.

In the following sections, the requirements and approaches for the detailed recording of the costs relevant for complaint management will first be described (Chapter 10.3.1). Chapter 10.3.2 deals with the operationalization and quantification of the benefit components of complaint management. The cost and benefit measurements will be combined for purposes of profitability controlling, where the "Return on Complaint Management (RoC)" will be calculated (Chapter 10.3.3).

10.3.1 COST CONTROLLING

10.3.1.1 BASIC CONCEPTS OF COST ACCOUNTING

Managers who work in complaint management usually have very little to do with cost accounting. They also will not be the ones who will be engaged in cost-accounting activities. However, in order for them to be able to request the relevant analyses from the cost-accounting department and to interpret the results, it is essential that they be familiar with some of the main concepts and methods that are relevant in cost controlling.

Direct Costs and Common Costs

Many costs can be directly assigned to a specific product, for example, the costs for the raw materials that are used for the production of the product. Such costs are called direct costs. Other costs are incurred in the general context of operational activities and cannot be assigned to an individual product, for example, the costs of the human resources department. These costs are common costs. Both types of costs are encountered in complaint management. Warrantee costs can, for example, be directly assigned to the product in question in each case and are therefore direct costs. Rental costs for the offices in which the employees of the complaint management department work are of common cost nature.

10.3.1.2 COST CONTROLLING FROM THE PERSPECTIVE OF TRADITIONAL COST ACCOUNTING

The main tasks of cost accounting include the differentiated documentation of the costs incurred (cost-type accounting), the analysis of their internal development (cost-center accounting), and the assignment to the products and services offered for purposes of price calculation (cost-unit accounting).

Cost-Type Accounting

Cost-type accounting answers the question "Which costs were incurred?"

Personnel costs, administrative costs, communication costs, and reaction costs are designated relevant cost types of complaint management.

- Personnel costs arise from the salaries (including employee benefit costs) of the employees working in a firm's complaint-management department.
- Administrative costs (office supplies, costs of the office space itself, and depreciation of the office equipment) make up another pool of costs.
- Communication costs include all the costs that are incurred in the context of the communication that takes place during the process of solving the customer's problem (e.g., telephone, fax, and postage costs).
- Included among the reaction costs are all the costs that arise from the solution offered, for instance, when the customer is granted a price reduction, provided a new product, or presented a gift. These costs are compensation or goodwill costs when they arise based on voluntary payments by a firm to which the customer has no legal claim. Warrantee costs arise in the case of solutions to which the customer has a legal or contractual right.

It is important to document compensation and warrantee costs separately, since only then is differentiated cost control possible. While a reduction of the compensation costs is possible immediately—although with negative consequences for complaint satisfaction—a cut in the warrantee costs can have grave consequences, since the firm must take into account the costs of judicial disputes and greater damage to its image, in addition to an increase in complaint dissatisfaction.

Cost-Center Accounting

Cost-center accounting analyzes the operational areas to which the costs can be assigned. It answers the question "Where were the costs incurred?"

If a complaint management department has been established as an independent organizational unit, it represents the relevant cost center.

Only the common costs (personnel costs, administrative costs, communication costs) are assigned to the cost center. The reaction costs are, for the most part, related to very specific products and services and are thus of a direct-cost nature. For this reason, they are directly assigned to the respective products and services (cost units) in the context of cost-unit accounting.

Figure 10.19 shows a simple example of an ideal type of complaint-management cost center, in which there is a differentiated documentation of the costs for a complaint-management department consisting of a complaint-management director, a complaint center with employees who receive and process customer complaints directly, and two complaint-management departments in regional subsidiaries.

Ideal Typical Structure of a Complaint-Management Cost Center

Cost position	Complaint-mangement department	Complaint center	Regional complaint units			Total
			North	South	Total	
Personnel costs	$78,000	$165,000	$20,000	$20,000	$40,000	$283,000
Administration costs	$15,000	$77,400	$6,550	$6,550	$13,100	$105,500
Communication costs	$2,200	$23,000	$3,150	$3,150	$6,300	$31,500
Total	$95,200	$265,400	$29,700	$29,700	$59,400	$420,000

Note: The reaction costs in the amount of $240,000 are direct costs and will be allocated directly to the cost object.

Figure 10.19

Cost-Unit Accounting

Cost-unit accounting assigns the costs to the respective causative products and services. It answers the question "For what were the documented costs incurred?"

In corporate practice, this allocation usually takes place using overhead allocation. This means that the common costs of complaint management are allotted to the cost units on the basis of production cost. The presented approach leads to the situation that costs are not allocated to products fairly according to input involved. Flawless products have to bear the costs of defective products, while the latter are not burdened with regard to costs. This represents a malfunction in cost accounting, which requires rethinking. This is the starting point of activity-based costing, which allows for a fair allocation of costs according to input involved.

10.3.1.3 COST CONTROLLING FROM THE PERSPECTIVE OF ACTIVITY-BASED COSTING

In the context of traditional cost accounting, the common costs of complaint management are assigned to the products or services using a specific allocation base, regardless of whether these products or services generated the complaint-management costs. This approach can lead to serious malfunctions, since products and services are charged with greater or lesser costs than they generated. Activity-Based Costing (ABC) avoids this problem by allocating common costs to individual items based on the resources they actually consume.

The basic principle of activity-based costing consists of four steps: (1) First, the business processes that generate the common costs must be defined. (2) Next, the cost drivers that generate these common costs must be identified. (3) These results then form the basis for the calculation of the process costs and process cost rates. (4) Using these figures, it is possible to charge the cost objects (products and services) with costs according to the processes they consume, which in turn allows for targeted planning and control of the common costs. The application of these fundamental steps to complaint management will now be presented.

1. Process Identification

The first step is to define the business processes that generate the common costs. This leads to a differentiation between core processes and support processes. Core processes deliver the output directly to external customers, and support processes deliver the output directly to internal customers. The classification of the overall complaint-management process into direct and indirect complaint-management processes reflects this differentiated perspective: (1) The direct complaint-management process is a core process that is aligned to external customers, since "complaint satisfaction" or "reestablishing customer satisfaction" and thus achieving higher customer retention should be the result. (2) In contrast, the indirect complaint-management process is a support process that supplies information to internal customers (e.g., other departments) in the form of complaint evaluations and analyses, as well as targeted reports.

A detailed process analysis is carried out for the direct and the indirect complaint processes by which the different activities (subprocesses) are identified for each cost center that participates in a process. For the direct complaint-management process, these could be the cost center "General Administration" that handles the incoming mail and the switchboard, the cost center "Complaint Management," and the cost centers of the departments that participate in complaint acceptance and complaint processing. Activities or subprocesses are, for instance, the opening and sorting of letters, the receipt or transfer of telephone calls, the structured documentation of complaint information, and the generation of receipt confirmations or reply letters. Such activity lists should be produced for all the departments within the firm that are integrated into the complaint-management process. If there is a central unit (e.g., a complaint center) in which all the operational activities of the complaint contact process are united, the majority of the relevant sub-processes will occur here.

A similar identification of cost centers and activities also takes place for the indirect complaint-management process. The cost center in question is either the complaint-management department itself or another functional area in which activities such as the performance of analyses or the moderation of quality circles takes place.

Figure 10.20 gives an overview of a possible systematization of the processes and activities of complaint management as the basis for the application of activity-based costing.

2. Determination of Cost Drivers

Activity-based costing also differentiates between direct and common costs. Direct costs are immediately allocated to the cost object; common costs are recorded at the place where they arise, and a differentiation is

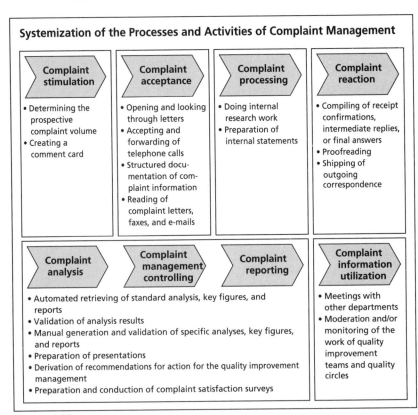

Figure 10.20

made whether those costs are activity-driven or activity-neutral. For the activity-driven costs, so-called cost drivers are defined that determine the usage of the corresponding activities. For the direct complaint-management process, these drivers are the articulated and documented, or processed, complaints; for the indirect complaint-management process, they are the business activities that are to be fulfilled, for example, analyses to be performed or reports to be produced. If the costs arising from a process—such as the costs for the executive in charge of complaint management—are not in direct proportion to the cost driver (e.g., the complaint volume), then these are activity-neutral costs.

3. Determination of the Activity-Based Costs and Process Cost Rates

Based on the cost drivers, a process cost rate (PCR) is calculated as the quotient of the costs determined for a process and the process quantity (e.g., the complaint volume). It is thus possible to account for the per-complaint costs immediately. In addition, the process cost rate provides precise insight into the cost structure of complaint management because it also takes into consideration all complaint-management activities in participating interface departments.

The process cost rate may either be calculated globally across all the activity-based costs of complaint-management or in a differentiated fashion for the direct and indirect complaint-management processes. The latter is especially advisable when an internal allocation of the services of the indirect complaint-management process is planned. At the same time, this approach brings about greater transparency with regard to the cost structure of complaint management.

Figure 10.21 shows a method of determining process cost rates. For the overall complaint-management process, total costs in the amount of $1,100,000 are projected for an estimated annual volume of 50,000 complaints. Of this total, $100,000 is incurred by departmental management as activity-neutral costs, $850,000 is incurred as activity-driven costs for the direct complaint management process (accepting and processing customer complaints), and $150,000 is incurred for the indirect complaint-management process (analyzing, preparing and supplying complaint information). The process cost rates for the activity-driven costs are determined by dividing the planned activity-based costs by the respective planned process quantities. The two process cost rates that result from this process are in the amounts of $17 for the acceptance and processing of a complaint and of $200 for complaint analysis and reporting. In order to calculate the apportionment rates for the activity-neutral costs, these costs ($100,000) are divided by the sum of the activity-driven costs of the two subprocesses ($1,000,000). From this, we obtain a ratio coefficient (0.10), which is multiplied by the respective process cost rate. For the subprocess "Accept and process customer complaints," we thus obtain an apportionment rate for the activity-neutral costs of $1.70 for the direct complaint management process and $20 for the indirect complaint-management process. If we then add the process cost rate per sub-

Determination of Process Cost Rates

Subprocess		Cost driver	Planned process quantity	Planned process costs	Process cost rate (ad)	Appor-tionment rate (an)	Total process cost rate
Accept and process customer complaints	ad	Articulated complaints	50,000	$850,000	$17.00	$1.70	$18.70
Analyze, prepare, and provide complaint information	ad	Requested analyses and reports	750	$150,000	$200.00	$20.00	$220.00
Manage the department	an	–	–	$100,000	-.--	-.--	-.--
Total				$1,100,000			

ad = activity-driven;   an = activity-neutral

Figure 10.21

process for the activity-driven costs to the respective apportionment rate, the result is the total process cost rate per subprocess. For the subprocess "Accept and process customer complaints," this rate is $18.70, and for the subprocess "Analyze, prepare, and provide complaint information," it is $220.

4. Determination of the Costs for Cost Objects

The activity-based costs of complaint management are allocated to the cost objects according to their usage of the two subprocesses "Accept and process customer complaints" and "Analyze, prepare, and provide complaint information."

To continue with our example, we assume that of the volume of 50,000 complaints anticipated for the next accounting period, a total of four products (A, B, C and D) are affected, and that 40,000 complaints with the following distribution were received in the previous accounting period: 10 percent were allotted to Product A, 35 percent to Product B, 40 percent to Product C, and 15 percent to Product D. If the same distribution is also assumed for the planning period, this means that Product A will cause the activation of the direct complaint process 5,000 times, Product B 17,500 times, Product C 20,000 times and Product D 7,500 times. By using the process cost rate of $18.70 that was ascertained for the direct complaint-management process, $93,500 (5,000 × $18.70) is assigned to Product A, $327,250 to Product B, $374,000 to Product C, and $140,250 to Product D, and subsequently taken into account in the calculation of their respective prices.

The internal allocation of the performances of the indirect complaint-management process is carried out in a similar way. In a parallel process, it is possible, in terms of a realistic customer valuation, to assign to complainants the costs that they generated.

10.3.1.4 PERFORMANCE FIGURES OF COST CONTROLLING

The most important cost-controlling performance figures can be considered on various levels. It must be decided whether the costs for the entire scope of complaint management or for the two subprocesses of direct and indirect complaint management will be considered. In addition, one must differentiate according to whether absolute cost measurements will be collected or whether ratios will be calculated. One must also look for performance figures that provide insight into cost-oriented relationships with other operational departments. The most important cost-controlling performance figures from complaint management are summarized in Figure 10.22.

With respect to the entire scope of complaint management, the absolute measurements of cost are of primary interest. A specific examination of the total costs with and without reaction costs is advisable. In many firms, reaction costs represent one of the largest cost blocks of complaint management, although they do not permit conclusions to be drawn about how profitably tasks are executed.

In the case of a relative evaluation, the complaint management costs are related to the number of complaints processed. This performance figure provides details about the costs resulting from the processing of a complaint. Here again, the total costs with and without the inclusion of the reaction costs are used as a basis. The first variation indicates which costs overall are triggered by a single complaint. The second variation is primarily relevant for the cost-related monitoring and controlling of complaint handling.

If an organizational separation exists concerning the perception of the tasks of the direct and the indirect complaint-management processes, it is obvious that absolute and relative cost performance figures should also be collected for these subprocesses in order to obtain detailed control measurements. In addition, other reference figures must be used for a specific analysis of the costs in the indirect complaint-management process, such as determining the costs per complaint report generated or per complaint satisfaction survey conducted.

If the costs of complaint management are further allocated between individual cost centers or process groups in the context of internal cost allocation, performance figures should be calculated that also provide information on ratios between the costs that are caused and those that are allocated further (Figure 10.22).

The calculations presented, using either the traditional overhead costs calculation method or activity-based costing, make the costs of complaint management transparent. This may have the effect that managers who are solely focused on the goal of reducing costs hastily intensify their efforts to minimize complaint-management costs in order to keep the price-increasing effects that accompany their allocation as low

---

Selected Key Figures of Cost Controlling

Referred to the total area of complaint management

- **Absolute cost**
  - **Total costs of complaint management**
    - Total complaint management costs
    - Complaint management costs without reaction costs
  - **Reaction costs of complaint management**
    - Total reaction costs
    - Compensation costs
    - Guarantee costs

- **Relative cost**
  - **Costs per employee (without reaction costs)**
    - Costs per employee
  - **Costs per complaint**
    - Total costs per complaint
    - Costs per complaint without reaction costs

Referred to subprocesses of complaint management

- **Absolute cost**
  - Total costs of the direct complaint-management process
  - Costs of the direct complaint-management process without reaction costs
  - Costs of the indirect complaint-management process

- **Relative cost**
  - **Costs per employee (without reaction costs)**
    - Costs of the direct-complaint management process per employee
    - Costs of the indirect complaint-management process per employee
  - **Costs per complaint**
    - Complaint management costs of the direct complaint process per complaint including reaction costs
    - Complaint management costs of the direct complaint process per complaint without reaction costs
    - Complaint management costs of the direct complaint process per complaint
  - **Costs per activity (without reaction costs)**
    - Costs of the indirect complaint management per complaint report
    - Costs of the indirect complaint management per complaint satisfaction measurement

---

Referred to the linkage with other departments

- Relation of the costs caused by the complaint-management department and the costs that are allocated to other departments

- Relation of the costs caused by the complaint-management department and the costs that are allocated by other departments to complaint management

- Relation of the costs that are allocated to the complaint management by other departments and the costs that are allocated to other departments by the complaint-management department

Figure 10.22

as possible. This attitude is dangerous because it can lead to a situation in which not only complaint-management costs are reduced, but also the firm's opportunities to achieve financially relevant goals related to customer retention and quality. In order to avoid this danger, complaint management must also successfully quantify the specific contributions to the company's value creation in the context of benefit controlling.

10.3.2 BENEFIT CONTROLLING

While complaint costs are recorded in many firms, only a relative few make an effort to identify and to quantify the benefit components of complaint management.

Four essential benefit components can be distinguished. Three of them are related to changes in customer attitudes and behavior that are brought about by complaint management: the attitude benefit, the repurchase benefit, and the communication benefit. The attitude benefit results from the reestablishment of customer satisfaction and the improvement of the customer's attitude. The repurchase benefit arises from the prevention of customer switching behavior, that is, the assurance of the customer's loyalty. The communication benefit describes the avoidance of negative word-of-mouth and the initiation of positive word-of-mouth. In addition to these, there is a fourth effect for the company: the information benefit is realized if companies use the information provided by complainants to eliminate errors, to reduce costs, and to improve the quality of products, services, and processes.

The challenge for complaint management then is to quantify the benefit components mentioned and to compare them to the cost components. The methodical difficulties associated with these tasks are great. This is certainly one reason why only sporadic systematic attempts of this type have been made so far (Fornell 1978; Kendall and Russ 1975; Blanding 1988; Goodman, O'Brien, and Segal 2000). Renewed efforts to quantify the benefit components are necessary, however, because only in this way can a rational basis for investment decisions in complaint management be established.

10.3.2.1 INFORMATION-BENEFIT CONTROLLING

If the information contained in complaints is systematically documented, edited in the context of complaint analysis, and regularly made available in complaint reports to the business units concerned, benefits accrue to the firm in many respects. One can expect that complaint information will bring about cost savings. This is the case when complaint information leads to an optimization of the internal processes, to time savings, and to increases in productivity, and when settlement costs in terms of warrantee and product-liability payments can be reduced with the help of such information. Furthermore, revenue increases can be expected, provided that product variations and product innovations that prove to be marketable result from complaint analysis. Complaint information can also be used to prevent sales decreases. Critical customer assessments with respect to all aspects of marketing and of the firm's perceived sociopolitical behavior give the firm the opportunity to optimize the implementation of the marketing mix and to adapt to new sociopolitical trends.

It will not always be possible to assess all of these effects. Nevertheless, realistic starting points that are available should be utilized. It is also possible to fall back on experiences from the employee suggestion system.

In handling proposals in the context of the suggestion system, the firm must distinguish between benefits that are monetarily ascertainable and benefits that are not monetarily ascertainable. In the case of suggestions with ascertainable benefits, the accounting balance between the costs of the previous procedure and those of the new procedure—the net savings in a particular period of time—are considered benefits. In order to quantify these benefits, various methods used in investment accounting can similarly be implemented here.

The simplest alternative is the cost-comparison method. It consists of comparing the costs of the previous process with those of the proposed process. The cost difference between the alternatives is regarded as the benefit of the suggestion for improvement. Here the approach is to determine

- which types of costs will change due to the new process
- which cost differences arise per type of cost, and
- how great is the overall sum of the cost differences.

In many cases, the benefit cannot be calculated in this way, for instance, with respect to the effects of changes in product design, promotional presentation, or usage instructions. In these cases, a scoring process can be used. Two criteria must be considered: (1) the importance of the suggestion, and (2) the degree of improvement.

Just as monetary values are assigned to particular point values in the employee suggestion system to offer premiums, values can also be assigned to the point values in the scoring matrix by assigning a hypothetical monetary value to a point. This can be done according to the company's willingness to pay. A piece of complaint information then obtains the value of the price that the firm would be prepared to pay for a similar suggestion from a consulting company.

10.3.2.2 ATTITUDE-BENEFIT CONTROLLING

The attitude benefit of complaint management comes about because an improvement in the attitudes of customers who complain can be achieved with the help of complaint management.

We can assume that the customer's attitude toward the product or the firm will worsen with the occurrence of a problem that results in a complaint. With the use of complaint management measures, it is possible to reverse this attitude decline, or even to bring about a more positive attitude than the one that existed before the problem occurred. This phenomenon ("complaint paradox"), which may at first seem surprising, can be explained because the customer experiences in a very tangible way the firm's ability, flexibility, and customer orientation during the successful processing of the complaint case so that the original, perhaps somewhat vague, attitude can then be strengthened in the long term as a result of the complaint reaction experienced.

The attitude benefit comes from the improvement in complainants' attitude values. Customers' attitudes after the complaint case has been concluded must be compared with their attitudes after the problem occurs. In order to obtain the most valid data possible, a double measurement would actually have to take place at the respective moments, which is impossible. For this reason, one must make do with surveying the complainants after the fact with respect to their attitudes in the context of a complaint satisfaction survey (see Question 14 in the questionnaire shown in Figure 10.8). The methodical problem here is, of course, that customers are required to reconstruct previous mental states at a later point in time. Since this is difficult, biases are very likely. In any case, the results still reveal the attitudes that customers had after their complaint experience and how they subsequently perceive the process of their attitude development. These assessments decisively influence their repurchase and communicative behaviors. The difference revealed can therefore be regarded as the quantification of the attitude benefit.

A direct monetary quantification of this benefit is not feasible. There is, however, the possibility of a comparative estimate if information is available from advertising effectiveness research about the advertising costs per customer that must be invested in order to achieve attitude improvements of the same scale value in the target group.

10.3.2.3 REPURCHASE-BENEFIT CONTROLLING

The focus of the financial quantification of the benefit of complaint management is the repurchase benefit, which is regarded as the key monetary measurement of the success of complaint management. This benefit effect is attained when complaint satisfaction is achieved and dissatisfied customers who would have switched to the competition and been lost indefinitely due to their negative experiences continue their association with the firm.

10.3.2.3.1 OPERATIONALIZATION OF THE REPURCHASE BENEFIT

A firm realizes a repurchase benefit when complaint management activities bring about the continuation of the business relationship that the complainant would otherwise have discontinued. The task here is to determine the number and value of those complainants for whom complaint management plays a decisive role in the continuation of the business relationship.

The starting point for the identification of customer relationships such as these is the customers who have cause for a complaint. At the same time, it must be determined how many of these dissatisfied customers actually make or waive making a complaint. This differentiated documentation of complaint behavior is important, since repurchase benefit effects can exclusively be realized with regard to the group of complainants.

Not all repurchases by complainants can be ascribed to complaint management as benefits, however. The following cases are to be excluded: (1) Complainants who are convinced by or satisfied with the type of complaint processing and continue the business relationship, but for whom the complaint reaction experienced does not play a decisive role. (2) Complainants who remain loyal despite their dissatisfaction with the complaint handling and engage in repurchases because other factors (e.g., price or existing contracts) have a binding effect.

Consequently, the realized repurchase benefit of complaint management is reflected exclusively in the purchase activities of complainants and the resulting sales and profits that can be traced back to a successful stabilization of the customer relationship due to convincing complaint processing. This benefit is also to be regarded as a direct performance figure for complaint management, since it—along with the realized communication benefit described below—represents the market success of complaint management. This benefit can be compared to the costs that arose in a period in question in order to calculate the profitability of complaint management.

The calculation of the realized repurchase benefit involves two steps. First, the number of customers retained through complaint management must be determined. Second, this number of customers is valued with regard to the related sales and profit contributions, and the result of this process is the monetary realized repurchase benefit.

10.3.2.3.2 DETERMINATION OF THE NUMBER OF CUSTOMERS RETAINED THROUGH COMPLAINT MANAGEMENT

Required Data

In order to determine the number of complainants retained through complaint management, it is necessary to have information about complaint behavior, about the purchase behavior of the complainant, and about the importance of complaint management in the continuation of the business relationship.

Representative customer and complaint satisfaction surveys make up the database for the collection of this information. On the basis of the results of customer satisfaction surveys, the firm determines how many customers are not convinced by its performances and have cause for complaint, and how many customers have actually complained. At the same time, the firm can find out whether and to what extent complainants have maintained the business relationship and what significance they ascribe to complaint handling in maintaining that relationship by looking at the results of complaint satisfaction surveys and the level of complaint satisfaction reached.

The relevant population for the question on the importance of complaint handling in maintaining a business relationship can be determined in two ways. First, it can be ascertained during the survey itself by asking complainants directly whether purchases took place after the complaint was processed. Second, it can be determined before the survey is conducted. In this case, the complainants who purchased again after the complaint was processed are verified in the customer database, and only these complainants are included in the survey.

Figure 10.23 provides an overview of the information to be elicited in the context of customer and complaint satisfaction surveys, which is

---

Overview of the Information that Is Necessary to Determine the Number of Retained Customers through Complaint Management

Customer satisfaction survey

Overall satisfaction
"How satisfied are you overall with the products/services offered?"

☐ completely satisfied ☐ very satisfied ☐ satisfied ☐ less satisfied ☐ dissatisfied

Complaint reason
"Did you experience a problem that gives you reason to complain?"
☐ Yes   ☐ No

Complaint behavior
"If so, did you complain?"
☐ Yes   ☐ No

Complaint satisfaction survey

Complaint satisfaction
"If you consider your overall complaint experience, how satisfied are you with the handling of your complaint case?"

☐ completely satisfied ☐ very satisfied ☐ satisfied ☐ less satisfied ☐ dissatisfied

Relevance of complaint handling
"Did you purchase a product or a service from our firm, or did you continue the business relationship respectively since the day you articulated your complaint?"
☐ Yes   ☐ No

If "Yes": "Which impact did the complaint experience for the continuance of the business relationship have?"
☐ Crucially or great impact
☐ Low or no impact

If "No": "Will you buy products or services from our firm, or will you continue the business relationship respectively in the future?"
☐ Yes   ☐ No
"Which impact did the complaint experience for your decision have?"
☐ Crucially or great impact
☐ Low or no impact

Figure 10.23

needed in order to be able to determine the number of customers retained through complaint management. We assume here that the complainants who will be surveyed have already purchased again, which means that actual customer behavior will be recorded. If appropriate data are not available, the firm must settle for complainants' declarations of intent with respect to their future repurchase behavior. However, great care must be exercised when basing further calculations on customers' statements about their future intended behavior, and these statements should be subsequently corrected, if necessary, after verification of how close they actually were to reality.

Calculation

The starting point for the calculation is the number of those customers from the total customer base who have experienced a problem and consequently had cause for a complaint. For this group of customers with a complaint cause, the firm must determine how many actually make a complaint or waive doing so. For the group of complainants, the next step is to segment them according to the level of complaint satisfaction reached and to determine the number of convinced, satisfied, and disappointed complainants.

Consequently, this segmentation process initially leads to a structuring of the group of customers with a complaint cause into four subsegments: convinced, satisfied, and disappointed complainants, as well as noncomplainants. For each of the three complaint satisfaction segments mentioned, a notation is made of how many have maintained the business relationship and for how many complainants the complaint handling experience was decisive or significant for the continuation of the business relationship. The number of complainants that continue the business relationship based on their positive experience with complaint handling is the basis for the calculation of the monetary realized repurchase benefit.

The determination of the number of customers retained through complaint management will be clarified with a specific example. Figure 10.24 gives an overview of the data required for the calculation and contains numerical data that form the basis for the sample examination that follows in Figure 10.25.

The starting point is the value for the number of customers who had cause for a complaint, which was determined in the context of a representative customer satisfaction survey. In our example, which assumes a customer base of 100,000 customers, the number of customers with cause for a complaint is 48,000. The complaint satisfaction survey shows that 50 percent of these customers (or 24,000 customers) have actually complained. The values for the complaint satisfaction rates and the corresponding numbers of convinced (7,200) and satisfied (6,000) complainants are derived from the complaint satisfaction survey. The complaint satisfaction survey also provides information about whether complainants have purchased again since the time that the complaint was made, thus continuing the business relationship, and about the importance of complaint handling in the continuation of that relationship.

To continue with the calculation, the only values that are relevant are those for the two segments of convinced and satisfied complainants who are still in the business relationship and ascribe great importance to complaint management with regard to the continuation of the relationship. In our example, 4,446 convinced complainants and 585 satisfied complainants (a total of 5,031 customers) attach great importance to

Overview of the Required Information for the Calculation of the Number of Retained Customers

Data from controlling			
Number of customers	Active customer base		100,000
Data from the customer satisfaction survey			
Complaint reason	Share of customers with a reason to complain		48%
Complaint behavior	Share of customers with a complaint reason who did complain		50%
	Share of customers with a complaint reason who did not complain		50%
Data from the complaint satisfaction survey			
Complaint satisfaction	Share of convinced customers		30%
	Share of satisfied customers		25%
	Share of disappointed customers		45%
Continuation of the business relationship	Convinced complainants	Share of convinced complainants who continue the business relationship	95%
		Share of convinced complainants who do not continue the business relationship	5%
	Satisfied complainants	Share of satisfied complainants who continue the business relationship	65%
		Share of satisfied complainants who do not continue the business relationship	35%
	Disappointed complainants	Share of disappointed complainants who continue the business relationship	0%
		Share of disappointed complainants who do not continue the business relationship	100%
Importance of complaint handling regarding the continuation of the business relationship	Convinced complainants who continue the business relationship	Share of convinced complainants to whom the handling of the complaint is of great importance	65%
		Share of convinced complainants to whom the handling of the complaint is of little importance	35%
	Satisfied complainants who continue the business relationship	Share of satisfied complainants to whom the handling of the complaint is of great importance	15%
		Share of satisfied complainants to whom the handling of the complaint is of little importance	85%

Figure 10.24

complaint management in their decision to hold on to the business relationship. The quantitative components of the calculation of the realized repurchase benefits, which form the basis of the monetary quantification of this benefit, are thus established.

10.3.2.3.3 MONETARY QUANTIFICATION OF THE REALIZED REPURCHASE BENEFIT

The monetary quantification of the realized repurchase benefit takes place with the turnover and contribution margins of customers that the

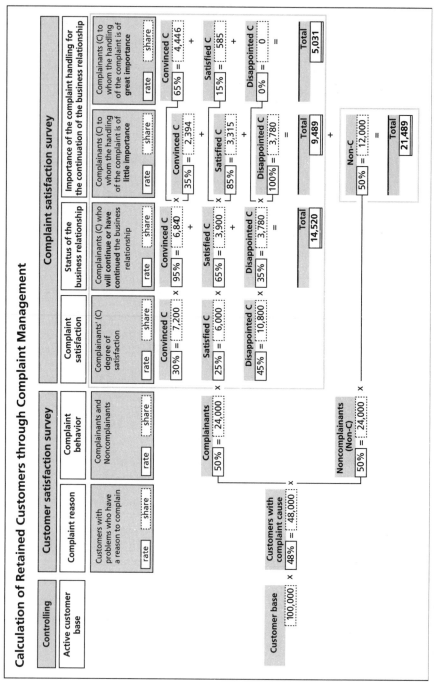

Figure 10.25

firm was able to retain through complaint management. In considering the Customer Lifetime Value, the firm takes into account that customers

Calculation of the Monetary Quantification of the Realized Repurchase Benefit in the Form of Annual Values Based on . . . Customer-Individual Revenue and Profit Data

Complainant	Average customer-individual annual revenue	Average customer-individual annual profit
Complainant A	$1,239	$247.80
Complainant B	$2,134	$533.50
Complainant C	$3,343	$668.60
Complainant D	$2,156	$646.80
Complainant E	$3,121	$780.25
Total	$11,993	$2,876.95

Figure 10.26

remain loyal for longer than one year. As far as the calculation itself is concerned, it may be necessary to proceed in different ways, depending upon whether customer-specific data or average values are available for use in the calculation.

Monetary Quantification in the Form of Annual Values on the Basis of Customer-Specific Data

If the firm has a customer database with information about the individual turnover and profit of customers, the realized repurchase benefit can be easily calculated. For all the customers retained through complaint management, the customer-specific turnover or profits over the duration of the business relationship to date are determined as an average annual value. If the customer-specific results are then added for all these complainants, we obtain the monetary realized repurchase benefit on an annual basis.

Figure 10.26 illustrates these approaches using a simple example. Here we assume that all complainants have been surveyed and that five of them have indicated that they attach great importance to complaint processing in the maintenance of the business relationship. On the basis of the customer-specific turnover and profits, we obtain a realized repurchase benefit of $11,993 based on turnover and $2,876.95 based on profits.

Monetary Quantification in the Form of Relationship Duration Values on the Basis of Customer-Specific Data

In many cases, however, annual observation is insufficient. A significant proportion of customers prove to be brand loyal and remain loyal for more than one year. In such cases, the Customer Lifetime Value—the value of the customer over the total duration of the customer relationship—should be used.

Usually, the Customer Lifetime Value is defined as the net present value of all profits that can be expected from a business relationship during the remaining duration of the relationship. The profits for the accounting period of the likely remaining relationship duration are then discounted back to the point of time in question, yielding the present value of the relationship. In practice, this approach usually proves to be either unworkable or highly problematic, because neither meaningful data about the in-payments and out-payments of future periods nor clear rules for the decision regarding the adequate internal rate of discount exist. For this reason, a greatly simplified and more practical approach, which settles for using rougher estimates, is recommended. According to this approach, the Customer Lifetime Value of the realized repurchase benefit is obtained by multiplying the number of periods remaining in the relationship duration by the customer's average profit during the relationship duration to date.

When referring to the remaining relationship duration, we mean the difference between the average total relationship duration for all customers and the previously realized relationship duration of customers who were further retained through complaint management. If we multiply the individual turnover or profits (annual values) with the respective number of periods remaining in the relationship duration for these customers, we obtain the Customer Lifetime Value of the realized repurchase benefit.

Figure 10.27 illustrates the calculation of the remaining relationship duration, as well as the determination of the monetary realized repurchase benefit as the Customer Lifetime Value. Once again, five complainants have indicated that they ascribe great importance to complaint processing in maintaining the business relationship. For each individual complainant, it was possible to obtain from the controlling department the average annual turnover (Column 1) and profit (Column 2) earned during the relationship duration to date, as well as the relationship duration to date in number of years (Column 3). In addition, it is already known that the average relationship duration for all customers is five years. By subtracting the respective customer-specific relationship duration from this value, we obtain the customer-specific remaining relationship duration for the business relationship (Column 4). If we now multiply the value for the remaining relationship duration by the average turnover or profit, we obtain the Customer Lifetime Value for customers who were retained through complaint management (Columns 5 and 6). If we add the Lifetime Values for all customers retained through complaint management, we obtain the monetary value of the overall realized repurchase benefit on the basis of customer-specific values—in our example, in the amounts of $39,763 (turnover) and $7,074 (profit).

Monetary Quantification in the Form of Annual and Relationship Duration Values on the Basis of Average Values

If customer-specific data for turnover and profit are not available, the firm must start with the average turnover and profit per period for all customers and assume that these values also apply to the customers who

Calculation of the Monetary Quantification of the Realized Repurchase Benefit in the Form of Relationship Duration Values

Average relationship duration across all customers: 5 years

Complainants	(1) Average customer-individual annual revenue	(2) Average customer-individual annual profit	(3) Customer-individual relationship duration to date (in years)	(4) Customer-individual remaining relationship duration (in years)	(5) Remaining customer lifetime value (revenue)	(6) Remaining customer lifetime value (profit)
Complainant A	$1,239	$247.80	1.50	3.50	$4,336.50	$867.30
Complainant B	$2,134	$533.50	2.00	3.00	$6,402.00	$1,600.50
Complainant C	$3,343	$668.60	1.60	3.40	$11,366.20	$2,273.24
Complainant D	$2,156	$646.80	2.60	2.40	$5,174.40	$1,552.32
Complainant E	$3,121	$780.25	1.00	4.00	$12,484.00	$780.25
Total	$11,993	$2,876.95	Ø 1.74	Ø 3.26	$39,763.10	$7,073.61

Figure 10.27

were retained through complaint management. The average remaining Lifetime Value must be estimated based on internal or external experience.

Monetary Quantification of the Realized Repurchase Benefit (based on Average Values)

Calculation (annual basis)	
Number of complainants who remained loyal due to complaint handling	5,031
x Ø monthly revenue	$200
x 12 months	12
= Secured revenue (annual basis)	$12,074,400
x Ø Profit margin	8%
= Secured profit (annual basis)	$965,952

Calculation (relationship basis)	
Number of complainants who remained loyal due to complaint handling	5,031
x Ø monthly revenue	$200
x Estimated remaining duration of a customer relationship	20
= Secured revenue (relationship basis)	$20,124,000
x Ø Profit margin	8%
= Secured profit (relationship basis)	$1,609,920

Figure 10.28

For the following sample calculation, we will refer to the values from Figure 10.25. Using these values, we can see that complaint management was successful in retaining 5,031 customers. If we assume that these customers have an average monthly turnover of $200, we then obtain a secured annual turnover of $12,074,400. With a profit margin of 8 percent, this corresponds to a secured annual profit in the amount of $965,952. Using an estimated remaining relationship duration of 20 months, we can anticipate secured turnover in the amount of $20,124,000 and a secured profit contribution in the amount of $1,609,920 for the entire remaining relationship duration (Figure 10.28).

Monetary Assessment When Data Regarding the Retention Effects of Complaint Management Are Missing

If there is no data whatsoever available regarding the retention effects of complaint management, the realized repurchase benefit obviously cannot be calculated. In such cases, it is advisable to change perspectives and to estimate, on the basis of assumptions, the market loss the firm suffers as a result of customer dissatisfaction and the size of the economic potential that can be tapped through complaint management. In this case, the focus of consideration is not on the realized repurchase benefit, but rather on the lost repurchase benefit that results when customers

Matrix for the Calculation of the Economic Effects of Possible Customer Switching due to Dissatisfaction

Customer base	100,000 customers	Ø revenue per customer p.a.: $1,000				
		Ø profit margin p.a.: 10%				

Share and number of disappointed customers	30.00 % (30,000 customers)					

Share and number of disappointed and potentially lost customers	0.003 % (1 customer)	0.50 % (150 customers)	1.00 % (300 customers)	5.00 % (1,500 customers)	10.00 % (3,000 customers)	20.00 % (6,000 customers)
6 months	$500 / $50	$75' / $8'	$150' / $15'	$750' / $75'	$1,500' / $150'	$3,000' / $300'
1 year	$1,000 / $100	$150' / $15'	$300' / $30'	$1,500' / $150'	$3,000' / $300'	$6,000' / $600'
2 years	$2,000 / $200	$300' / $30'	$600' / $60'	$3,000' / $300'	$6,000' / $600'	$12,000' / $1,200'
3 years	$3,000 / $300	$450' / $45'	$900' / $90'	$4,500' / $450'	$9,000' / $900'	$18,000' / $1,800'
4 years	$4,000 / $400	$600' / $60'	$1,200' / $120'	$6,000' / $600'	$12,000' / $1,200'	$24,000' / $2,400'
5 years	$5,000 / $500	$750' / $75'	$1,500' / $150'	$7,500' / $750'	$15,000' / $1,500'	$30,000' / $3,000'

(Vertical axis label: Ø lost relationship duration)

$4,500'	⟵ Upper cell: lost repurchase benefit (revenue)
$450'	⟵ Lower cell: lost repurchase benefit (profit)

Figure 10.29

terminate the business relationship because they are dissatisfied and thus do not engage in additional purchase activities.

For this analysis, the firm must have at its disposal information regarding the customer base, the average turnover per customer, and the average profit margin. It can be assumed that these data come from controlling. The information about the percentage of nonconvinced customers should be taken from a customer satisfaction survey. If this information is not available, an alternative would be to refer to estimates, for example, the results of corresponding industry analyses. On the basis of this information, the market loss (the lost repurchase benefit) can then be calculated.

Figure 10.29 shows a corresponding matrix for the calculation of the lost repurchase benefit that can arise when dissatisfied customers switch. The basis for this calculation are internal data regarding the customer base (100,000), the percentage of nonconvinced customers (30 percent), the average annual turnover per customer ($1,000), and the average profit margin (10 percent). The vertical axis of the matrix indicates different values for the length of the possible remaining relationship duration; the horizontal axis indicates different percentages of disappointed customers who will switch because of their dissatisfaction with a product or service. The corresponding values in the matrix indicate the market loss (lost repurchase benefit) as well as the lost turnover and profit that the firm will suffer due to customer dissatisfaction.

The firm must then make assumptions—based on the estimates of experts in marketing, sales, service, and controlling—about the potential probable remaining relationship duration and the percentage of nonconvinced customers who will switch. The corresponding amount of market losses can then be taken directly from the matrix. If, for example, the experts come to the conclusion that 5 percent of 30,000 dissatisfied customers (1,500 customers) will switch to the competition because of their dissatisfaction and further assume that these customers would have remained in the business relationship for another three years, the result is a lost repurchase benefit of $4,500,000 in terms of lost turnover, and of $450,000 in terms of lost profits.

Based on the values determined for the lost repurchase benefit due to customer dissatisfaction, the firm can consider whether it is possible to achieve retention effects that will lead to a reduction of the customer losses indicated by introducing or optimizing complaint management. If we assume in the sample calculation above that the firm could have kept 30 percent of the 1,500 lost customers with adequate complaint management, the result is a potential realized repurchase benefit of complaint management in the amount of $1,350,000 (turnover) and $135,000 (profit).

The calculation of the lost repurchase benefit is based on assumptions and thus does not provide a secure foundation for more wide-ranging conclusions. Nevertheless, it does provide an impression of the lost turnover and profits that the firm will have to accept in the absence of professional complaint management and the repurchase benefits that could be realized. Calculations such as these are also helpful in making an initial assessment about whether investments in complaint management are economically justified.

10.3.2.4 COMMUNICATION-BENEFIT CONTROLLING

The communication benefit is closely related to the repurchase benefit. Based on their experiences with complaint handling, customers not only draw consequences for their repurchase behavior, but also make their experiences the topic of conversations with friends, relatives, or colleagues. Depending on whether they assess their complaint experience as positive or negative, they recommend the firm to others or advise them against purchasing from it. This action also strongly influences the attitudes and behavior of other current and potential customers. Empirical studies prove that personal communication has a substantially greater impact than does advertising that is initiated by the firm itself. The reason for this is because the communicant is not viewed as being commercially motivated, but rather as a neutral source of information, an advisor, or a referee.

Operationalization of the Realized Communication Benefit

The communication benefit of complaint management can come about in indirect and direct ways. An indirect communication benefit is achieved when the complaint handling is so convincingly designed that customers who were dissatisfied are deterred from reporting negatively to friends, relatives, or colleagues about the problem that is the basis of the complaint, or from expressing a warning against purchasing from the firm. Complaint management brings about a direct communication benefit when complainants make positive complaint experiences the subject of their communication and in this way recommend the firm and its products and services to others. We will restrict ourselves in the following sections to the observation of this direct communication benefit, which is termed the realized communication benefit.

According to an approach proposed by the consulting firm TARP, the realized communication benefit is calculated as follows: First, the number of persons to whom complainants have expressed a purchase recommendation and whose purchase behavior was positively influenced by this recommendation is determined. Then, by assessing these business relationships that were initiated due to positive word-of-mouth, as well as the corresponding turnover and profits, the monetary realized communication benefit can be obtained (TARP 1979; Goodman, O'Brien, and Segal 2000).

Calculation of the Number of Business Relationships Initiated Due to Positive Word-of-Mouth

The necessary information regarding the number of people who have been approached comes from representative complaint satisfaction surveys. In these surveys, complainants are asked whether and (if yes) with how many people they have spoken about their complaint experience.

Figure 10.30 gives an overview of the information that should be collected in the context of a complaint satisfaction survey in order to be able to calculate the number of business relationships that were influenced by positive word-of-mouth.

There are two versions shown of how to determine whether positive or negative word-of-mouth was practiced. In the first version ("positive communication behavior"), the respondents are only requested to indicate whether they have expressed a positive opinion about the products or the firm. In the second version, information is collected about whether they have taken on a more active role and expressed deliberate buying recommendations ("recommendation behavior"). In either case, the survey asks about actual communication behavior in the past. Questions that are aimed at collecting customers' intended communication behavior are problematic because the number of prospective communication partners is not consciously planned by complainants and thus is not predictable.

The number of positively addressed people that is determined by asking these questions forms the basis for the calculation of the number of people who actually base their buying behavior on the contents of the word-of-mouth. Here we can refer to the empirical results of TARP from more than 1,000 projects and studies (Goodman, O'Brien, and Segal 2000). According to these results, it can be assumed that in the case of positive word-of-mouth, approximately 1 percent of the persons con-

---

Required Information from Complaint Satisfaction Surveys for the Calculation of the Number of Customers who Were Influenced through Positive Word-of-Mouth

- **General communication behavior of complainants**
"Did you talk about your complaint experience to other people?"
☐ Yes ☐ No If "Yes," to how many people?   Approx. _____ People

- **Differentiated communication behavior of complainants**
"Did you talk about your complaint experience to other people (friends, relatives, colleagues)?"
☐ Yes ☐ No If "Yes," to how many people?
  - In the circle of family and relatives: ... Approx. _____ People
  - In the circle of colleagues: .... Approx. _____ People
  - In the circle of friends/acquaintances .. Approx. _____ People
  - In the circle of club colleagues: .... Approx. _____ People

- **Positive communication behavior**
"Did you recommend to other people (friends, relatives, colleagues) to buy products/services of our firm due to your complaint experience?"
☐ Yes ☐ No If "Yes," to how many people?
  - In the circle of family and relatives: ... Approx. _____ People
  - In the circle of colleagues: .... Approx. _____ People
  - In the circle of friends/acquaintances .. Approx. _____ People
  - In the circle of club colleagues: .... Approx. _____ People

- **Recommendation behavior**
"Did you discourage other people from buying products/services of our firm due to your complaint experience?"
☐ Yes ☐ No If "Yes," to how many people?
  - In the circle of family and relatives: ... Approx. _____ People
  - In the circle of colleagues: .... Approx. _____ People
  - In the circle of friends/acquaintances .. Approx. _____ People
  - In the circle of club colleagues: .... Approx. _____ People

Figure 10.30

tacted entered into a business relationship based on the positive description of the complaint case or on the articulated buying recommendation. If we accept this measurement as a rule of thumb, this 1 percent of all the people addressed with buying recommendations represents the number of business relationships initiated or strengthened through positive word-of-mouth.

As in the case of the calculation of the realized repurchase benefit, the convinced and satisfied complainants are the basis for determining the business relationships initiated through positive word-of-mouth. It is irrelevant whether these complainants view the complaint processing as particularly meaningful in the continuation of the business relationship or not, because positive descriptions of one's own complaint experience and buying recommendations can also be expressed when the complaint handling has no particular relevance for customer retention.

Figure 10.31 provides an overview of the information needed for the calculation. The values for the number of people addressed by convinced and satisfied complainants are to be derived from the complaint

Overview of Required Information for the Calculation of the Number of Customer Relationships Initiated or Intensified through Positive Word-of-Mouth

Data from the complaint satisfaction survey	
Reference behavior of complainants	
Number of people addressed by convinced complainants	14
Number of people addressed by satisfied complainants	9
Estimated value of the buying effects of positive word-of-mouth	
Share of people addressed who actually became buyers or intensified their purchases as a result of the positive word-of-mouth	1%

Figure 10.31

satisfaction survey. With regard to the buying effect of communication behavior, we will refer to TARP's rule of thumb.

Using this information, the realized communication benefit can be calculated. In Figure 10.32, the approaches to the calculation are illustrated, and we also refer to the results from Figure 10.25.

The 13,200 customers convinced by (7,200) and satisfied with (6,000) the complaint processing form the starting point for the calculation of the realized communication benefit. If we follow the steps presented, it appears that a total of 154,800 people were addressed by the

Calculation to Determine Those Customer Relationships Initiated or Intensified through Positive Word-of-Mouth

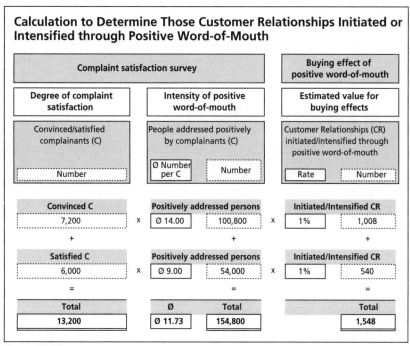

Figure 10.32

convinced and satisfied complainants. If we assume that of these persons, 1 percent actually entered into a business relationship with the firm or intensified an existing relationship due to the positive description of the complaint case, this means that a total of 1,548 customer relationships could be gained or strengthened as a result of the positive communication effects brought about by complainants.

Monetary Quantification of the Realized Communication Benefit

For the monetary quantification of the realized communication benefit, the number of customers who enter into a new business relationship or intensify an existing relationship based on positive communication is evaluated along with the average turnover or average profit of customers from the present customer database.

Just as was the case with the realized repurchase benefit, the realized communication benefit can be economically quantified not only on an annual basis, but also from the perspective of the relationship duration. The average relationship duration of current customers is the basis for all initiated or intensified customer relationships.

For our sample calculation (Figure 10.33), we start with the values upon which the calculation of the realized repurchase benefit was based.

The average monthly turnover of a customer is $200, an average relationship duration of 60 months is assumed for current customers,

---

Calculation of the Monetary Quantification of the Realized Communication Benefit (TARP Approach)

Calculation (annual basis)	
Number of customer relationships initiated by positive word-of-mouth	1,548
× Ø monthly revenue	$200
× 12 months	12
= Initiated revenue (annual basis)	$3,715,200
× Ø Profit margin	8%
= Initiated profit (annual basis)	$297,216

Calculation (relationship basis)	
Number of customer relationships initiated by positive word-of-mouth	1,548
× Ø monthly revenue	$200
× Estimated relationship duration in months	60
= Initiated revenue (relationship basis)	$18,576,000
× Ø Profit margin	8%
= Initiated profit (relationship basis)	$1,486,080

Figure 10.33

and the profit margin is 8 percent. The monetary realized communication benefit for the 1,548 newly gained or intensified customer relationships, when considered for the year, is $3,175,200 (turnover) and $297,216 (profit), or considered in terms of the Customer Lifetime Value, $18,576,000 (lifetime turnover) and $1,486,080 (lifetime profit).

The calculation approach presented has the advantage that it can be easily implemented. There is, however, a problem with this approach, which is that an assumption must be made regarding the probability that a person who is positively influenced by word-of-mouth will in fact become a buyer. The 1-percent variable specified by TARP is based on the analysis of a large number of empirical studies; nevertheless, there is no guarantee that this variable would also apply to an individual case. Therefore, if firms do not want to rely on this estimated variable, they must attempt to conduct an independent survey among their current customers to determine the extent to which positive word-of-mouth by complainants directly influences the decision to commence or intensify a business relationship. Specifically, information must be collected on whether people were informed within their social networks by complainants concerning their complaint experience, and what role the positive description of the complaint handling played in their behavior. Such surveys are, however, not only costly, but also difficult, because customers are rarely in a position to understand and to report their own purchase decision-making processes. For this reason, it is more practical to forego a separate survey and calculate using the 1-percent rule of thumb. In this case, however, one must be aware that the value determined for the realized communication benefit represents only a rough starting point, and not an exact variable.

10.3.2.5 REPURCHASE AND COMMUNICATION BENEFITS AS THE MARKET SUCCESS OF COMPLAINT MANAGEMENT

With the information, attitude, repurchase, and communication benefits, the key benefit components of complaint management were defined and their operationalization described. Because of their particular importance and due to the existence of realistic approaches to their calculation, monetary quantification was only shown in the cases of the repurchase and communication benefits. The sum of the monetary realized repurchase benefit and the monetary realized communication benefit is defined as the market success of complaint management. This variable is compared to the costs as a corresponding variable in the context of profitability controlling.

It stands to reason that the market success should be calculated both as a quantity-related and as a value-related variable. The monetary market success is determined as a turnover and profit variable, on an annual basis as well as with respect to the remaining relationship duration. Figure 10.34 summarizes the calculation of the market success of complaint management, using the results of the sample calculations carried out in each case as a basis.

For this assessment of the market success, it should be remembered that the value determined should be regarded more as a lower limit, since the monetary effects resulting from the attitude and information benefits are not considered.

10.3.3 PROFITABILITY CONTROLLING

In order to be able to make statements about whether and to what extent the targeted monetary market success can be justified by the costs involved and in order to be able to judge the success of complaint management from an economic point of view, it is necessary to compare the monetary benefits achieved with the costs involved and consequently to obtain insights into the profitability of complaint management. This applies to the overall domain of complaint management, as well as to individual subprojects or measures planned to optimize complaint-management processes.

10.3.3.1 PROFITABILITY OF THE COMPLAINT-MANAGEMENT DEPARTMENT

One of the key approaches to calculating the profitability of the complaint-management department is to compare the monetary market success determined for complaint management with the costs caused by this department and thus to determine the profit or loss earned by complaint management in the period.

Profit Calculation

Figure 10.35 shows the structure of a profit calculation for complaint management. In this statement, the personnel costs are first subtracted from the market success of complaint management. The result is the gross profit of complaint management, from which—in a next step—the administrative, communication, and reaction costs are deducted, which yields the profit of complaint management.

In our sample calculation, we refer to the realized market success from Figure 10.34, specifically to the relationship profit. This variable should be given priority over the annual profit, since the total duration of the customer relationship is expressed here. If instead the annual profit is used as the market success of complaint management, only the minimum profit level of complaint management can be ascertained.

With respect to costs, we will refer to the values from Figure 10.19. After deducting the personnel costs from the market success of complaint management, the result we obtain is a gross profit in the amount of $2,813,000. After further subtracting the administrative, communication, and reaction costs, the profit of complaint management comes to $2,436,000.

Profitability of the Market Success and Return on Complaint Management

The variables underlying the profit calculation form the basis for the calculation of two relevant return figures of complaint management: the

Calculation of the Market Success of Complaint Management

Quantity-related market success of complaint management					
Quantity component	Customer relationships retained through complaint management	+	Customer relationships initiated through positive word-of-mouth	=	Market success of complaint management
Number of retained or initiated customer relationships	5,031	+	1,548	=	6,579

Value-related market success of complaint management					
Reference value of market success	Realized repurchase benefit	+	Realized communication benefit	=	Market success of complaint management
Annual turnover	$12,074,400	+	$3,715,200	=	$15,789,600
Annual profit	$965,952	+	$297,216	=	$1,263,168
Relationship turnover	$20,124,000	+	$18,576,000	=	$38,700,000
Relationship profit	$1,609,920	+	$1,486,080	=	$3,096,000

Figure 10.34

profitability of the market success and the Return on Complaint Management.

The profitability of the market success of complaint management can be expressed as the quotient of the profit earned due to complaint management and the market success generated by complaint management. For our calculation example, the result is a value of 78.68 percent (Figure 10.34).

Profit Calculation for Complaint Management

Position		% of market sucess
Realized repurchase benefit (profit)	$1,609,920	52.00
+ Realized communication benefit (profit)	$1,486,080	48.00
= Market success of complaint management	$3,096,000	100.00
− Personnel costs	$283,000	9.14
= Gross profit of complaint management	$2,813,000	90.86
− Administration costs	$105,500	3.41
− Communication costs	$31,500	1.02
− Response costs	$240,000	7.75
= Complaint management profit	$2,436,000	78.68

Figure 10.35

In many firms, the Return on Investment (ROI) is used as another performance figure with which to judge the profitability not only of the entire firm, but also of individual departments. This performance figure is calculated by dividing the profit earned by the "capital invested." If the costs incurred by complaint management in the accounting period are interpreted as "capital invested," the performance measurement of the "Return on Complaint Management" is the result of the quotient of the profit of complaint management and its costs in the same period. Figure 10.36 shows an example of the calculation of the Return on Complaint Management based on the numerical values from the profit calculation above. In this sample calculation, complaint management has earned a return of 369.09 percent.

Return on Complaint Management

$$\text{Return on Complaint Management} = \frac{\text{Complaint management profit}}{\text{Investments in complaint management}} = \frac{\$2{,}436{,}000}{\$660{,}000} = 369.09\%$$

Figure 10.36

10.3.3.2 PROFITABILITY OF MEASURES INTENDED TO OPTIMIZE COMPLAINT MANAGEMENT

Profitability calculations should also be performed to assess investments in projects intended to optimize complaint management, such as introducing a complaint management software system or conducting a training program. Investments such as these are always associated with out-payments and are made in order to earn the largest possible profit in terms of an in-payment surplus. Evaluating whether and to what extent the projected investment satisfies goals such as these is the task of investment calculation. At the same time, investment calculation methods provide decision rules to select the optimal alternative when several possible measures are available.

In the following sections, the evaluation of investments in complaint management will be described using a simple example in which techniques from the cost comparison, profit comparison, and return comparison methods are applied.

We assume that the firm's initial situation is correctly described in Figure 10.25. The firm has a customer base of 100,000 customers, 48,000 of whom have cause for a complaint. Of this number, only a small percentage (5,031 customers) can be retained through complaint management.

Definition of Measures

In this situation, consideration is made for which specific measures should be taken in order to retain more dissatisfied customers for the firm in the future. There are three key drivers of customer retention:

- Reducing the extent of the problem's occurrence. The fewer customers who are confronted with a problem that gives rise to a complaint, the smaller the probability that customers will switch providers because of the problem, and the smaller the lost repurchase benefit will be.
- Increasing the articulation rate. The more dissatisfied customers who complain, the more complaint management can influence the elimination of the dissatisfaction and prevent intended switching.
- Increasing complaint satisfaction. The more satisfied complainants are with the processing of their complaints, the smaller is the probability that they will terminate the relationship.

These drivers of customer retention point simultaneously to specific starting points for the establishment of measures designed to maximize the number of customers retained through complaint management and minimize the loss of customers. Quality improvement measures that are implemented reduce the probability of the occurrence of problems and thus the number of customers who are confronted with a problem. The direct communication of a newly established telephone complaint channel would greatly increase the number of dissatisfied customers who complain. Employee training programs, a reorganization of the complaint processing procedures or a reworking of the reaction alternatives have an immediate impact on the satisfaction of the complainant.

Similar considerations are expressed in the following example case. In order to illustrate the different impacts of the three drivers of customer retention described, an appropriate optimization measure is given in each case: The first, Measure A, includes a sensitivity training program for all customer-contact employees in order to improve the satisfaction level of complainants. Measure B is intended to increase the articulation rate by increasing the communication of a central telephone complaint channel. Measure C has to do with the implementation of a quality improvement program for a problem area and targets the goal of reducing the percentage of nonconvinced customers.

Planning the Customer Retention Effects per Measure and Calculating the Results Achieved

The first step is to make specific assumptions about the expected impact of the individual drivers of customer retention—the extent of the problem's occurrence, complaint behavior/articulation rate, and complaint satisfaction. Figure 10.37 shows that the percentage of convinced and satisfied customers should increase as a result of the sensitivity training program (from 30 percent to 37 percent, and from 25 percent to 30 percent, respectively). The number of dissatisfied customers who complain should increase from 50 percent to 60 percent as a result of increased communication of the central telephone complaint channel, and the percentage of customers who have cause for a complaint should decrease from 48 percent to 41 percent as a result of the quality improvement program. The extent of the reduction in customer switching is used to evaluate the success of these measures. For each measure, the

Calculation for the Evaluation of the Profitability of Different Measures for the Optimization of Complaint Management

		Initial situation: Current complaint management	Measure A: Training program for customer contact personnel	Measure B: Intensified communication of the telephone complaint channel	Measure C: Identification/implementation of a quality improvement program
Customer base					
Current customer base		100,000	100,000	100,000	100,000
Assumptions regarding the expected customer retention effects					
Degree of problem occurrence	Nonconvinced customers with complaint reason	48,000 : 48 %	48,000 : 48%	48,000 : 48%	41,000 : 41 %
Complaint behavior/ articulation rate	Nonconvinced customers with complaint reason who complain	24,000 : 50 %	24,000 : 50 %	28,800 : 60 %	20,500 : 50 %
	Nonconvinced customers with complaint reason who do not complain	24,000 : 50 %	24,000 : 50 %	19,200 : 40 %	20,500 : 50 %
Complaint satisfaction	Convinced complainants	7,200 : 30%	8,880 : 37%	8,640 : 30 %	6,150 : 30 %
	Satisfied complainants	6,000 : 25 %	7,200 : 30 %	7,200 : 25 %	5,125 : 25 %
	Disappointed complainants	10,800 : 45 %	7,920 : 33 %	12,960 : 45 %	9,225 : 45 %
Lost repurchase benefit					
Lost repurchase benefit (Quantity component)	Convinced complainant	360 : 5%	444 : 5%	432 : 5%	308 : 5%
	+ Satisfied complainant	2,100 : 35%	2,520 : 35%	2,520 : 35%	1,794 : 35%
	+ Disappointed complainant	6,480 : 60%	4,752 : 60%	7,776 : 60%	5,535 : 60%
	+ Noncomplainant	12,000 : 50%	12,000 : 50%	9,600 : 50 %	10,250 : 50%
	= Overall lost repurchase benefit	20,940	19,716	20,328	17,886
	− For complaint behavior not accessible repurchase potential (switched convinced and satisfied complainants)	2,460	2,964	2,952	2,101
	= Lost repurchase benefit	18,480	16,752	17,376	15,785

Figure 10.37 Part A

Calculation for the Evaluation of the Profitability of Different Measures for the Optimization of Complaint Management continued

		Initial situation	Measure A	Measure B	Measure C
Lost repurchase benefit					
Monetary evaluated lost repurchase benefit	Profit contribution based on the relationship duration revenue per month: $200; remaining relationship duration: 20 months; profit margin: 8%	$5,913,600	$5,360,640	$5,560,320	$5,051,200
Through measures A, B and C realized effects					
Secured customer relationships	Additional secured customer relationships		1,728	1,104	2,695
Secured monetary lost repurchase benefit	Additional secured monetary lost repurchase benefit		$552,960	$353,280	$862,400
Costs of measure					
Average costs p.a.			$69,000	$51,500	$111,667
Evaluation of the profitability of the specific measures					
Cost comparison calculation	Costs per secured customer		$39.93	$46.65	$41.43
Profit comparison calculation	Profit per measure		$483,960	$301,780	$750,733
	Profit per customer		$280.07	$273.35	$278.57
Return calculation	Return on investment per measure		807%	878%	563%

Figure 10.37 Part B

199

accompanying quantitative components of the lost repurchase benefit are calculated on the basis of the target values that were formulated. As was the case in the firm's initial situation, we assume an average monthly turnover of $200 per customer, an estimated remaining relationship duration of 20 months and a profit margin of 8 percent for the monetary assessment of the number of lost customers per measure. The monetarily valued lost repurchase benefit is stated as a relationship profit.

The values determined for the lost repurchase benefit for the individual measures are then compared to the corresponding variables from the firm's initial situation. The changes brought about in each case are then calculated with regard to additionally secured customer relationships and additionally secured monetary lost repurchase benefits. In comparison to the firm's initial situation, it is clear that each measure can help to reduce the lost repurchase benefit significantly. If the firm had to decide on a measure based exclusively on these results, it would choose Measure C, since it brings about the greatest reduction in the lost repurchase benefit as compared to the firm's initial situation, with 2,695 additionally secured customer relationships and an additionally secured monetary lost repurchase benefit in the amount of $862,400.

Calculation of the Costs per Measure

In order to be able to make a choice, however, it is necessary to include in the decision-making the costs incurred by the three measures. In order to do this, the average costs caused in a period are calculated for each individual measure. For the sensitivity training program (Measure A), these costs total $69,000 per year; for carrying out a campaign to communicate the central telephone complaint channel (Measure B), $51,500 per year is estimated; and for the quality improvement program, an amount of $111,667 per year is projected.

Together with the values for the secured monetary lost repurchase benefit, the average annual costs now form the basis for evaluating the individual measures from an economic perspective by means of cost, profit, and return comparisons.

Evaluating the Efficiency of the Individual Measures

In the context of the cost comparison, preference is given to the alternative that incurs the least costs. If we use the absolute values based on the average annual costs as an assessment criterion, the decision falls in favor of Measure B ($51,500). If the average costs are calculated per additionally secured customer relationship, preference will be given to Measure A ($39.93). Only when the latter decision-making criterion is applied is it guaranteed that the firm will choose the measure with which the preventable customer losses in each case can be achieved in the most cost-effective way.

The overall goal, however, is to cover the costs incurred by a measure through the profits initiated by this measure. For this reason, it is advisable to apply the profit comparison method. Using this approach, one can determine and select the alternative that will earn the highest profit. The profit per measure is computed by subtracting the average annual costs from the additionally secured monetary lost repurchase benefit. In our example, the decision again falls in favor of Measure A, which shows the highest profit value overall with $483,960 ($ 552,960 – $69,000), as well as the highest profit value per additionally secured customer relationship with $280.07 ($483,960/1,728 additionally secured customer relationships).

Since even the amount of profit does not allow conclusive statements to be made regarding which investment is most profitable, it is advisable to perform a return on investment calculation as the last step. The return on investment that is calculated here provides the information about how much the capital yields that is invested in the different measures. Thus, it is calculated as a ratio of the annual profit per measure and the respective average fixed capital. This variable takes into consideration that the capital is depreciated little by little in the course of using the investment, and that over the course of time, less and less capital is fixed. If the initial investment, as in our example, is depreciated linearly, the average fixed capital can be ascertained by adding the initial investment and the depreciation amount for the last year of use, as well as the remaining residual value and dividing the result by 2. For Measure A, we assume an average fixed capital in the amount of $60,000, for Measure B, $34,375, and for Measure C, $133,333. By dividing the profits per measure by the values for the fixed capital, we obtain the rates of return shown in Figure 10.37. It is clear that from the standpoint of profitability, preference will no longer be given to Measure A, but rather to Measure B, which has the highest rate of return with 878 percent, since both of the other measures tie up too much capital.

Weighing the Decision

It would be erroneous to make decisions regarding measures for the optimization of complaint management based exclusively on profitability. In our sample calculation, everything in this regard would speak for Alternative B, and Alternative C would come off the worst. Solely on the basis of the rate of return, however, it would be overlooked that with the implementation of Measure C, a substantially greater effect with respect to the additionally secured customer relationships and with respect to the additionally secured monetary lost repurchase benefit can be achieved. At the same time, the cost and profit values determined for all three measures are very close to one another, and the rates of return for Measures A and C are also impressive values. In a case like this, the basic goals that are being pursued must be weighed out: If the firm is exclusively focusing its attention on profitability aspects, the decision should be made in favor of Measure B. If the firm is striving for a clear increase in the absolute number of additionally retained customers, preference should be given to Measure C. Furthermore, the effects with respect to a measure's external and internal impacts should be kept in mind. Measure A underlines the seriousness of the subject and has a direct announcement effect for all employees. The firm's endeavors are also visible and comprehensible to all its customers. The latter also applies to Measure B, which presents the firm as customer-oriented, especially in problem situations. Measure C, however, has probably the least external and internal impact.

This evaluation shows that a firm should by no means confine itself to calculating only the return on investment of individual measures when upcoming investments in complaint management are to be made. Since it is always necessary to determine the respective cost and profit variables in order to calculate this rate of return, it is fundamentally advisable to use the approaches of the cost comparison and profit comparison methods for well-founded decision-making. Measures that are identified as being inefficient should not be pursued any further. Profitable measures should be evaluated in comparison to one another with respect to the aspects shown above.

After the selected measure has been implemented, the firm should verify, after an appropriate period of time, the extent to which the projected improvement was achieved and whether the profitability calculated in advance was actually attained. It is necessary to collect again the data upon which the profitability calculation is based and to calculate the amount of projected costs that were actually incurred and the extent to which the lost repurchase benefit was actually reduced.

11

Complaint Reporting

Complaint reporting pertains to the regular and active reporting of complaint-relevant facts to internal target groups. This process is primarily concerned with significant results from complaint analysis, but the focus is also on information from complaint-management controlling about the efficiency and effectiveness of complaint management itself. In addition to this active reporting (Information Push), other activities that belong to the task spectrum of complaint reporting are carrying out special analyses at the request of internal customers and making available all the complaint-relevant information so that authorized internal customers have direct access to it or are able to carry out independent analyses (Information Pull).

11.1 ACTIVE REPORTING OF THE RESULTS OF COMPLAINT ANALYSIS AND COMPLAINT-MANAGEMENT CONTROLLING (INFORMATION PUSH)

A central task of complaint reporting is to determine which analyses (quantitative and qualitative) should be prepared and actively transmitted at which time intervals (daily, monthly, weekly) for which internal customers (upper management, quality control, marketing department).

11.1.1 THE TARGET-GROUP-ORIENTED DIMENSION OF COMPLAINT REPORTING

The first step is to make a general decision about the people or departments to whom or to which complaint information should be made accessible. All those who are responsible for customer management, as well as departments that can derive direct benefits from the results, should be accommodated. Numbered among these are top management, quality management, controlling, marketing and marketing research, customer relationship management, and the customer care department. In addition, all organizational units whose field of responsibility includes the problems articulated by dissatisfied customers are to be informed. These could be specialist departments that are involved in complaint processing and complaint reaction (e.g., the legal department). Furthermore, in firms with decentralized distribution structures, these decentralized units require appropriate feedback.

Another decision is which results from complaint analysis and complaint-management controlling should be made accessible to all the employees in the firm, for instance, in the context of specific, regular contributions in employee magazines or in specially designed complaint-management intranet pages.

Depending on the corporate function, the extent of responsibility for complaints, or the communication goal, the individual target groups make different demands on the information in the reports, specifically with respect to the contents and level of abstraction of the presentation.

11.1.2 THE CONTENT DIMENSION OF COMPLAINT REPORTING

Once the individual target groups of complaint reporting have been determined, the next step is to decide which contents must be made available to the respective groups of people, in which form and with which level of detail. In terms of content, one must distinguish between complaint-related and complaint-management-related information.

Complaint-related information provides details about the complaint volume and the consequences that result from complaint cases. Essentially, it is a matter of information on weaknesses in products, services, and processes, as well as the failure costs that arise from these weaknesses.

- **INFORMATION ON COMPLAINT VOLUME.** The reports need to give a quick overview of the development of the total complaint volume. The focus lies on the volume of the received complaints (number of complaints). Moreover, it should be visible to which extent customers had multiple reasons for complaints and in how far there were several problems articulated in one complaint. Therefore, the number of complainants and the number of problems articulated has to be displayed next to the number of complaints.
- **INFORMATION ON WEAKNESSES IN PRODUCTS, SERVICES, AND PROCESSES.** A majority of the complaint information is related to the errors perceived by customers with respect to the firm's performance. First among these are frequency distributions about the complaint objects, the type of problem, the location of the problem, and the complaint category (first or follow-up complaint, guarantee/ goodwill). Equally significant is information about the complainant, for example, the distribution of complaints across specific customer segments. In addition, selected cross-tabulations should be provided, which point out the relevant relationships between the variables, such as between the type of problem and the customer's behavioral intentions, or between the product in question and the extent of guarantee or goodwill cases. Furthermore, each report must not only contain time period analyses for the respective reporting period, but also time series analyses that make clear the chronological development. If such matters are actively communicated to the respective target groups, these groups will be able to carry out quality improvement measures in a targeted fashion.
- **INFORMATION ON THE FAILURE COSTS ARISING FROM COMPLAINT CASES.** The willingness to take serious consequences on the basis of complaint information increases significantly when the failure costs asso-

ciated with the respective problems are simultaneously accounted for in the reports in a differentiated manner. Here it is a matter both of internal failure costs (e.g., for duplicated work or investigations) and of external failure costs (e.g., guarantee and goodwill costs). It is important that the customer switching costs, that is, the lost sales/profit contributions that result from customer dissatisfaction, are also included in the reporting. For the most part, these data are available in complaint management because they are recorded in the context of task controlling. They may, however, be supplemented through the use of other sources, for example, through an appropriate recourse to failure-cost calculations of quality management or migration analyses from analytical CRM.

Complaint-management-related information refers to complaint management itself and provides details about the strengths and weaknesses of this area of activity and its successes with respect to customer retention and also with respect to financial success.

- **INFORMATION ON THE STRENGTHS AND WEAKNESSES OF COMPLAINT MANAGEMENT.** A content focus of complaint-management-related reporting pertains to the achievement of its goals. Complaint handling information and all the performance figures from task controlling provide information important in the identification of strengths and weaknesses. On this basis, one should engage in considerations for improvements in the complaint-management processes. The primary addressees of the contents are the directors of complaint management or Customer Care, but the superior organizational unit is also included, for example, the directors of Customer Relationship Management or company management.

- **INFORMATION ON CUSTOMER RETENTION.** A key goal of complaint management is the stabilization of endangered business relationships. For this reason, providing information about the number of customers retained due to complaint management must also be an important element of complaint reporting. Customers' statements about the behavioral intentions that they have considered in the context of complaint acceptance, as well as the details about their current or planned behavior in the course of follow-up interviews and complaint satisfaction surveys, provide the information necessary for this task. The information value is even higher, however, when it is possible to include results from customer database analyses, which provide unambiguous details about the factual purchase behavior of complainants.

- **INFORMATION ON THE PROFITABILITY OF COMPLAINT MANAGEMENT.** Cost-benefit controlling provides the basic input for the calculation of the profitability of complaint management. This calculation is based on customer statements about behavioral consequences that have already occurred or are planned for the future (from task controlling), and also on information that does not come directly from complaint management, but rather is derived from the customer database. Included in this information are data on customer sales and profit contributions, as well as on actual customer migration due to customer dissatisfaction. The comparative observation of these values from various time periods permits the calculation of the financial benefit of complaint management, or its profitability, when the financial benefit is compared to the corresponding costs.

With respect to the formal presentation, we can distinguish among the following possibilities:

- Detailed lists and tables on the level of classification characteristics, standards/performance figures, and complaint processes
- Aggregate results and performance figures, for example, at higher hierarchical levels or at the level of the respective overall results, and
- "Hit Lists" that provide a concise summary of the key information (e.g., top complaint objects, top problem categories, top complaint methods). The extent of the hit lists depends upon the number of classification characteristics of the individual information concerned; however, care must be taken to ensure that the information remains easily comprehensible.

With regard to the format, one must also decide how the lists, tables, and target figures contained in the complaint reports should be prepared. This applies to the structure of the contents of the tables and lists, the selection of the appropriate graphics, and the way in which the results are communicated. Moreover, the report medium must be determined. Usually, reports are distributed in written form or sent electronically as data.

Figure 11.1 provides an overview of the connections between the target-group-oriented and the textual dimensions of complaint reporting.

There can be no universally applicable statements made regarding the reporting contents or form; rather, the Process Owner has the responsibility of jointly determining the content and form of the information requirements with the representatives of the target groups and making sure that the necessary data is generated in the form desired and transmitted to them. As a general tendency, nevertheless, it can be said that it is usually sufficient to supply firm management with basic facts and figures that have global information value. It is essential, however, that other departments such as quality management receive detailed information about the problems that have occurred with individual products or product components. In every case, though, it would be wise to supplement the numerical data with examples of selected original quotes from the complaint articulations in order to present the customers' perception of the problem and their irritation to the internal target groups in a vivid fashion.

11.1.3 THE TEMPORAL DIMENSION OF COMPLAINT REPORTING

With respect to the different reports, the frequency with which the defined contents are sent to the individual target groups (e.g., daily, weekly, monthly, quarterly, or yearly) must be established. The reporting

Overview of the Relation between the Target-Group-Oriented and the Textual Dimensions of Complaint Reporting

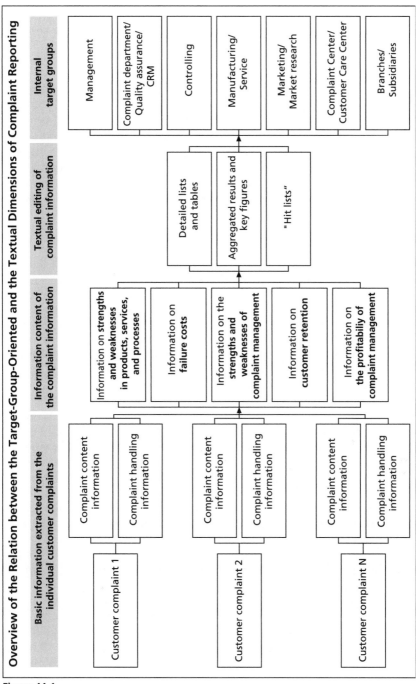

Figure 11.1

intervals are dependent upon the complaint volume and the informational requirements of the internal customers. In addition, the contents of the analyses that are to be presented suggest differing reporting intervals. Problems with especially high reaction urgency, for instance, serious health damage resulting from product use, require daily reporting. It is also advisable to generate frequency distributions and cross-tabulations of problem types and complaint objects more frequently (e.g., weekly) than corresponding analyses of first and follow-up complaints (e.g., monthly). A uniform recommendation cannot be provided. On the contrary, here again it is the responsibility of the Process Owner and the internal target group to determine what information must reasonably be made available at what intervals.

Spotlight 8 shows an excellent example of how a complaint reporting system can be set up (compare also Wirtz and Tomlin 2000).

SPOTLIGHT 8

Based on an analysis of the information requirements of internal customers, the complaint management department of a supermarket chain decides to generate six different types of complaint reports, whose target groups, reporting frequency, goals and basic contents are summarized below in Figure A.

Senior management receives a monthly overview of the most significant problems perceived by customers and of the key performance indicators of the complaint management department. It thus has the information basis with which to make fundamental decisions for customer retention management from a truly customer-oriented perspective and to steer important business processes in a customer-oriented way (Report I). Furthermore, management receives, as do departments that are directly affected, a weekly report on particularly serious problems and unusual developments in complaint frequency (Report II). Marketing and Customer Management are likewise monthly provided with complaint information, on the basis of which the marketing mix can be improved and endangered business relationships stabilized (Report III). The central divisions responsible for causing the problems, such as purchasing or quality control, as well as regional and branch managers, are in turn supplied on a monthly basis with the information that is relevant for eliminating the causes of the problems and controlling the branches. At the same time, each branch has access to comparative information from other branches (Reports IV and V). The last report pertains to all the information relevant for complaint management, which gives a differentiated overview of the quality of task fulfillment and of the cost and benefit effects of complaint management and makes it possible to optimize the individual subprocesses (Report VI).

Report	Recipient	Time frame	Objective	Content*
Report I	Senior management	Monthly (plus corresponding quarterly and annual reports)	- Customer-oriented decisions - Customer-oriented controlling of the firm	- Number of complaints and articulation rate/complaint evidence rate - Repeat, multiple, and follow-up complainants (incl. top 5 problems) - Problem responsibilities (including top 10 branches) - Top 5 complaint objects and problems (with regard to frequency and relevance) - Problems having the character of mass complaints - Top 3 complaint stories - Core dimensions of complaint satisfaction - Unfulfilled customer expectations - Complaint management index - External and internal failure costs (total and for the top 3 problem categories) - Efficiency of quality improvement measures - Costs of complaint management - Repurchase benefit of complaint management - Return on complaint management - Comments and recommendations for action with decisional character (including assessment of profitability)
Report II	Senior management and affected departments	Weekly and as required	- Targeted and systematic handling of the occurrence of especially serious problems and/or exceptional developments	- New problems with high frequency and/or high relevance perceived by customers - Exceptional increase of problems - Exemplary "complaint stories" for the affected categories - Comments and recommendations for action
Report III	Marketing and customer management	Monthly (plus corresponding quarterly and annual reports)	- Customer-oriented improvement of the marketing mix - Initiation of customer individual measures for the stabilization of endangered business relationships	- Differentiated consideration of the number of complainants (single, repeat, multiple, and follow-up complainants) - Top 10 problems of repeat complainants - Top 5 complaint objects and problems (with regard to frequency and relevance) - Problems having the character of mass complaints

Spotlight 8, Figure A

Overview of Complaint Management Reports, continued

Report	Recipient	Time frame	Objective	Content*
Report III	Marketing and customer management	Monthly (plus corresponding quarterly and annual reports)	- Customer-oriented improvement of the marketing mix - Initiation of customer individual	- Exemplary "complaint stories" for the top problem categories - External (and internal) failure costs for the top problem categories - Efficiency of quality improvement measures - Comments and recommendations for action
Report IV	(Other) central departments responsible for problem causes (procurement, quality assurance) Each report refers to the complaint volume relevant for the respective department.	Monthly (plus corresponding quarterly and annual reports)	- Minimization of the causes relevant for perceived customer problems	- Number of complaints - Top 10 problems of repeat complainants - Top 20 complaint objects and problems (with regard to frequency and relevance) - Problems having the character of mass complaints - Exemplary "complaint stories" for the top problem categories - External (and internal) failure costs for the top problem categories - Comments and recommendations for action
Report V	Regional and branch manager Each report refers to the complaint volume relevant for the respective department.	Monthly (plus corresponding quarterly and annual reports)	- Regional manager: Customer-oriented controlling of branches (internal benchmarking) - Minimization of the causes relevant for perceived customer problems	(per region and branch, respectively and top 10 branches per sales region) - Number of complaints - Top 10 problems of repeat complainants - Top 20 complaint objects and problems (with regard to frequency and relevance) - Problems having the character of mass complaints - Exemplary "complaint stories" for the top problem categories - External (and internal) failure costs for the top problem categories - Comments and recommendations for action

Spotlight 8, Figure A, continued

Overview of Complaint Management Reports, continued

Report	Recipient	Timeframe	Objective	Content*
Report VI	Director complaint management (This report refers to the problems accounted for complaint management itself.)	Monthly (plus corresponding quarterly and annual reports)	- Optimization of complaint management processes	- Top 10 problems for follow-up complaints (with regard to frequency and relevance) - Problems having the character of mass complaints - Top 3 follow-up complaint stories - Realization rates for objective quality standards - Delays in complaint processing - Realization rates for subjective quality standards - Observance of productivity standards in the complaint management process - Unfulfilled customer expectations - Complaint management index - External and internal failure costs (with regard to frequency and relevance) - Efficiency of quality improvement measures - Costs of complaint management - Repurchase benefit of complaint management - Return on complaint management - Comments and recommendations for action

* The contents relevant for the individual reports are displayed as values for each period, together with a percentage development over the period under consideration (compared to the previous month as well as cumulated for the respective quarters).

Spotlight 8, Figure A, continued

Excerpts from two of these reports are presented below. Here we have the complaint report for senior management and the specific report for the Head of Complaint Management, both of which deal with the time period from January 1 to June 30 of a particular year.

The senior management report (Figure B) first gives an overview of the complaint volume—differentiated according to the number of complainants, the complaint processes, and the number of problems articulated. The "Total Articulation Rate" and the "Complaint Evidence Rate" facilitate the actual assessment of the complaint volume. Moreover, the complaint development with respect to the different types of complainants (Follow-Up, Repeat, and Multiple Complainants) is indicated. The top five problems reflect the key issues, which represent 53 percent of all the problems perceived by complainants. In addition, the top complaint stories of the top two problem categories are presented in order to illustrate customers' specific problem situations. A problem prioritization of the five most frequently occurring problems on the basis of the Frequency Relevance Analysis of Complaints (FRAC) shows that the perceived urgency of eliminating the problem shifts in comparison to an exclusive examination of the problem frequency when the relevance ascribed by customers to the problems is taken into consideration. Furthermore, it becomes clear at a glance that two types of problems among the top five ("Insufficient Quantity of Advertised Articles Available" and "Waits at Register Longer than Ten Minutes") account for 73 percent of the total problems perceived by customers. Excerpts of the cost/benefit effects of complaint management are presented here by presenting the development of the Return on Complaint Management.

The report for the Head of Complaint Management (Figure C) first shows the degree to which selected quality standards from objective and subjective task controlling are fulfilled, as well as the development of the Complaint Management Index over time. With respect to the cost-benefit effects of complaint management, the costs per complaint process are prepared in a differentiated manner for the reaction costs and for the pure processing costs. The report contains an excerpt from the status report regarding the progress and the performance results of quality-improvement measures in complaint management. Recommended actions are subsequently derived from the key aspects of analysis, which form the basis for customer-oriented decision-making and controlling of the complaint management processes. In a more detailed version of this report, these recommendations are to be supplemented by a specific consideration of the profitability in each case. Assessments of the progress of implementation and the efficiency of individual quality-improvement measures are also components of continuous reporting.

Senior Management Report [Cut-out]

Complaint volume

1,200

1,000

400

Jan Feb Mar Apr May Jun

- S 6,400 [+ 11%]
- S 6,100 [+ 17%]
- S 5,700 [+ 15%]

Total Articulation Rate [Jan. – Jun.]: 53% [+ 7%]
Complaint Evidence Rate   [Jan. – Jun.]: 34% [+ 5%]

The growth rates refer to the comparison period of the previous year.

Articulated problems   Complaint cases   Complainants

Main problems

Top 5 problems [53%]

Problem categories	Jan. – Jun.	D prev. year
1 Insufficient quantity of advertised article	1,090	-25.1%
2. Unfriendly service personnel	893	-11.8%
3. More expensive than regional suppliers	621	+29.9%
4. Products were charged twice	400	-29.4%
5. Waiting time at cash desk exceeds 10 min	388	+290.1%

Problem priorization [FRAC]

100%

80%

60%

40%

20%

0%

Top 2 customer complaint stories

Insufficient quantity of advertised article
The special offer was already sold out 15 minutes after the opening of the supermarket. The customer was very disappointed about this incident. She neither received background information regarding the incident nor was she informed if and when the desired article will be available again. In the future the customer will not try to buy any special offers in this market again. She will also discourage other people from buying special offers in this market.

Unfriendly service personnel
The customer had given a bag to the customer information desk for them to keep it until she was done with her shopping. In exchange for her bag she received a ticket. When she wanted to re-exchange this ticket for her bag the person at the desk told her that there was no bag and that she must have picked it up already. The general manager of the store did not believe the customer either. The customer was mortified and felt put in the position of a cheater. The situation was especially humiliating due to the fact that other customers were able to overhear and witness this incident. The customer will never visit a subsidiary of this supermarket chain again.

Types of complainants

400

200

Jan Feb Mar Apr May Jun

- 1,900 [+ 3%]
- 1,350 [- 14%]
- 625 [- 24%]

The growth rates refer to the comparison period of the previous year.

Multiple complainants   Repeat complainants   Follow-up complainants

Cost-benefit effects of complaint management

Return on Complaint Management [RoCM]

100%

50%

0%

-25%

-50%

-31%   10%   42%   108%   115%   100%

Jan   Feb   Mar   Apr   May   Jun

Spotlight 8, Figure B

213

Head of Complaint Management Report [Cut-out]

Performance of objective quality indicators

Quality Indicators	Target value	Actual value	Realization degree
Addressee rate [ADR]	80%	95%	119%
Information completeness rate [ICR]	75%	60%	80%
First-time fix rate [FFR]	50%	50%	100%
Reminder rate [RR]	10%	5%	200%
Processing time < 7 days	90%	80%	89%
......	...%	...%	...%

Performance of subjective quality indicators

Quality indicators [Satisfaction with ...]	Target value	Actual value	Realization degree
Overall complaint experience	55%	40%	73%
Complaint process	70%	55%	79%
Complaint result	40%	25%	63%
Reaction time	85%	65%	76%
Empathy	75%	80%	107%
Active approach to the customer	80%	55%	69%
......	...%	...%	...%

Complaint management index

1.00
0.80
0.60
0.40
0.20

Jan Feb Mar Apr May Jun

Cost-benefit effects of complaint management

Costs per complaint case

200 $
150 $
100 $
50 $

Jan Feb Mar Apr May Jun
62 41 40 88 92 100

Reaction costs per complaint case [warranty, goodwill, compensation]
Process costs per complaint case

Efficiency of quality improvement measures

Realized quality improvement measures

Customer problem	Improvement measures		
Span until the first reaction to written complains too long	Every customer whose written complaint cannot be closed immediately receives a telephonic confirmation of receipt regarding the arrival of the complaint.	142	12
......	......		

* The complaint volume is measured on a monthly basis.

Recommendation for action

Complaint volume
- Establishment of [complaint relationship desks] in every branch
- Conducting focus-group interviews with repeat and follow-up complainants

Problem responsibility
- Initiation of monthly meetings with the department managers
......

Spotlight 8, Figure C

11.2 PROVISION OF COMPLAINT-RELATED INFORMATION (INFORMATION PULL)

The scope of activity of complaint reporting includes not only the target-group-oriented distribution of previously defined reports, but also the provision of complaint-oriented information for special, irregular information wishes of internal customers. Due to the initiative required from the internal customers with respect to the acquisition of information, we can speak of information pull here. From complaint management, relevant information from complaint analysis and complaint management controlling can be supplied in two ways—on stock and on demand.

On-stock supply of information is available when complaint management establishes a pool of information to which authorized internal customers have access. First, this pool of information should include the original documents so that members of the departments involved can also gain insight into the complainants' original descriptions. Second, all the detailed analyses should be available, even when they are not part of the standard program of the reports. This makes it possible for the members of internal target groups to consolidate their activities using complaint information in a more detailed and extensive manner. Through the provision of simple tools of analysis, the information users also have the opportunity to generate their own analyses in an easily manageable way.

On-demand supply of information is provided when analyses are carried out based on the individual demands of internal customers. This is relevant if specific cases (e.g., complaints with a high problem or customer risk) are investigated at the request of internal target groups, or there are deviations from the stipulated frequency.

The supply of information on an on-stock and an on-demand basis is an important internal service of complaint management that contributes to increasing the use of complaint information and thus to achieving the goals of quality improvement and customer retention.

12

Utilization of Complaint Information

A key goal of complaint management is to make a substantial contribution to quality management by guaranteeing an active utilization of documented complaint information for measures of improvement. In this way, a reoccurrence of customers' problems will be avoided in the future, and customer retention will be realized by means of customer satisfaction. In order to reach this goal, specific management measures and instruments must be employed. Three relevant aspects will be considered in greater detail in the following chapter: the application of a specific quality planning technique to the development of problem solutions (12.1), the use of complaint information in quality improvement teams and quality circles (12.2) and the leveraging of complainants' problem solving competency (12.3).

12.1 UTILIZATION OF COMPLAINT INFORMATION BASED UPON THE FAILURE MODE AND EFFECT ANALYSIS (FMEA)

For many years, the application of planning techniques has been proven valuable in quality management. Among these techniques are base methods that can be summarized under the term "Seven Tools of Quality." They serve primarily in failure mode documentation and failure mode analysis. Three important representatives of this group of methods—the histogram, the Pareto diagram, and the cause-and-effect analysis—were already introduced in connection with quantitative and qualitative complaint analysis. In this chapter, one more complex instrument with applications for complaint management will be presented—the Failure Mode and Effect Analysis (FMEA).

The FMEA is a formalized analytical method for the systematic recording and prevention of potential failure modes in the development of products and services. It was developed in the mid-1960s in the American aeronautics industry and since that time has been among the key methodological instruments in quality management (Stamatis 1995).

The FMEA is a method of preventative quality assurance, since it is concerned with the timely identification, rating, and prevention of potential failure modes. For this reason, its use in the context of complaint management might at first appear to be unsuitable, because complaints contain information about failure modes that have already occurred and can no longer be prevented. Closer examination reveals, however, that very practical applications are nevertheless conceivable, specifically through the supply of complaint information for use in the FMEA and also the prevention of failure modes in complaint management itself.

The Use of Complaint Information in the Context of the FMEA Application

An essential area of application for the FMEA is the new development or modification of products and services. Here it is necessary to recognize and reduce the risks of potential failure modes by taking a structured approach. This occurs when a team of experts from different departments carries out the discussion and assessment of failure modes, using a specific form (Figure 12.1).

The approach can be characterized in ten steps:

1. The initial discussion is about which failure modes could actually occur, and the potential failure modes identified are listed in the first column "Potential Failure Modes."
2. For each potential failure mode, the problems that could result are recorded in the column "Potential Effects of Failures."
3. Subsequently, for each failure mode, the causes that are responsible for its occurrence must be found.
4. Next, the risks associated with the failure modes are assessed on the basis of this information. For this purpose, it is first estimated in the column "Occurrence" how probable it is that this failure mode could occur. The rating is based on a scale that ranges from "unlikely" (1) to "highly likely" (10).
5. After that, the gravity of the effects of the failure mode is analyzed from the customer's perspective. The rating is again based on a ten-point scale that ranges from "hardly noticeable" (1) to "serious failure mode" (9 or 10). The respective value is entered in the column "Severity."
6. The column "Detection Ratings" is used to express an estimate of how likely it is that the failure mode can be detected before the product reaches the customer. Since the risk of a failure mode is greater, the later it is detected, the rating scale ranges from "highly likely" (1) to "unlikely" (10).
7. The Risk Priority Number (RPN) is the result of multiplying the values for Severity, Occurrence, and Probability of Detection. It is the standard that permits a comparison of the risks of various potential failure modes and thus is also an essential variable in prioritizing failure mode prevention measures.
8. The causal analysis is the basis for the recommendation of actions that should prevent the occurrence of the failure mode.
9. Subsequently, the effect of these measures is to be discussed and evaluated by making a new risk assessment. Taking the corrective measures into consideration, Occurrence, Severity, and Probability of Detection are assessed anew, and the residual risk is expressed in a new Risk Priority Number.

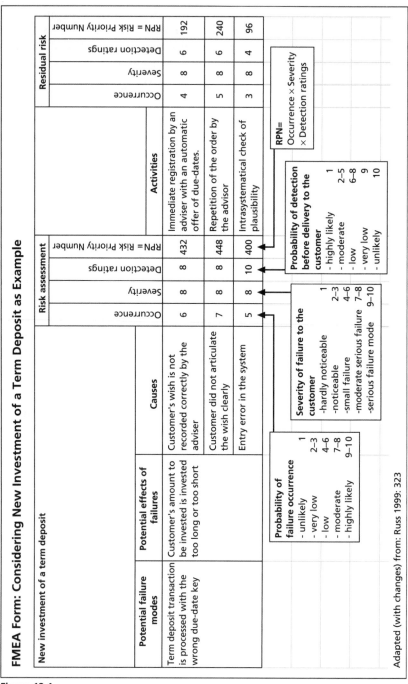

FMEA Form: Considering New Investment of a Term Deposit as Example

New investment of a term deposit			Risk assessment				Activities	Residual risk			
Potential failure modes	Potential effects of failures	Causes	Occurrence	Severity	Detection ratings	RPN = Risk Priority Number		Occurrence	Severity	Detection ratings	RPN = Risk Priority Number
Term deposit transaction is processed with the wrong due-date key	Customer's amount to be invested is invested too long or too short	Customer's wish is not recorded correctly by the adviser	6	8	8	432	Immediate registration by an adviser with an automatic offer of due-dates.	4	8	6	192
		Customer did not articulate the wish clearly	7	8	8	448	Repetition of the order by the advisor	5	8	6	240
		Entry error in the system	5	8	10	400	Intrasystematical check of plausibility	3	8	4	96

Probability of failure occurrence
- unlikely — 1
- very low — 2–3
- low — 4–6
- moderate — 7–8
- highly likely — 9–10

Severity of failure to the customer
- hardly noticeable — 1
- noticeable — 2–3
- small failure — 4–6
- moderate serious failure — 7–8
- serious failure mode — 9–10

Probability of detection before delivery to the customer
- highly likely — 1
- moderate — 2–5
- low — 6–8
- very low — 9
- unlikely — 10

RPN= Occurrence × Severity × Detection ratings

Adapted (with changes) from: Russ 1999: 323

Figure 12.1

10. A comparison of the Risk Priority Numbers before and after the planned measures is therefore possible, and in this way, measures with the greatest influence on the reduction of risk can be selected.

This approach shows that the FMEA can be used not only for failure mode prevention, but also for the assessment of failure modes that are documented in complaints and for the development of corrective measures in the context of quality management. But even if one clings to the preferred FMEA application—in the context of new developments—the recourse to information from complaint management makes a great deal of sense.

As the presentation of the FMEA process has shown, the team must constantly make valuing decisions. They must determine the likelihood with which failure modes occur and are detected in a timely manner, and they must perform an assessment of the failure mode's consequences from the customers' point of view. There is a great danger here that the team members will rely on their personal evaluations and come to the wrong conclusions. The recourse to complaint information can reduce this danger by permitting a customer-oriented and factually supported assessment. This applies particularly in the vast majority of cases in which, instead of a completely new product being developed, a product relaunch is to be made:

- Quantitative and qualitative complaint analysis provide a number of indications of failure modes that have actually occurred and could reoccur in the changed product, or that contain suggestions valuable in the detection of other possible failure modes.
- The information from complaint management concerning complainants' intended actions and actual behavior after the failure mode has occurred provides specific insights into the failure mode's consequences and relevance from the customer's perspective.
- Quantitative complaint analysis permits definite conclusions with respect to the probability of occurrence and the probability of detection. Failure modes that lead to complaints are obviously detected too late by the firm, and the failure mode statistic shows differences in the probability of occurrence. It makes sense to use this information in the risk assessment.
- Qualitative complaint analysis in particular offers valuable indications of the causes of problems and possible measures that can be used to combat those causes.

It is therefore advisable to integrate information from complaint management much more systematically into the traditional failure mode and effects analysis.

Use of the FMEA for the Improvement of Complaint-Management Processes

Complaint management does not merely provide valuable input for the application of the FMEA planning instrument in the development process. It can also use this instrument to subject its own processes to a failure mode analysis. In this case, the FMEA serves to prevent failure modes in complaint management.

Gierl (2000) provides an example of this when he applies the FMEA to complaint stimulation, a task area of complaint management. He interprets a low number of dissatisfied customers who complain to the firm as a failure mode. Along the lines of the approach presented above, it is then recommended that a working group with members from the marketing, sales, and customer service departments be established so that this failure mode can be addressed more closely. The team describes the failure mode's consequences, analyzes the causes, performs a risk assessment, and develops proposed solutions. Taking these measures into account, the new risk priority numbers are calculated, which permits the selection of the measures that will be implemented first. Figure 12.2 shows an appropriate form for this hypothetical example.

The FMEA is a recognized systematic method whose general application can be improved in its informational content by the utilization of complaint information and can reasonably be used in the improvement of complaint-management processes. What is essential is not the filling out of the form, but rather the structured guidance of preventative thinking, the inclusion of experts across departmental boundaries, and the structured documentation of the problem solution process.

12.2 USE OF COMPLAINT INFORMATION IN QUALITY IMPROVEMENT TEAMS AND QUALITY CIRCLES

The systematic analysis and evaluation of complaint information and the development of possible solutions cannot be carried out by individual experts exclusively. The problems must be considered in all their various aspects, the causes must be analyzed in their complexity, and the influencing variables must be thoroughly documented. A similar principle applies to the generation of ideas for solutions and their assessment with respect to their ability to prevent future failure modes. Thus, one of the requirements for the application of methods such as FMEA is the formation of teams that allow for the creative process and the use of diverse expert know-how.

The teamwork in quality improvement utilizing complaint information may be structured and designed differently, depending on the firm's situation and on the problem. Two different kinds of team concepts can be primarily differentiated with regard to the permanence of their existence and the structure of their membership: quality improvement teams and quality circles.

Quality Improvement Teams

Quality improvement teams are charged, on a short-term basis, with formulating a solution for a specific quality problem that has previously been clearly defined. Quality improvement teams are assembled across departmental boundaries. They can be identified by the following characteristics:

- The task is clearly defined. Depending upon which weak points are highlighted in the context of quantitative complaint analysis and com-

FMEA in the Context of Complaint Stimulation

Complaint stimulation			Assessment of residual risk				Activities	Residual risk			
Potential failure modes	Potential effects of failures	Causes	Occurrence	Severity	Detection ratings	RPN = Risk Priority Number		Occurrence	Severity	Detection ratings	RPN = Risk Priority Number
Dissatisfied customers who do not complain	High rate of customer switching and negative word-of-mouth	High perceived complaint costs	4	9	10	360	Installation of a hotline	2	9	9	162
		Success probability assumed to be low	8	9	7	504	Introduction of service guarantees	2	9	6	108

Adapted (with changes) from: Gierl 2000: 170

Figure 12.2

plaint management controlling, a very specific problem becomes the focus of the work of a quality improvement team.

- The quality improvement team is composed of those people with the highest potential for formulating solutions and implementing measures. The crucial factor is that all the required expertise is represented so that the problem that needs to be solved can be addressed effectively. All departments that may have contributed to the occurrence of the problem or can make a contribution to the solution should be represented. The involvement of all those concerned should reduce interdepartmental conflicts, and realistic solutions that can be supported by all those involved in the new process should be developed.

- The work in quality improvement teams is an essential component of the work performed by employees. Many efforts to improve quality fail due to the fact that employees only grudgingly take part in the meetings, believing that the real work is being left undone. Not until this attitude that "quality is outside the job" is overcome and the efforts to improve quality are seen as part of the corporate performance requirement, and not as a burdensome additional task, can the firm count on successful teamwork and the necessary commitment from the employees.

- Quality improvement teams disband after the problem is eliminated. They exist during the time in which the quality problem is being processed and are disbanded when it is solved. They are not a permanent structure.

Quality Circles

Quality circles are a special form of quality improvement teams. They are also dedicated to the systematic elimination of failure modes and the creative search for new solutions to problems. Their distinctiveness comes from being designed for regular meetings on a continuing basis, operating on a volunteer basis, and principally being concerned with problems in the more immediate work environment.

Quality circles have proven their worth in many companies as an important instrument for the improvement of product quality and process flow. It has been shown that they can greatly contribute to increasing motivation, improving internal communication, continuing job-related training, and strengthening employees' identification with their company. There are relatively few barriers to their implementation, since the establishment of quality circles is not associated with structural changes in terms of the operational and organizational structure of the firm.

So that quality circles can serve as an important committee for the use of complaint information, a series of requirements must be fulfilled:

- The results of the quantitative complaint analysis are to be forwarded to all quality circles in the context of complaint reporting.
- Part of the standard procedure of the work of quality circles must be to analyze complaint reports with the objective of identifying possible

causes within one's own field of activity and making these causes the object of improvement activities.

- If the qualitative complaint analysis takes place elsewhere (e.g., in quality improvement teams), insights into possible sources and causes of problems are to be forwarded immediately to the quality circles. A link between the work of the quality circle and more comprehensive improvement activities should also be established.
- For an exact analysis of the problem and a targeted development of solutions, members of quality circles must have access to the complaint database, and they must be trained to work with problem solution techniques.

Employees from complaint management play a key role in the fulfillment of these requirements. Not only must they carry out analyses and supply information in the context of reporting, but they must also become active internally as stimulators of quality improvements by purposefully approaching the quality circles, supplying additional information on customers' problems and requests for change, and providing training for the application of customer-oriented methods of information use.

12.3 CUSTOMER PANELS AS AN INSTRUMENT OF QUALITY IMPROVEMENT

Quality improvement teams and quality circles are forms of teamwork in which the creative potential of employees is used to arrive at solutions for problems. Another approach is to enlist the complainants themselves in developing these solutions.

Customer panels are an important instrument in this process. In the following section, the basic value of customer panels with complainants will be discussed first (Chapter 12.3.1). Then it will be shown how the creative potential of customers can be increased through the use of specific methods in customer panels (Chapter 12.3.2). In a third section, the advantages and disadvantages that result when the dialogue with complainants takes place in virtual customer panels (e-customer chats) will be demonstrated (Chapter 12.3.3).

12.3.1 GENERAL GOALS OF CUSTOMER PANELS WITH COMPLAINANTS

Customer panels, also known as customer conferences or customer focus groups, are group discussions with a circle of selected customers with whom certain topics related to the business relationship are discussed in detail.

Customer panels are established in pursuit of the following goals:
- Gaining deeper insights into the desires, motives, and assessments of customers
- Identifying spontaneously expressed criticism and suggestions for improvement
- Achieving a greater understanding of problems observed in the provider's behavior from the customer's point of view

- Signaling customer orientation
- Enhancing customer retention
- Sensitizing employees to customer concerns and supporting efforts directed toward customer-oriented change in the firm.

Experience shows that these goals can for the most part be reached when customer panels are used professionally. The group discussions give customers the opportunity to present their perspectives extensively. They are also stimulated by the contributions of other participants to reflect on their desires and to evaluate their experiences so that the information gain is greater than it is in individual interviews, due to the group dynamic.

The opportunity to have an extensive discussion of the problems often makes it possible to obtain not only detailed information about the problems observed, but also about the causes of the problems and the dynamic of annoyance in the customer's experience process. In this way, valuable indications concerning possible corrective actions and new solutions can be extracted.

This effect is particularly to be expected when complainants are invited to the customer panels. Complainants have already taken a critical look at the problem in their minds and frequently have developed ideas for alternative pathways. They prove, therefore, to be especially critical and valuable advisors. Customer panels thus not only have a complaint-stimulating function, but also can be regarded as an important instrument for using the creative potential of customers in the improvement process.

12.3.2 USE OF METHODS IN CUSTOMER PANELS

The stimulation of creative processes among customers begins when joint deliberations on problem solutions are started with them after the actual and extensive phase of criticism. This can already occur by requesting that customers speak out about the changes they would like to see in the future and, in their opinion, the steps the firm should take. The suggestions must then be collected and logged by the moderator. At the end of the session, the participants may be requested to weight the different suggestions in terms of their preferences.

An alternative to having this rather intuitive type of conversation in customer panels is to apply simple creativity and planning techniques for the generation of proposed solutions, which does, however, require adequate skill on the part of the moderator.

The first technique is the application of brainstorming, which usually produces a variety of ideas within a short period of time if the rules established by Osborn (1953) are observed. Principal among these are the following:

- Criticism is ruled out. Adverse judgment of ideas must be withheld until later.
- "Free-wheeling" is welcomed. The wilder the idea, the better; it is easier to tame down than to think up.
- Quantity is wanted. The greater the number of ideas, the higher the likelihood of useful ideas.

- Combination and improvement of ideas are sought. In addition to contributing ideas of their own, participants should suggest how ideas of others can be turned into better ideas, or how two or more ideas can be joined into still another idea.

Sympathizing with the customer's experience once more during the group discussion and making it the cause for reflecting on new ideas can also stimulate the generation of creative ideas. This can take place with the aid of the Sequential Incident Technique for Innovations (SITI), which itself is especially designed for extracting ideas for improvements in services or in the complaint process.

When using a service (e.g., that of a hotel), customers go through a sequence of individual episodes at a variety of contact points (e.g., arrival, check-in, stay in the room, restaurant visit, check-out). Their quality perceptions thus consist of a series of partial experiences. Quality perception takes place at each contact point, and the quality impression at the end of a transaction is the result of a cumulative process of perception. The SITI takes this circumstance into account and has as its aim the collection of customers' positive and negative quality experiences on the basis of a visualized customer pathway in personal interviews.

The basis and the main component of the method is the determination of the path customers typically take in using a service, as well as its graphical representation in a customer path or blueprint (Shostack 1987; Zeithaml and Bitner 2003). On this basis, the customers are then requested to go through the process of the service experience in their minds and to describe the individual contact situations in detail (Stauss and Weinlich 1997).

This process can very reasonably be applied to customer panels and simultaneously developed further—with respect to exploiting the customer's creativity—into a SITI. Decker and Meissner (1999) demonstrated this with an example of customer panels in car dealerships. In these panels, initially the typical customer path taken in having a car repaired was developed. The customers were not solely requested to describe their respective experiences with regard to each episode (e.g., making an appointment, driving onto the premises, conversing with the customer-service employee). They were also asked to reflect on possible improvements or to describe whether they had noticed superior solutions in the case of other providers—even in different sectors. The result showed that customers are in an excellent position to make a number of very specific suggestions for improvement.

The application of these methods in customer panels with complainants is suitable above all for situations in which customers who have experienced their problems during a similar customer process are invited. This principle applies to a majority of purchase and service processes. The direct complaint-management process experienced by the customer can itself be made the subject of the discussion when it is intended to improve this process and to increase the complaint satisfaction of the customer.

For this type of application of the SITI in the context of customer panels, one should proceed as follows:

- The complainants invited are each initially requested to list the individual contact points in the course of a normal service transaction with the firm in chronological order.
- In the joint discussion, the progression of a typical customer path is recorded and visualized.
- Based on this customer path, the customers describe what they experienced at each point and evaluate the experience they had.
- Finally, suggestions for improvement are developed and recorded for each contact point on the customer path.

The use of methods such as these not only improves the chances of using the creative potential of customers, but it also signals the firm's earnest desire to learn from the customer. This even increases the willingness of very critical customers to work constructively with the firm after they articulate their criticism. In doing so, a corporate feeling actually develops in many cases during the discussion of the problem and the possible solutions, which includes not only the customer group, but also the employees and the firm collectively. One experiences the community of the efforts toward improvements for the customer, which stresses the firm's proximity to its customers and contributes to the development of a true customer relationship.

Customer panels have not only external functions directed toward customers, but also internal functions. The participation of employees gives them an immediate impression of the perceived quality experience of customers. Even employees who otherwise have no contact with customers now receive the complaint information directly, rather than in aggregate form and as a written document. In this way, they are directly confronted with the customers' opinion and trained by the customers themselves with respect to customer-oriented behavior. With adequate preparation and post-processing, customer panels thus represent an essential instrument of employee coaching and of organizational change toward customer orientation.

12.3.3 VIRTUAL CUSTOMER PANELS WITH COMPLAINANTS—E-CUSTOMER CHATS

The rapid proliferation of the Internet has made new forms of customer dialogue available. Among these is the possibility of hosting customer panels virtually as chats (online focus groups), rather than in person (Sterne 2000).

Similar to the approach taken in "traditional" customer panels, complainants are requested to participate in a dialogue. This dialogue, however, takes place over the Internet and mostly in written, not verbal, form. The participants interact with one another and with a moderator by sending and receiving messages. The following sequence of events is typical.

After entering their names and a previously disclosed password, the participants arrive in a "virtual lobby." Here, the participants are introduced to one another. After that, the participants appear on the interaction surface ("interface screen"), on which the course of the discussion is recorded visually. Moderator and participants type their contributions in a "comment box" on the screen and send them to a server. Each message received is immediately displayed on all the participants' screens, and the participants can spontaneously react to them.

The moderator has at her disposal a number of ways to direct the discussion. She can copy prepared questions from a text file in the comment box, and she also has other means of intervention at her disposal. Among these is the "whisper mode," which allows her to address individual participants without the other participants noticing, for example, in order to ask that dominant participants restrain themselves. Live links to other Web sites and the transmission of multimedia data files are also possible during the discussion. Since the time and sender of each answer and of the links to external sources are recorded, the entire chronicle of the customer panel is available as a transcript immediately after the conclusion of the "round of talks."

Compared to traditional focus groups, virtual focus groups have a number of advantages. Experience shows that the quality of the answers is higher. The participants do not spend a long time with the social processes of getting to know one another and exchanging pleasantries. They devote more time to the answer and give answers that are more thought-out. The greater anonymity of the situation also appears to promote a frank articulation of opinions. In this way, both the participants and the firm can realize significant savings in time and costs. Another advantage for the firm in terms of time and costs is that the content of the dialogue is immediately available as a data file and can be directly analyzed and entered in the customer database.

Nevertheless, these advantages are also somewhat balanced out by several disadvantages. The moderator and participating observers from the firm have access only to the written messages. Forms of nonverbal communication that can be observed in the context of traditional customer panels are not visible, which means that a related information loss is incurred. Moreover, the information exchange proceeds in a more controlled and less spontaneous fashion.

The use of customer panels with complainants shows, however, that even this less elaborate version of feedback is a good instrument of information utilization. The participating complainants give detailed information about their experiences and their ideas with regard to improvements. At the same time, they see the opportunity they are offered for feedback and cooperation as an expression of the firm's interest and appreciation so that retention effects can be expected. This holds true even more when the firm informs them at a later time about how the information has been used internally.

13

Human Resource Aspects of Complaint Management

13.1 THE IMPORTANCE OF EMPLOYEE BEHAVIOR IN COMPLAINT CONTACT

The way employees react to customers' complaints plays a significant role in whether customers feel that they are being taken seriously, whether a consensual solution can be reached, and whether complaint satisfaction is created. Practical experience shows that extreme customer irritation often arises in the complaint acceptance and reaction process itself: "Angry customers are created by the firm itself" (Blanding 1991: 94). The majority of customers state their concerns calmly and constructively; however, when they are simply turned away, put off with false information, or constantly transferred to other departments within the firm, then irritation and anger are the results. The following example from corporate practice confirms this observation.

The manager of the R&D department of a large pharmaceutical corporation, a chemist, the prototype of the rational thinking person, orders an analysis device from a well-known manufacturer. About three months later, the device fails. But the defect is due to a little part costing only about three dollars. After sending a claim to the manufacturer, a letter comes back from the engineer responsible. In this letter, the engineer blames the researcher for not using the device properly and states that therefore his company is not responsible for the defect. The following return letter stays unanswered. Instead, three experts of the manufacturer behave arrogantly and insensitively in three subsequent telephone conversations. That becomes the last straw for the manager. He gives the instruction never to buy from this particular manufacturer again. Since then, ten years have passed, and the decision remained final (Scheerer 1994: 10).

Conversely, experience has proved over and over again that the occurrence of an error in the core performance is not assessed as being overly negative if employees behave appropriately. Not only must the employees in customer care departments be aware of this, but also all employees in contact with customers, because the majority of complaints will be articulated to them. Only a relatively small share of customer dissatisfaction is reflected in written complaints. Most of the criticism is expressed in person, for instance, to salespeople or to other customer-contact employees. According to a study, 65 percent of complaints were initiated with front-line workers (Tax and Brown 1998; Brown 2000). Only a few complainants who are not satisfied with the results of the first encounter demand to speak with a manager. Letters to the board of directors, the CEO, or corporate headquarters are comparatively rare. In a survey by Adamson and Goodman (1992), only 2.5 percent of complaints were directed to top management. Articulations to third-party institutions (consumer organizations, media, federal agencies) represent the absolute exception. Usually, this method is only chosen when all other efforts have been in vain (Adamson 1993).

In view of these insights, the central importance of customer-contact employees for the implementation of active complaint management becomes clear:

- They have direct contact with customers who complain and thus the first opportunity to reduce dissatisfaction.
- They can potentially bring about an immediate solution to the problem and thus, in many cases, provide especially rapid and cost-effective processing.
- They have an important function in accepting information about customer problems that are not made the subject of written complaints.
- They can significantly ease processing, solution, and analysis by recording additional information (about the complaint case or the solution desired by customers).

Therefore, an essential task of human resource management is to prepare all customer-contact employees for complaint situations and provide them with the skills necessary for successfully coping with these contacts.

13.2 NECESSARY EMPLOYEE SKILLS

The attributes that complainants use to evaluate the firm's reaction provide important indications about the skills that should be demanded of complaint-contact employees. Generally, what customers expect from the firm is a high degree of accessibility, friendliness/politeness, empathy/understanding, effort/helpfulness, activity/initiative, reliability, reaction speed, and appropriateness/fairness of the solution offered. Accordingly, in the specific complaint situation, customers must observe employee behavior that can be characterized by these attributes. There are, however, essential requirements that must be fulfilled so that employees will be able to display this behavior. First, employees must possess the adequate motivation toward service orientation, as well as social, emotional, and professional competence. Second, using internal marketing measures, the firm must see to it that employees with appropriate skills are attracted and retained, and that employees are able to strengthen their competencies. Through these measures and the goal-oriented design of the corporate culture and the infrastructure, the firm must further guarantee that employees actually translate their skills into corresponding behavior.

Service Orientation as the Basic Motivation

The basic requirement for any successful action by service-contact employees is distinct service orientation. The employee must have the fundamental willingness to be a problem solver for customers and the desire to serve them.

Service orientation has two motivational roots—motivation to help and achievement motivation. Motivation to help includes the desire and the willingness to take care of customers' problems. Achievement motivation refers to an inner drive to fulfill a task in an excellent way, to be involved, and to learn in order to be able to meet the requirements even better in the future. In this sense, service orientation is the motivation to be a problem solver for customers to the best of one's ability and to serve them in an excellent way. Only employees who display this service orientation are also prepared to use their skills to find the best possible solution to the complaining customer's problem.

Social Competency

Social competency is the ability to pursue one's own goals during the interaction process, while also taking into account the goals of one's interaction partner. This type of competency primarily includes the abilities to observe and to assess the partner, the situation, and one's own possible actions correctly. Employees who speak with complainants must be able to put themselves in the customers' place and to relate to their view of the situation. Employees must keep an eye on the complaint situation and recognize factors that would have a disturbing influence, in order to be able to reduce or eliminate them. It is also necessary that they correctly recognize the impact of their own behavior on their conversation partners—that is, correctly picking up on the words, gestures, and measures that would have a calming effect on customers, or those that would annoy them even further. In order to be able to draw the right conclusions from these perceptions and act as a conflict solver, however, it is necessary that employees possess sophisticated communication abilities. Only with the correct use of verbal and nonverbal instruments—such as wording, tone, facial expression, and gestures—is the employee's social competency noticeable to and effective for the partner. A broader understanding of social competency also includes additional key skills such as flexibility and creativity, which permit employees to act in a way that is appropriate to the situation and fair to customers, that is, to be prepared for customers' different expectations and to develop problem solutions that correspond to those expectations.

Emotional Competency

To a certain extent, customers who complain experience strong negative emotions. They feel harmed and hurt, are annoyed and angry. These negative emotions are partly expressed by the type of complaint articulation, when customers "let off steam." But even when they express their concerns in a more composed manner, customers are negatively affected. For this reason, dealing with complainants demands that employees perform not only a technically defined task, but also "emotional labor" at a particularly high level. Emotional labor is the modulation and control of feelings by service-contact employees with the goal of evoking those specific emotions that are desired by the firm and/or the customers (Hochschild 1983).

Regarding the ability to fulfill these requirements, a great deal has been said in recent years about "emotional intelligence," the ability of a person to perceive and express feelings, to comprehend and control their impact, and consciously to influence them in oneself and in others (Goleman 1997, 1998). A broader understanding of this construct also includes the motivational dimensions of service orientation and the interpersonal abilities of social competency previously presented. For this reason, we will speak here of emotional competency in a more narrowly defined sense, which focuses on the "intrapersonal" competencies of self-awareness and self-control. Self-awareness includes the ability to recognize and understand one's own feelings and their impact on others. Self-control is the ability to master abrupt emotional impulses and moods, or to be able to focus them in another direction.

To a great extent, complaint-contact employees must perform emotional labor in the sense of managing their own emotions, as well as the emotions of others. They have to use their emotions to satisfactorily demonstrate empathy. They must be in a position to influence customers' emotional sensitivity—to reduce their annoyance, for example, and to put them at ease. This requires that employees be capable of emotional self-perception and able to influence the interaction systematically by employing their own feelings. A high degree of emotional self-control is also required so that they will not react aggressively to unjustified criticism, for instance, and make the situation worse. It is exactly this emotional self-control that in many cases represents an especially high mental burden for the employee.

Professional and Methodological Competency

In the specific situation of complaint acceptance, the service orientation and the social and emotional competency of the employee accepting the complaint are particularly critical. Nevertheless, an efficient and satisfactory solution will not be reached if employees do not also have the necessary professional and methodological competency. In order to be able to record the complaint contents precisely, employees must know which information to collect and in what way, and how the internal complaint-processing procedures are organized. Moreover, precise knowledge of the products in question is necessary for accepting and processing complaints. Broader and more sophisticated professional and methodological competencies are required when the overall spectrum of complaint management tasks is taken into consideration. Employees in the customer care department must, for example, have detailed knowledge of the software that is being used, a good command of internal processes and methodological knowledge of quantitative and qualitative complaint analysis, and be able to implement processes of task and cost-benefit controlling.

Figure 13.1 provides a summary view of the requirements for employees in complaint management and reveals the range of necessary skills. Individual skills frequently encompass a whole array of requirements. Communication ability, for example, includes the ability to express oneself in a language that is appropriate to the addressee and to gather the necessary information using techniques of questioning and analytical reasoning. The figure also shows that service orientation and social and emotional competence skills are more urgent, the more employees are occupied with tasks of direct complaint management, that is, the more they have direct contact with customers. In contrast, the share of professional and methodological competency required grows with respect to tasks of indirect complaint management, which in essence demands that methods be implemented within the firm. This should, however, be understood only as a rough assignment. Without professional competency, social and emotional competency do not lead to successful conduct, and even the highest professional and methodological competency of internal employees will not lead to the desired result if these employees are unable to configure the interactions with their internal partners in a socially and emotionally competent fashion.

13.3 PERSONNEL-ORIENTED INTERNAL MARKETING AS A CONCEPT FOR SECURING THE REQUIRED EMPLOYEE SKILLS

Fully aware that the quality perception of service customers is substantially determined by the behavior of service-contact employees, service firms have generally come to believe that customer-contact employees are a key internal customer group whose skills should be designed in a systematic manner. In order to highlight the similarity of this task to external marketing, we speak of internal marketing. The application of the internal marketing concept aims to make sure that employees conduct themselves in such a way that customers are acquired, satisfied, and retained (Berry and Parasuraman 1992). The target groups of internal marketing in the context of complaint management are managers and employees of all hierarchical levels and employees that are occupied specifically with complaint management tasks, particularly complaint acceptance.

First, employees at all hierarchical levels, primarily also top management, must be convinced that complaints contain business opportunities and are not to be interpreted as dangers to be averted. This basic message should be disseminated through different instruments of internal communication. What is even more important, however, is that it is effectively supported and authenticated through an appropriate corporate culture, consistent actions, and an appropriate incentive structure.

The introduction of professional complaint management is commonly associated with difficult learning processes, especially in the case of managers. They must

• be able to acknowledge their own mistakes

Essential Qualifications of Employees for Complaint Management

Service Orientation

Professional and methodological competency	Social and emotional competency
• Expertise regarding the main features of complaint behavior • Knowledge of guidelines • Proficiency in communication techniques • Knowledge of complaint processing procedures and their steps • Proficiency in complaint-management software • Methodological skills regarding complaint analysis and complaint management-controlling	• Sensitivity • Communication skills • Flexibility and creativity • Emotional self-awareness • Emotional self-control • Coping with criticism • Conflict resolution skills • Coping with pressure

Direct complaint-management process

Complaint stimulation ⟩ Complaint acceptance

Complaint processing ⟩ Complaint reaction

Complaint analysis ⟩ Complaint management controlling

Complaint reporting ⟩ Complaint information utilization

Indirect complaint-management process

Figure 13.1

- make the importance of complaints clear by scheduling personal management time for reading and answering complaint letters
- prove on an everyday basis that they are not interested primarily in naming culprits, but in analyzing the causes of problems and developing solutions to those problems
- give employees responsibility and grant them decision-making authority
- correct employees who made a mistake in their efforts to find a customer-oriented solution and help them with their future behavior, but not "punish" them
- honor exemplary reactions to customer complaints.

Learning processes such as these should be initiated and promoted with the aid of information, feedback, and behavioral training.

For the personnel of the complaint-management department, the goal of personnel-oriented internal marketing is to attract, develop, and retain service-oriented employees for the firm—employees who demonstrate a high degree of service orientation, as well as emotional, professional, and methodological competency, and are willing and able to fulfill the goals of complaint management and the expectations of complaining customers in the best possible way.

The entire array of measures that can help to influence the service orientation, the various skills, and the behavior of employees are available for use as instruments of personnel-oriented marketing. In the following sections, we will address in more detail the instruments that are given particular importance in the context of complaint management: the recruiting of service-oriented and qualified employees, employee communication and training, incentive systems, burnout prevention measures, and empowerment.

13.3.1 RECRUITING SERVICE-ORIENTED AND QUALIFIED EMPLOYEES

A fundamental goal of internal marketing is to select the most suitable candidates during the recruiting process. This requires a systematic approach, which in many cases is disregarded with respect to the recruiting of customer-contact employees (Berry and Parasuraman 1992). Special care is required when recruiting employees who will constantly be dealing with dissatisfied customers in customer care centers, for example, because the demands on the employee's social and emotional competency are especially high in these cases.

Among the crucial steps in a systematic selection process are task analysis, the resulting personal attributes analysis, the development and implementation of a selection system design strategy, and the continuous validation of the recruiting process (Schneider and Schechter 1991).

In the context of task analysis, what is important is to describe in detail the specific tasks to be performed by the prospective employee. By surveying current employees and supervisors and by observing their work, the specific activities that applicants will have to perform in the future can be determined. For instance, for an employee in a customer care center, these activities may include the following:

- Greeting the customer in a friendly manner
- Asking questions designed to encourage the customer to describe the circumstances precisely
- Entering the complaint content and complaint processing information quickly and correctly in the system
- Calming distressed complainants
- Determining the solution desired by the customer
- Developing one's own suggestions for solutions
- Making independent decisions while keeping in mind both the customer's desire and the organizational rules
- Explaining to the customer the solution being offered
- Using the customer's name during the conversation
- Listening, accessing the available information in the database, and entering new information during the conversation

- Initiating the appropriate processing procedure when an immediate solution is not possible
- Informing the customer about further procedures
- Thanking the customer and ending the conversation on a friendly note.

The insights from this task analysis form the basis for the personal attributes analysis, which is the specific description of skills that employees must possess. The approach is to ask employees and supervisors with appropriate experiences to indicate the characteristics that employees must possess in order to fulfill the requirements well, as far as the individual job tasks are concerned.

According to a study by Schneider and Schechter (1991: 223), a specific telephone job with sales and service responsibilities requires the following competencies:

- **PERSUASION** = the ability to influence the opinions and attitudes of others through the skillful use of information.
- **COMPREHENSION AND MEMORY** = the ability to understand the written and spoken language of others; skilled at listening; the ability to learn, understand and remember large numbers of facts, rules and procedures, and codes.
- **REASONING** = the ability to apply learned rules and procedures, use judgment, combine pieces, and make decisions.
- **SOCIAL SENSITIVITY** = the ability to act enthusiastically in interpersonal situations. Involves skillful adjusting of behavior to fit demands of a call and requires figuring out how others are likely to react. Involves the skillful use of control and assertion.
- **UNDERSTANDABILITY** = the ability to express oneself through written and/or spoken language so that others will understand.
- **CLERICAL SPEED AND ACCURACY** = the ability to quickly and accurately look up, write down, and/or key in facts, codes, data, numbers, and so forth that are heard, looked up, or already in memory.
- **DEALING WITH PRESSURE** = the ability to act and react without losing effectiveness given the very strong requirements on rapid, efficient, and courteous sales and service.

A list of characteristics generated in this manner must then be evaluated in two respects—first, with respect to the importance of the characteristics, and second, with respect to the extent to which the employees must already possess these characteristics during their first day on the job.

Among the characteristics that employees absolutely must possess when they are hired are those that the employees must apply very quickly in order to fulfill their tasks and that are difficult to convey. It is primarily the differing degrees of difficulty between conveying social and emotional competency compared to professional and methodological competency that must be taken into account. Professional and methodological knowledge can be learned much more easily when the employee possesses adequate perception than can basic aspects of social and emotional competency. Because of this reason, the department store

235

Nordstrom's basic principle when recruiting employees is that the important behavioral characteristics must be observed and technical deficits compensated for in on-the-job training: "Nordstrom hires the smile and trains the skill" (Spector and McCarthy 2000: 180).

If, based on the assessment of the necessary characteristics, the desired requirements are firmly established, the third step is to develop and implement suitable selection methods. These methods are those that measure the relevant characteristics, that can be easily applied by the selection team, and that are insightful from the applicants' perspective with regard to their importance in the workplace.

For the characteristics of comprehension and memory, as well as understandability, speed and accuracy, which belong more to professional and methodological competencies, the firm should administer standardized tests that permit it to make a judgment of the extent to which applicants possess the required cognitive abilities. In terms of the characteristics that are classified under social and emotional competency, primarily interactive selection methods are suitable, which include interviews and work simulations. What is most important in the interviews is achieving clarity regarding the applicant's motivation, particularly the degree of service orientation. In work simulations, applicants are faced with a task whose accomplishment demands the required characteristics, without the applicants themselves having to be familiar with the specific job. Applicants are then confronted with a fictitious complainant on the telephone, for example, and are assigned the task of accepting the complaint, calming the caller down, and correctly recording the circumstances in writing. In carrying out this task, the candidates obtain information about responsibilities, deadlines, and decision rules. Using checklists, observers and evaluators can then perform an assessment of the applicant. Figure 13.2 shows an example of a checklist for telephone contact and the written documentation of the complaint incident (Schneider and Schechter 1991).

Aided by methods such as these, the selection team is not dependent on the answers of applicants in the context of interviews, but rather can observe them in realistic scenarios in which they must actually apply the abilities relevant to the job.

Every recruiting process to be developed on a firm-specific basis must of course be validated with regard to efficiency on an ongoing basis. The combined implementation of three different methods is advisable. First, the firm must investigate the extent to which the recruited applicants actually fulfill the requirements as defined. For this purpose, supervisors should reevaluate the employees after a certain period of time based on the criteria laid out when they were hired. Second, the firm should supplement the internal perspective with an external assessment from the customer's point of view. Analyses of customer satisfaction surveys, praise and complaint analyses, and the use of professional testers who monitor the observance of predefined standards as pseudo-customers ("Silent Shoppers," "Mystery Callers") are recommended. Third, it is a good idea to increase employee satisfaction and loyalty

Checklist for Behavioral Characteristics of the Candidate in the Context of Work Simulation

Behavioral characteristic	Indicator The candidate. . .	Evaluation true false
Comprehension and memory	. . . records all important aspects of the complaint incident	⬜1 ⬜2 ⬜3 ⬜4 ⬜5
	. . . refers correctly to responsibilities, time standards, and decision rules	⬜1 ⬜2 ⬜3 ⬜4 ⬜5
Reasoning	. . . properly classifies the complaint as a routine case and initiates the adequate complaint process . . . applies correctly the designated decision rule	⬜1 ⬜2 ⬜3 ⬜4 ⬜5
Social sensitivity	. . . is able to put himself/herself in the complainant's position and to express his/her understanding . . . expresses his/her regret for the customer's annoyance . . . avoids rash problem diagnosis	⬜1 ⬜2 ⬜3 ⬜4 ⬜5
Understandability	. . . clearly expresses himself/herself, provides clear-cut information about the corporate standards . . . concentrates on the facts . . . rarely makes verbal and written mistakes	⬜1 ⬜2 ⬜3 ⬜4 ⬜5
Clerical speed and accuracy	. . . needs few further inquiries to resolve the case . . . assimilates quickly the facts of a case . . . needs little revision	⬜1 ⬜2 ⬜3 ⬜4 ⬜5
Persuasion skills	. . . is able to persuade the caller that the problem remains in good hands . . . is able to argue the caller out of engaging the supervisor without the caller being dissatisfied	⬜1 ⬜2 ⬜3 ⬜4 ⬜5
Coping with pressure	. . . reacts objective to customer reproaches . . . maintains the performance level even during multiple consecutive conversations . . . keeps calm even under time pressure	⬜1 ⬜2 ⬜3 ⬜4 ⬜5

Adapted from: Schneider and Schechter 1991: 228

Figure 13.2

constantly in order to have starting points for determining from the employees' perspective whether the general organizational conditions tend to encourage or to hinder them from applying their own skills in an appropriate fashion.

13.3.2 EMPLOYEE COMMUNICATION AND TRAINING

Particular importance is given to employee communication in the context of the internal implementation of complaint management. Everyone associated with the firm must be informed of the importance of customer satisfaction for customer loyalty, for corporate profits, and for their own job security. It is necessary, especially in the cases of customer-contact employees, to create acceptance with respect to the maxim of consistent orientation toward customers' wishes, to motivate the customers, and to make them see themselves as problem-solvers for customers. In addition, the employees must be informed of all the principles of a customer-oriented complaint policy, as well as the codes of behavior, and be in a position to fulfill these principles and standards.

Generally speaking, the firm's internal communication policy serves the following purposes:

- Creating a fundamental appreciation of the importance of customer satisfaction for the economic success of the firm
- Conveying and increasing the awareness of the potential opportunity for achieving customer loyalty and improving performance quality that is found in complaints
- Illustrating the significance that top management attributes to complaint acceptance in the corporate goal system
- Ensuring the identification of employees with their complaint tasks
- Increasing the feeling of responsibility for the accurate fulfillment of all complaint-management tasks
- Contributing to a corporate culture that is characterized by customer-orientation, error prevention, and the constant search for better solutions for customers
- Pointing out examples of excellent employee conduct in complaint situations
- Conveying factual information in order to achieve complaint-management tasks in the best possible way
- Systematic informational promotion of professional, methodological, social, and emotional competency
- Providing feedback information for specific employee behavior in complaint management.

A considerable number of instruments are available to help the firm achieve these goals. These instruments can be analyzed according to their focuses by using two criteria. The first criterion pertains to the question of whether the communication predominantly takes place through various media or by personal interactions. The second criterion makes a distinction based on whether the instrument is directed more toward conveying information or more broadly toward training certain skills.

Media-supported instruments of corporate mass communication are the primary instruments that serve to convey information about the fundamental importance of complaint management, to sensitize employees, and to show the corporate importance. Through posters, for example, the fundamental ideas of complaint management can be strikingly expressed, and prejudices can be reduced. In contributions to the employee newsletter, top management can express its personal commitment to the goals of complaint management. Persuasive examples of exemplary employee behavior may also be presented. Circulars, brochures, and handbooks are suitable for the communication and documentation of behavioral rules and processes. Actuality, completeness, and access to the appropriate information at any time are assured when the information is placed on the intranet.

In addition to media-supported information, a great deal of importance is also placed on direct personal communication. Management can emphasize the importance of customer satisfaction for the firm in specific information events. Meetings provide an opportunity to obtain detailed information and exchange ideas on current developments and challenges in the area of complaint management. Feedback sessions with supervisors are more critical for the behavior of individual employees, however. These sessions may concern either customer complaints about the employee's behavior or about the performance of complaint-management tasks by the employee. Customer complaints about a specific employee should be discussed between the supervisor and the employee. In order to avoid jeopardizing the basic goals of complaint management, however, supervisors must observe important rules of conduct during such discussions. The type of approach they use must creditably demonstrate that they see the incident primarily as an opportunity for improvement and not simply as a chance to denounce the culprits. They must allow for a factual explanation of the case and, based on this explanation, develop ideas about future approaches in cooperation with the employee. These ideas may also include decisions concerning necessary qualification measures. A similar principle applies to feedback sessions that pertain to the performance of given complaint-management tasks. In jointly conducted discussions between employers and employees, the parties must agree on goals, determine and analyze the level of achievement, perform deviation analyses, and draw consequences for activities. These conversations must take place in an atmosphere of trust that is unmistakably supported by the common desire to improve performance for the customer. In the case of feedback like this, the line has been crossed from pure information to coaching, and thus to a guided and systematic improvement process.

While media communication is primarily used by management to propagate its own perspective in the firm in a type of top-down communication, the various forms of personal communication provide many more opportunities for a dialogue in which employees can also bring in their perspectives. This perspective is explicitly requested when standardized methods of employee surveys are used as a form of bottom-up communication. As far as complaint management is concerned, what is important is to survey the employees' expectations regarding active complaint management, their own roles as complaint managers, and management's support. The results of the survey then form the basis for the collective identification of deficits and the development of problem solutions.

Even between the regularly administered surveys, however, the firm must see to it that the idea potential of customer-contact employees be utilized to analyze the current situation and to stimulate ideas for improvements. A possible consideration would be the promotion of ad

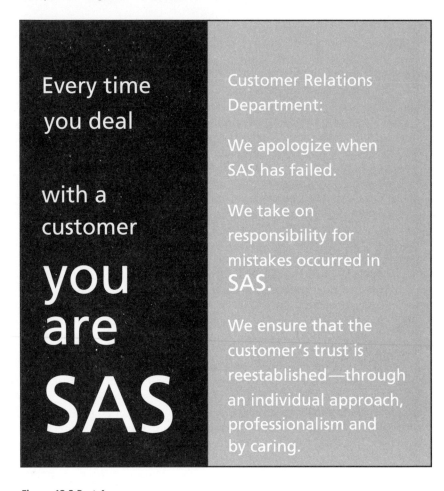

Every time you deal

with a customer

you are SAS

Customer Relations Department:

We apologize when SAS has failed.

We take on responsibility for mistakes occurred in SAS.

We ensure that the customer's trust is reestablished—through an individual approach, professionalism and by caring.

Figure 13.3 Part A

hoc conversations between customer-contact employees and management. These conversations may include, for example, establishing round-table discussions with top management (e.g., a "breakfast with the boss") (Furlong 1993: 82). Informal communication in terms of "management by walking around" or of "open house" days or hours, in which top managers are available to talk, should also be initiated.

The personal forms of communication include not only the interactions between managers and employees, but also the interactions among the employees themselves. Employees need opportunities to exchange ideas with one another, to eliminate information deficits on a spontaneous basis, and to pass on their own experiences and knowledge to others. It is the task of management to give ample time for informal employee contact and for formal team meetings. The latter also include the quality improvement teams and quality circles described in Chapter 12.2.

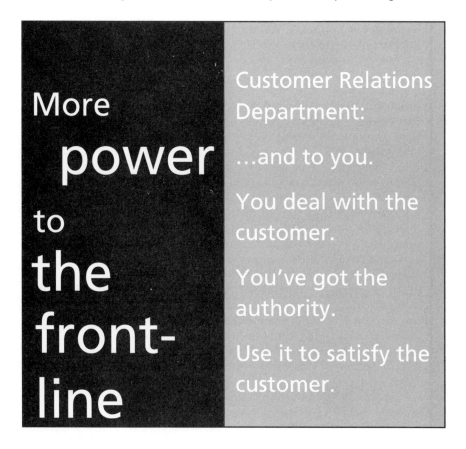

Figure 13.3 Part B

Training programs for all customer-contact employees and the employees in Customer Care Departments are of special importance. Specific courses are to be offered to all customer-contact employees in order to acquaint them with the philosophy of active complaint management, train the appropriate behavior during complaint acceptance, and illustrate the function and mode of operation of a Customer Care Department. Figure 13.3 gives examples taken from the training material of Scandinavian Airlines. In the upper part of the figure, it is made clear to the employees that they are representing the company during each customer contact ("Every time you deal with a customer you are SAS"). In addition, the message is delivered that it is part of the company's policy to take responsibility for errors occurring in the service process, to apologize, and to win back the customer's trust with "an individual approach, professionalism and by caring." The problem-oriented and individual reaction calls for empowered frontline personnel. This becomes clear in Part B of Figure 13.3. Here the company commits itself to the concept of empowerment ("More power to the frontline") and encourages employees to use the options open to them, keeping the best interests of the customer in mind, to secure a competitive advantage ("You deal with the customer. You've got the authority. Use it to satisfy the customer").

A broad spectrum of media and measures are available for specific training programs designed to impart and increase professional, methodological, social, and emotional competency. Written and especially multimedia learning materials, as well as forms of e-learning offered over the Internet and the intranet, can be made available in order to convey the specific content of the individual complaint-management tasks in different modules and to provide opportunities to practice behavior patterns.

These media-supported practice opportunities are to be supplemented by forms of personal training, in which employees have the opportunity to reflect on and to improve their behavior in actual or simulated situations. These training forms include workplace instruction by experienced colleagues and the employment of trainers who observe the behavior of employees and subsequently talk with them about their strengths and any adjustments that need to be made. If supervisors possess adequate qualifications, especially observational ability and intuition, the coaching should be assigned to them. They would then observe the behavior of their employees and help them with individual improvements by providing constructive feedback (Bell and Zemke 1990).

In order to test specific behavior and bring about permanent changes, however, it is necessary to create opportunities for practice independent of the real-world situation at the workplace. It is advisable to offer workshops using simulations and role-playing on specific topics, which make it possible to do away with reactions that are ingrained but ineffective and to practice the desired new behavior patterns.

13.3.3 INCENTIVE SYSTEMS

Normally, it is not sufficient simply to nurture the desired competencies through information and training programs. The willingness of employees to utilize their competencies on a long-term and independent basis must also be supported by appropriate incentive mechanisms. Goal-oriented behavior must be rewarded, and counterproductive incentive structures must be abolished.

The entire spectrum of tangible and intangible incentives can be used to reward excellent employee behavior in the fulfillment of complaint tasks. Employees might be rewarded individually or as a team for fulfilling or exceeding agreed-upon objectives or when they have been especially successful (e.g., as in solving an extraordinarily difficult complaint case) with financial bonuses or other tangible benefits, such as the occasional use of company vehicles. In addition to these tangible rewards, there are intangible incentives such as certificates, public distinctions, complimentary portrayals in firm communications, and membership in a "Best Service Club." In making a decision regarding the incentive system, it is necessary to verify the reward character of the individual incentives with the respective employee segment in advance and to leave the employees opportunities to choose their rewards where appropriate. The firm must also make sure that a direct connection exists between performance and reward, and that the practice of rewarding is transparent.

Just as important as the existence of a goal-oriented reward system is the abolishment of counterproductive incentive structures that lead employees in a direction other than the one desired. Firms frequently expose their employees to conflicting expectations by simultaneously demanding unequivocal customer orientation, strong turnover growth, and consistent cost reductions, for instance. If the reward system provides for bonuses that are dependent only upon turnover growth or cost reductions, it is implicitly made clear to employees that these goals, not customer satisfaction, are the only ones that really count; and they will behave accordingly. Paying employees in telephone centers based solely on their productivity will lead, for example, to a tendency to interrupt customers, not to clarify the facts thoroughly, or to transfer the customer unnecessarily in order to stay within the time limits set (TARP 1988). If firms want to remain true to the goals of active complaint management, they must design their incentive system in a way that such counterproductive conflicts are prevented.

13.3.4 MEASURES TO PREVENT BURNOUT

Specific personnel-related activities are needed in the case of customer-contact employees who not only accept complaints on an occasional basis, but constantly encounter complaint information in the course of their jobs in a customer care center or a telephone complaint department. The mental stress that is associated with managing conflict situations and uninterrupted "emotional labor" in terms of having to respond emphatically to another person's feelings while simultaneously suppressing one's own must be taken into account. Especially these employees are in great danger of suffering from "burnout syndrome." This syndrome is a form of emotional exhaustion that is expressed in an employee's reduced productivity and indifferent behavior toward the person receiving the service. This emotional exhaustion shows when these employees feel emotionally overwhelmed and inwardly burned out when dealing with customers. They think their competence is decreasing, feel worn out and dispirited, and see themselves less and less in a position to provide the emotional care demanded by customers. They tend to perceive the customer relationship more anonymously and to find fault for most of the problems with the customers themselves. In order to avoid these serious consequences, management must proceed in an active and preventative manner.

Bowen and Johnston (1999) propose a type of support concept for employees involved in direct complaint acceptance to which they apply the term "internal service recovery." They emphatically point out the stresses and strains that are associated with negative experiences in complaint situations. Such experiences include not only discrepancies between one's own feelings and the feelings that must be expressed in a given situation, but also doubts in one's own abilities to satisfy customers completely and resentment for having to bear the consequences of mistakes for which the individual employee is not responsible. In order to cope with this situation, the authors recommend that managers take care of their employees and behave the way that they would want employees to behave toward customers. They should take time for the employees, recognize that they have a difficult job, and demonstrate a great deal of empathy and social support. In addition, they must ask employees how the management of complaint contacts can be improved from their perspective.

The firm must make practical arrangements to make sure that the constant burden of stressful emotional labor is interrupted. Measures of "job rotation" are particularly suitable for this purpose. These may include, for example, directing employees in the complaint department to alternate the performance of complaint acceptance tasks and indirect complaint management activities (those without customer contact) such as in the areas of complaint analysis and controlling.

It is necessary to prevent feelings of helplessness and lack of control over the situation from emerging among employees. This can be achieved primarily by allowing them more responsibility and decision-making authority in solving customers' problems ("empowerment").

13.3.5 EMPOWERMENT

By "empowerment," we mean shifting the right to make decisions and transferring autonomy to employees at lower levels of the hierarchy (Brymer 1991), an approach that has attracted great interest in the corporate world as the importance of customer-contact employees in complaint situations has increased.

The basic idea is that customer satisfaction can be reestablished especially quickly when the first contact person has the ability and expertise to solve the problem without having to call in a supervisor. Customers should be spared the experience of having to deal with employees who claim not to be responsible and being referred to other people without recognizing an immediate effort to handle the case.

For this reason, the central goal of empowerment is to increase customer satisfaction by solving the problem quickly and to improve the process and reduce costs by saving processing time (especially management time). Moreover, the firm can strive to increase motivation on the part of its personnel, based on increased responsibility and improved communication between customer-contact personnel and management (Brymer 1991; Bowen and Lawler 1995; Rafiq and Ahmed 1998).

Within the framework of the empowerment concept, a distinction must be made between two versions that differ with regard to the degree of autonomy given to employees and with respect to the breadth of discretion they are allowed—structured empowerment and flexible empowerment (Brymer 1991). Structured empowerment refers to guidelines that are specified in a relatively clear manner and allow customer-contact personnel the opportunity to propose or select certain solutions independently or to decide between specified versions. Brymer (1991: 60) gives examples for such a structured empowerment by presenting sample guidelines developed by the Hilton Hotel at Walt Disney World Village. If a guest experienced a room-related problem (e.g., no hot water, poor television reception) and complains about it at checkout, the front-desk clerk is authorized to offer an upgrade for the next visit or adjust the current bill by as much as $100. If a guest complains about something unrelated to the room (e.g., luggage was delivered late), the front-desk clerk is supposed to offer a compensation of $50 for the inconvenience.

There are also comparable examples known from the restaurant industry. A regulation at Satisfaction Guaranteed Eateries, for instance, stipulates that guests who have to wait between 10 and 20 minutes for their reserved table are to be offered a free drink; but if they have to wait more than 20 minutes, the entire meal may be complimentary. Employees are nevertheless encouraged to decide for themselves, based on what is appropriate in the situation, what they consider necessary in the interests of satisfying the customer, rather than to follow the rules blindly (Firnstahl 1989). An approach such as this marks the transition to a more flexible form of empowerment.

Flexible empowerment allows customer-contact personnel greater discretion in their behavior. The guidelines are established more broadly, and the employees are asked to react flexibly and creatively to customers' desires and demands. Not only should they have a standard repertoire of behavior ready to use in a given situation, but they should also increase customer satisfaction with customized reactions. Offers of price reductions represent only one of many action alternatives. Even guidelines for flexible empowerment can be specified to differing degrees. Nordstrom, the department store known for its service policy, simply formulates the general basic rule "Use your good judgment in all situations" (Spector and McCarthy 2000: 180). In the majority of cases, however, the rules refer to specific problem situations. Figure 13.4 shows an example of solving complaints upon checkout from a hotel.

Guidelines for Resolving a Complaint During Checkout

If the guest is uncertain how she or he would like the problem to be resolved, the employee should ask if the guest is planning a return visit in the near future. If so, offer to her or him an upgrade at no additional charge. If the guest does not plan to return soon, the employee may ask again of the guest, "What may I do to help make up for the inconvenience you experienced?" Follow through with the guest's suggestion or propose to the guest one of the company's approved adjustments, including making changes to the current room bill.

Adapted from: Brymer 1991: 61

Figure 13.4

Guidelines and action alternatives may be generated and put in concrete terms by the employees themselves. This is—to some extent, at least—the case at the hotel group Marriott Corporation, where employees discuss typical complaint situations among themselves and come up with appropriate possible courses of action and the competencies associated with them (Furlong 1993).

The "complaint ownership" approach is also an integral part of the empowerment concept. Employees to whom a complaint is expressed or who even just accidentally find out about a customer problem then "own" this problem and must bring about a solution. They may not claim that they are not responsible for the problem. Instead, they should ask themselves, "What can I do for the customer in order to remedy this problem?" Within broad limits, they also have the expertise to solve the problem in the way the customer desires; otherwise, they must see to it that more qualified employees carry out a settlement that suits the customer. When, for instance, a guest dining in the hotel restaurant mentions that the television reception in his room is poor, the waiter must inform the repairperson and attend to the problem until he is certain that it is actually solved (see also Chapter 6.1.1).

Flexible empowerment and the "complaint ownership" approach place increased demands on employees. They must think and act more independently and creatively and, in doing so, keep an eye on customers' needs while also considering the corporate interests. Therefore, the granting of responsibilities and competencies is also associated with certain risks (Bowen and Lawler 1992). Implementing the empowerment concept demands greater investments in the personnel selection process and in employee training, may involve higher personnel costs, and may lead to other cost-intensive consequences if employees make decisions and incorrectly assess the consequences of those decisions. Nevertheless, this latter risk should not be overestimated. Against the background of their many years of experience in complaint consulting with TARP, Goodman and Grimm (1990: 52) report that they have never encountered a case in which employees "have given away the store," while a reduction of the processing costs by 30 to 50 percent through empowerment could be observed.

The risks can be avoided and the advantages realized when management makes sure that the necessary qualifications are established with respect to leadership and organization. These qualifications include the following (Bhote 1991; Brymer 1991; Furlong 1993; Venkatesan 1993):

- A basic trust in employees that they will not exploit the demand for consistent customer orientation in a way that is irrational and damaging to the firm.
- The involving, informing, and winning over of middle management at an early stage. These managers fear loss of power, competence, and authority the most and may obstruct the introduction of empowerment. These managers must be won, for their support is imperative for the guidance and training of contact personnel.

- An information system that allows employees fast, direct access to all the data needed for their decisions.
- The overcoming of reservations on the part of the employees themselves, who do gain a measure of responsibility but lose a certain amount of comfort, and only really use the new level of discretion they enjoy when they are convinced that the advantages associated with it outweigh the risks.
- The establishment of empowerment teams in which fundamental principles can be clarified, specific behavior patterns discussed and developed further, and barriers removed.

We can see that empowerment is a long-term oriented concept for firms that consider themselves learning organizations (Venkatesan 1993). For this reason, it is also advisable to proceed with the implementation in manageable steps, while taking into account the situational conditions. Flexible empowerment is especially appropriate in the context of a corporate strategy that is geared toward differentiation and customized performance, whose goal is long-term business relationships, where complex and changing customer demands are typical and there are a large number of interactions between customers and employees (Bowen and Lawler 1995; Rafiq and Ahmed 1998). In situations that can be characterized by contrary characteristics (a cost-leadership strategy in bulk business, a short-term transactional relationship with customers, relatively rigid customer desires, no customer contact or temporary customer contact), it seems advisable to use a more structured form of empowerment and to regulate the respective courses of actions in a differentiated and detailed fashion. The success of the largest fast-food chains is based at least partly on the employees being provided explicit scripts for everything from the greeting to the farewell and are monitored for compliance, all of which results in uniform performance and gives the customer a great deal of security regarding the expected service.

13.4 DESIGN OF THE FRAMEWORK FACTORS

The appropriate framework conditions must be created in firms so that employees can use their abilities, and first to be considered here are the infrastructure and the corporate culture.

Securing a quantitatively sufficient and adequately qualified workforce and providing suitable hardware and software are the two most important items in terms of infrastructure.

The existence of a customer-oriented corporate culture is an even more important requirement. The corporate culture is the entire range of ideals and ways of thinking and acting that are present in a firm and that shape the attitudes and the behavior of those affiliated with that firm. This corporate culture is expressed in various forms such as formal mission statements, unwritten rules, beliefs regarding corporate reference groups, patterns of success that have been passed down, and traditions.

Active complaint management in the form presented here is not compatible with every corporate value system, but instead demands a specific corporate culture. In public pronouncements, in internal statements, and in actual behavior, it must be unmistakably clear that customer orientation is at the core of the value system. It is only when the firm does not simply proclaim customer satisfaction as a goal, but rather strives consistently to achieve it, that a climate develops in which complaints are seen as customers' natural right and as an opportunity for the firm. In a corporate culture like this, however, complaint management itself then becomes a symbol of customer-oriented goals. Top management underscores the strategic importance of complaint management through organizational closeness, informational involvement, and the provision of the necessary resources.

In addition to consistent customer orientation, a specific way of dealing with failures (a type of "no-blame culture") (Johnston and Mehra 2002:149) is also necessary for complaint management. First, in the context of preventative quality management, this culture involves making every attempt to prevent failures in the first place. Second, one must be realistic about a zero-defects concept representing a goal that is not fully achievable in the service sector. It is necessary to correct these defects in the way that is best for the customer and to make certain that they do not reoccur in the future. Errors that do arise are viewed with regard to their informational value for possible improvements, and not primarily as indicators of employee weaknesses.

14

Organizational Aspects of Complaint Management

There are a number of organizational questions that must be clarified when an active complaint-management system is established. With respect to the company's organizational structure, decisions must be made about the assignment of responsibilities to particular organizational units (positions, departments). The primary question that must be answered is related to the degree of centralization or decentralization of complaint management. If a complaint-management department is established, the extent of conceptual-strategic control and operative tasks in the complaint center should be clarified. The firm must also decide how the complaint-management department will be integrated into the corporate structure and the extent to which tasks can be outsourced to external service providers.

14.1 CENTRALIZED, DECENTRALIZED, OR DUAL COMPLAINT MANAGEMENT

The alternative organizational structures are frequently limited to the extremes of centralized and decentralized complaint processing. In the case of purely centralized complaint management, a central complaint unit single-handedly administers all the tasks. Customers who complain to decentralized units (branch offices or subsidiaries) are consistently referred to the central complaint location, or complaints received at decentralized locations are immediately forwarded to the head office. Purely decentralized complaint management implies that complaint cases are independently processed by the decentralized sales units without the involvement of the head office. If complaints are received at the central level, they are forwarded to the proper organizational units, and the complainants are then referred to these units. This ideal type of dichotomy, however, unduly simplifies the complex decision problem, because for many firms it is either absolutely necessary or more efficient to establish a solution with centralized and decentralized elements—a dual complaint management system.

The decision regarding the design of the organizational structure of complaint management must be made in accordance with the specific corporate environment, which can vary widely from firm to firm. Consequently, for small businesses that market a limited product range directly to a small clientele, the problem is usually limited to determining the complaint-related responsibilities for customer-contact employees and for company management. Large companies that market a broad range of products through various distribution channels to a large number of geographical locations face the much more complex task of how to implement customer-oriented complaint management with the involvement of their distribution partners and/or through the establishment of a direct complaint channel. Therefore, there is no one organizational solution that is optimal for all firms. Rather, the particular situational factors, which place different demands on the complaint management process, should be identified.

Factors Influencing the Choice of Centralized, Decentralized, and Dual Complaint Management

A number of factors influence the choice of organizational form. Chief among these factors are the type of product, the number of customers, the type of distribution, and the centrality of customer contact.

TYPE OF PRODUCT. The product essentially determines the categories of possible problems and the necessary actions resulting from those problems, which raise organizational questions of their own. Services (such as those of a restaurant or a hotel) are rendered in direct contact with the customer. Based on the customers' involvement in the production of services, they have the opportunity to voice complaints directly to customer-contact personnel; and in many cases, employees have the chance to eliminate the problem immediately. Therefore, the possibility of a decentralized complaint solution must be envisioned for this problem. In the case of tangible goods that often have technical problems, it is necessary to establish rapid access to technical information, as well as to service and repair facilities.

NUMBER OF CUSTOMERS. If a firm has only relatively few customers who are significant to its bottom line, each individual complaint becomes very important. For this reason, the firm must make sure that the complaint is handled immediately. This handling should take place either centrally or decentrally, in the same way that the customer contacts are organized. Regardless of whether sales and service employees or members of company management are involved, the person addressed by the customer in each case is the "Complaint Owner" and must see to it that the problem is solved. In order to put this Complaint Owner in a position to solve the problem quickly, it is most important that competencies are conferred and that direct paths of communication with top management are established. When the number of customers is very large, the firm should establish its own department for complaints and customer communication, which can professionally manage the large numbers of complaints according to a uniform principle.

TYPE OF DISTRIBUTION. Different challenges must be met, depending on whether the firm is in direct contact with the customer or is distributing the products by means of other institutions (e.g., wholesale and retail distributors). In the case of direct distribution, the firm can design its complaint-management system autonomously. In terms of indirect forms of distribution, the problem that often arises is how to integrate the market partner in the firm's own complaint-management system in order to be able immediately to record and eliminate the customers' dissatisfaction with the product. This integration in vertical distribution systems is more difficult, the more independent the partners are legally and financially, and the greater their market power is.

CENTRALITY OF CUSTOMER CONTACT. Even in the case of firms that distribute their products directly, it frequently happens that customers have multiple decentralized contacts with the firm or with operational subsystems. For example, one may think about the hotels of an international chain, which are built in a multitude of different locations. Customers experience the quality decentrally in each hotel visited. It is thus extremely important for the management of the hotels to obtain information about the problems customers experience by way of their own complaint-management systems. Nonetheless, the customer's perception of quality is not related to the individual hotel alone, but rather influences his assessment of the entire brand and other hotels of the chain. For this reason, it is necessary for the management of the hotel chain to be informed about customers' problems with all system units, to establish a dual complaint-management system.

The Importance of These Factors for Selected Types of Firms

Depending on all the factors mentioned above, a multitude of situations is conceivable, each of which places specific demands on the organizational design of the complaint-management system. These situations cannot be presented here in full detail. Instead, we restrict the discussion to four typical cases:

- For Type A firms, the criteria named above have the following characteristics: tangible good, low number of customers, direct distribution, centralized customer contact. We will cite the example of a manufacturer of durable goods that sells drilling machines to a relatively small group of well-known industrial customers through a centralized distribution network (mechanical engineering firm).
- Type B firm has the following characteristics: tangible good, large number of customers, indirect distribution, and decentralized customer contact. A representative of this type of firm is an industrial consumer-goods manufacturer of packaged foods that distributes its products nationally through retailers to an anonymous mass market. The customers come into contact with the product in a multitude of different purchase locations that are distributed across a wide geographical area. The retailer only distributes the product; product-specific and customer-oriented services (such as consulting services) are not involved.
- Type C firms have the following characteristics: tangible good, large number of customers, distribution through retailers that perform additional services related to the particular tangible good, decentralized customer contact. As an example of this type of firm, one may think of a car manufacturer whose products are sold through dealer-

ships that are closely connected to the firm by contract. The dealers not only sell the automobiles, but also offer a number of product-relevant services, such as repairs, maintenance, leasing, and parts sales. Since the dealers also use the manufacturer's brand name, the customers' perceptions of the quality of the product and the service are not independent from each other; instead, there are carry-over effects, and service failures can also lead to customers' switching from the manufacturer.

- The characteristic features of Type D firms are as follows: service offering, large number of customers, direct distribution, and decentralized customer contact. Representative of this type of firm is a bank that has direct business relationships with a large number of known customers. Customer contact is primarily maintained through local branch offices.

The specific tasks of complaint management turn out to be different, depending on the type of firm, which gives rise to varying organizational consequences with respect to the question of centralization versus decentralization.

In Type A firms (mechanical engineering firms), all employees must be aware that the firm's survival can depend on the consistent support of each individual customer. Customer orientation in this case means individual customer care. It is necessary to maintain a permanent dialogue with customers in order to notice changes in the structure of their needs and expectations, as well as the degree of their satisfaction or dissatisfaction. Every dialogue partner in the organization—be it a sales associate, a customer service representative or a member of company management—thus has the task of encouraging customers to express their dissatisfaction and of accepting and forwarding complaints. As "Complaint Owners," they must provide a rapid solution, which requires wide latitude to act, clear competencies, and direct communication channels. The complaint processing and complaint analysis tasks can be assigned to the customer-contact departments (sales or service). It is frequently advisable, however, to have a central complaint-management department monitor the processing and analysis and take over essential controlling and reporting functions. In this way, the firm can make sure that those who are directly affected by complaint management become actively involved and that the management concept is internally enforced with the necessary emphasis.

Type B firms (manufacturers of packaged foods) do not have direct contact with customers, since the products are exclusively sold through retailers. When customers experience problems with a product, they do not have a strong incentive to complain. The items are usually sold at low prices, and it seems to be less effort for the customers to switch to a competitor when they make their next purchase than to take on the stress of an additional visit to their retailer just to make a complaint. Another factor is that discounters in particular, who sell at very low prices, do not dispose of sufficient quantitative or qualitative resources for product information and customer service. Thus, they are hardly in a position to take over complaint acceptance and processing functions, as manufacturers would like them to do. Manufacturers usually work out an agreement with retailers to replace defective items that are returned. Nevertheless, the number of these exchanged products is usually the only information that the firm can expect from the retailer regarding customers' problems with the product. More detailed descriptions of the negative customer experience rarely become the subject of complaints with the retailer and are not usually forwarded to the manufacturer (Halstead 1993). Even specific efforts on the part of the manufacturer to implement systematic complaint acceptance at the retail level (e.g., by providing complaint forms) do not seem to be worthwhile, given the differing interests of the parties involved, the human resources policy in discount businesses, and the market power of the retail chains.

Consequently, the manufacturer must centralize all complaint-management tasks in-house, especially complaint stimulation. Information requesting that customers seek direct contact with the manufacturer in case of a problem should be printed on the product packaging, and an easily accessible channel for that contact must also be communicated. In this way, all customer-initiated communication comes together at one organizational unit in the firm. It is also advisable to assign tasks of complaint processing and reaction, complaint analysis, controlling, and reporting to this unit.

For Type C firms (car manufacturers), the situation is similar to that presented in the preceding case, because a tangible good is sold decentrally to a large number of customers through retailers. There is, however, one essential difference. The car dealers influence the quality perception of the customer because they themselves render their own automobile-related service. The car manufacturers are faced with the task of directing the members of their distribution network in such a way that the dealers ensure manufacturer- and retail-oriented customer satisfaction and loyalty.

The complaints that arise at car dealerships may cover different product- or service-related customer problems. For the dealers, the relevant questions are whether they themselves caused the problem or whether the manufacturers did, and who is responsible for the costs. The dealers' contracts obligate the retail businesses to accept complaints about car problems caused by the manufacturer, to process them on the basis of defined guarantee and goodwill guidelines, and to bring customer complaints to the attention of the car manufacturer. This approach guarantees that the manufacturer at least receives information about customer problems that the retailer views as relevant and originated by the manufacturer. These problems encompass only a fraction of the automobile-related customer problems:

- Product-related problems that the retailer assesses as being irrelevant or that do not fall under the guarantee and goodwill conditions are either not forwarded to the manufacturer or are forwarded incompletely so that the manufacturer only receives an extremely imperfect view of the product-related problems experienced by customers.

- Complainants predominantly express their complaints to the dealer in person. Since the majority of these complaints are not recorded as complaints, but instead are processed in the context of routine procedures, not even the dealership itself has a systematic overview of the articulated customer complaints.

- The manufacturer finds out about dealer-related customer problems if the customer informs them about these problems. This only happens when the dealer, despite repeated efforts on the customer's part, fails to solve a serious incident satisfactorily. For this reason, the manufacturer faces the problem that shortcomings in the dealer's complaint-management system can lead to customer switching without the manufacturer itself receiving any information about the causes of this switching.

For the manufacturer, a series of difficult tasks arise from this situation:

- With respect to product-related complaints, the dealer must be fully integrated in the complaint-management system. A uniform system of complaint stimulation, acceptance, processing, and reaction is needed.

- Part of this system is that complaints brought forward in person are also documented as thoroughly as possibly and forwarded from the dealer to the manufacturer.

- With regard to dealer-related complaints, the dealership should be able to practice complaint management according to the manufacturer's conceptual understanding. This also includes training the customer-contact personnel appropriately. All dealer-related complaints must be processed, categorized, and analyzed according to a system approved by the manufacturer.

- The necessity of acknowledging great importance to complaint stimulation arises from the manufacturer's insufficient overview of customers' problems. A significant increase in product-related articulations is to be expected only if customers are provided an easily accessible (e.g., telephone) channel to the manufacturer. If, however, customers are requested to direct their complaints to a centralized customer care department of the manufacturer, an increased number of dealer-related articulations will also be received there. For the manufacturer, this has the advantage that the information level related to dealer-oriented customer problems will increase, and they can become active toward both the dissatisfied customer and dealerships that are reacting incorrectly. Nevertheless, this approach will encounter reservations and resistance from the dealers if they suspect that another instrument of control is being established.

Therefore, a certain amount of fine-tuning with respect to the execution of tasks is required between the manufacturer and the dealership, in terms of vertical cooperation. The focus of this version of complaint

management, which is at the same time dual and vertical, is the determination about
- which complaint stimulation measures are to be implemented
- which type of complaint should be forwarded to which department
- which complaints should be resolved on-site
- which alternative solutions are practical and acceptable
- how the information regarding complaints decided on-site should be collected and forwarded
- how the dealerships should receive feedback from analysis and controlling of comparative information and information relevant to their operations
- how the system of incentives for the execution of tasks should be designed.

The situation for Type D firms (banks) is similar to that previously discussed, in that the question of controlling decentralized systems is also an issue. There is, however, some difference because here the good in question is a service and the firm is set up as a branch operation, which makes it easier to take control of the decentralized units.

Banking services are performed primarily decentrally in a multitude of branch offices that are scattered across a wide geographical area and in direct contact with known customers. Many bank customers have contact only with the employees at "their" branch bank and turn to these employees when they have a problem. A number of the problems experienced by customers are also caused on-site. The result is that many customers encounter barriers to complaint articulation, while bank employees encounter obstacles to complaint stimulation and forwarding. If customers complain at the branch office, employees are frequently confronted with errors that they caused themselves, which brings about the danger of suppressing the facts of the complaint case.

In this situation, a dual (both centralized and decentralized) complaint-management system is required. In order to eliminate customer dissatisfaction immediately, the employees in the decentralized branch offices must be trained to deal with dissatisfied customers, equipped with competencies, and directed to accept complaint information. In order to combat the tendency of contact personnel to suppress, distort, or select complaints expressed by customers in person, branch managers must also be present on a regular basis during the service process and question the customers regarding their satisfaction. In addition, a central customer care department must be established, which allows each customer to articulate dissatisfaction centrally. In a dual system like this one, both centralized and decentralized tasks of complaint stimulation, acceptance, processing, and reaction come up. Moreover, analysis, reporting and complaint-management controlling functions must, to differing extents, be carried out.

Spotlight 9 provides an insight into the dual complaint-management system of McDonald's Germany, in which the national central customer service department supports the complaint management of the franchisees through internal services.

SPOTLIGHT 9

Complaint Management as a Service for Franchisees of McDonald's Germany

About 65 percent of the more than 1,200 McDonald's Restaurants in Germany are operated by franchisees. Their legal status as independent corporations requires that they are responsible for complaints: The affected franchise partners thus process complaints directly.

As a result of this decentralized organization, McDonald's can on the one hand ensure the intended closeness to its customers—but must on the other hand make sure that universal quality standards and the uniform appearance of the McDonald's brand are guaranteed, even in the case of a complaint, through appropriate measures.

Therefore, the central customer service department in Munich offers its franchisees—supported by regional franchise consultants—a comprehensive package of services and consultation for customer-oriented complaint processing:

- Each franchisee obtains a "Complaint Management" CD-ROM as a handbook from the head office. This CD-ROM provides checklists and form letters for dealing with critical situations.

- The offer of information is supplemented by workshop offerings for franchisees and their colleagues: They practice dealing with complaints; crisis situations are simulated.

- The legal department of the head office offers expert support for all problems for which complainants engage the services of a lawyer.

- Upon request, the service specialists of the head office support the franchisees in formulating reply letters or conduct conversations with customers on-site, in order to bring about a solution to the problem.

A substantial role in coordination and processing is accorded the regional franchise consultants. A list of outstanding complaints articulated to the head office is generated weekly by the complaint-management system, which goes to the employees in the five regions.

The franchise consultants then have the job of "aftercare": They talk with the affected franchisee and clarify whether there is a need for support in the outstanding complaint cases.

An example case: A guest calls the head office in Munich and complains of stomach problems after visiting one of the restaurants; he suspects food poisoning. The customer-service employee records the facts with the help of software and then refers the customer to the affected franchisee. At the same time, the regional franchise consultant is informed.

Using the guidelines for wording in the case of claims, the franchisee composes a letter to the customer: This letter explains to the guest, for instance, the strict requirements and quality measures to which McDonald's has committed itself in order to protect the health of its guests. At the same time, the franchisee informs the complainant that no other customers have complained—a clear sign that this is not a case of food poisoning that was caused by the consumption of a McDonald's product.

If the guest threatens to take legal measures, the franchisee can call on the head office legal department, from which he receives the necessary legal information, as well as a draft letter that has been verified by legal experts.

A copy of the correspondence goes to the head office so that the employees there are informed about follow-up contacts.

In order to continuously maintain the quality standards in dealing with complaints in the area of franchisees, the following measures are taken by McDonald's:

- Franchisees and franchise consultants obtain analyses of complaint causes, frequency of the causes, etc., in the form of quarterly reports, semiannual reports, and comprehensive yearly reports.

- Based on the reports, the franchise consultant analyzes trends and offers his franchise partners targeted support if it is required, for example, in the area of employee training, if complaints about unfriendly, unmotivated personnel accumulate for a certain location.

- In addition, the consultants in the field ensure through aftercare that the procedures are processed and closed within a recommended time period.

- The annual survey of franchisees helps determine on a regular basis the areas in which the entrepreneurs desire further service support from the head office.

As far as the guest is concerned, the decentralized processing of complaints by franchisees—supported and controlled by the head office—offers a dual advantage:

Whereas the franchise can investigate and solve the complaint cause in an effective and customer-friendly manner on-site, the head office contributes the complaint management know-how of its service specialists. At the same time, the head office ensures that the McDonald's Corporation faces its guests consistently and in accordance with the firm's basic principles, even in the case of a complaint.

Uta Reimer
Manager Customer Service
McDonald's Germany

14.2 THE COMPLAINT-MANAGEMENT DEPARTMENT

If firms make the decision to integrate the centrally performed tasks in a specific organizational unit, it should be designated as the complaint-management department. Often, however, it is not advisable in practice to limit the responsibility very narrowly to the issue of complaint-articulation. The integration of the different customer-initiated forms of communication in one unit and the necessary coordination between the different measures in dealing with customer concerns makes it seem practical to expand the scope of responsibility to all types of customer-initiated communication: that is, to notices of amendment, praise, requests, and ideas or suggestions for improvement. If the organizational unit acquires such comprehensive competency for all the relationship-oriented customer articulations, it would seem appropriate to label it as a customer care department. For the following section, we will assume that firms have opted to establish a customer care department. Since the discussion here—as elsewhere in this book—is restricted to presentations of complaint-management tasks, we subsequently will only speak of the complaint-management department.

In order to implement the tasks of complaint management efficiently, this department should be divided into the operative component of contact handling (complaint center) and the conceptual-controlling component (direction of complaint management).

14.2.1 RESPONSIBILITY FOR THE OPERATIVE PROCESSING OF COMPLAINTS BY THE COMPLAINT CENTER

The direct corporate interface with customers, in which the essential operative tasks of the direct complaint-management process are accomplished—especially complaint acceptance, processing, and reaction—is the complaint center.

Complaint Center, Customer Care Center, Customer Interaction Center

In practice, different terms can be found for this operational organizational unit, such as "Customer Service Department" or "Customer Interaction Center." In terms of the differentiation made in Chapter 1.3, it is advisable to designate this unit in different ways, depending on how broadly the fields of action and responsibility are set for this unit that accepts and processes customer concerns:

- If the range of activity consists primarily of accomplishing tasks of complaint management, then the term "Complaint Center" (CC) should be used. A Complaint Center focuses predominantly on complaint-related inbound activities and carries out outbound activities only to the extent that they serve the goals of complaint management (e.g., follow-up surveys of complainants).
- If the unit is placed in charge of handling all the relationship-oriented forms of communication (notices of amendment, praise, complaints, requests), the designation "Customer Care Center" (CCC) is appropriate. The emphasis of the tasks here is also clearly on

inbound activities; however, the scope of activities—even in terms of potential outbound contacts—extends to customer concerns of all kinds.

- If all customer-initiated inbound activities are included, regardless of whether they are purchase- or relationship-relevant, and if marketing- and sales-oriented outbound activities are also integrated, it is appropriate to speak of a "Customer Interaction Center" (CIC) in the comprehensive sense.

The use of the term "Center" makes it clear that a centralization of customer communication occurs in each case. A call center, where the customer contact that takes place over the phone is centralized, is usually the heart of this centralization. Complaint centers, customer care centers, and customer interaction centers comprise call centers, but complement the concept by consistently bundling all communication channels. Regardless of whether the customer contacts the firm by letter, fax, e-mail, or telephone, the customer articulations in each case arrive at a single organizational unit. For the customers, this has the advantage that they have to contact only a single department with all of their concerns. Consequently, the firm has the chance to have the current status of all customer data at its disposal at all times and thus to increase the quality of addressing those concerns. Furthermore, significant cost advantages can be realized, due to the synergy effects and the high degree of professionalism achieved.

Operational Units of a Complaint Center

The organization of complaint centers is basically oriented to that of call centers. Simply put, all calls are taken by employees of the "Front Office" (1st level). If customers' calls cannot be closed during the initial telephone contact, they are turned over to employees at the 2nd level for further processing by experts. In addition to the customer contact units, which deal exclusively with the processing of customer concerns by telephone, the "back office" takes responsibility for customer concerns articulated in writing. This office also takes over extensive investigational activities and takes care of processing complex customer concerns. For this purpose, it is necessary to integrate the expertise of specialist departments or individual sales units (3rd level) in addressing and resolving customer concerns.

In the following section, we will expand on this perspective, which is based on traditional concepts of call centers, and briefly characterize the individual operational units of a complaint center.

- **INBOUND CALLS (1ST LEVEL).** This team is responsible for the direct acceptance of customer complaints articulated by telephone.
- **2ND LEVEL (FOR INBOUND CALLS).** Complaints articulated by telephone that exceed the expertise and/or decision-making authority of the "inbound calls" (1st level) team can be forwarded on a "stand-by" basis during direct contact with the customer to a group of employees at the 2nd level (for inbound calls) who are equipped with adequate competencies and skills. The necessity of installing such a team primarily results from the complexity of the contents of the complaint

and the urgency of resolving the problem. This approach also guarantees the continuous accessibility of the 1st level, since its employee resources are not tied up with time-consuming investigational activities. If it is not necessary to establish a 2nd level (for inbound calls), a callback is arranged with the customer if complaints are not resolved during the initial contact at the 1st level, and the concern is turned over to the back office, where appropriate investigations are carried out and contact is again made with the customer.

- **INBOUND MAIL (1ST LEVEL).** This function is unprovided for in conventional concepts of call centers. Traditionally, it is located in the back office. The establishment of an inbound-mail team (1st Level) becomes relevant, however, when the volume of written complaints is high, but a large percentage of these customer concerns do not require specific expert knowledge, and when these processes can be standardized. Keeping in mind that expensive know-how regarding complex problem solutions is available in the back office, it is advisable from a financial standpoint to establish a 1st level for complaints that can be easily processed when the complaint volume is high.

  The direct acceptance and processing of all written complaints is the focus of this team. Taking into account the complaint volume, it may be advisable to set aside special groups to answer complaints expressed in e-mails and faxes, since complainants expect faster reaction times in these cases than they do when they articulate their complaints in letters (or on comment cards).

- **BACK OFFICE.** This team is traditionally responsible for processing customer correspondence. If, however, an "Inbound Mail (1st Level)" unit exists, the back office is primarily responsible for customer complaints that cannot be processed at this level. The same applies to telephone complaints forwarded from "Inbound Calls" (1st level) or "2nd level (for Inbound Calls). Employees who are especially skilled should be available in the "back office."

  Depending on how heterogeneous the expertise required in the back office is, it may be wise to compose this unit of several teams with differing emphases in terms of know-how. If the utilization of the telephone capacity is low, it is conceivable that the back office also executes the 2nd level (for Inbound Calls). In this case, however, the firm must take into account that the employees should be systematically trained with respect to the different demands. This is also necessary if employees carry out not only customer-contact tasks but also indirect complaint-management tasks as a consequence of a "job rotation" concept in order to reduce the employee's burden of permanent critical customer contacts and to increase the task variety.

- **3RD LEVEL (SPECIALIST DEPARTMENTS).** If the back office cannot solve the problem, it is necessary to involve specialist departments within the firm that possess detailed expertise (3rd level) in examining and resolving cases. Here the firm must be careful not to burden these departments with too many customer complaints, since the efficiency gains that would normally be achieved by establishing a customer care center are lost. In order to avoid this possible danger, it is recommended that the firm constantly monitor the quantitative volume of forwarded complaints and the employed resources of the specialist departments. If these departments reach the limits of their capacity, adequate capacity should be built up in the back office at the customer care center level.

- **OUTBOUND CONTACTS—ACTIVE COMPLAINT CONTACTS.** This unit, which is not taken into account in traditional concepts of call centers, takes responsibility for carrying out active complaint contacts. Actions and measures that serve the accomplishment of complaint management and are initiated by the firm take place here. Among these actions and measures are the processing of follow-up complaints (Chapter 8.4.1.4) and the conducting of complaint satisfaction surveys in the context of performance measurement (Chapter 10.2.1.1).

In the lower part of Figure 14.1, a typical organizational structure for the operational units of a complaint center is presented with its interfaces to the specialist departments and sales units of the firm.

The Management of the Complaint Center and Its Tasks

In order to guarantee and maintain operational complaint handling, the management of the complaint center has to perform a series of executive and managerial functions, specifically on a strategic and operational level, as well as on the personnel management level. Referring specifically to complaint management, the following tasks are of primary importance:

- **DIRECT COMPLAINT-MANAGEMENT PROCESS.** The main responsibility is to implement the targets for complaint stimulation, acceptance, processing, and reaction and to ensure the quality of task performance. The quality and productivity standards that have been defined must be communicated to the employees and must be measured. The Complaint Management Index described in Chapter 10.2.4 offers a suitable starting point.

  In order to secure the competence of the operational complaint centers for the smooth handling of customer contacts, it is advisable to establish an "Information Management" unit. The central task of this team is to request and to process current information from other departments or branch offices (e.g., about new prices, products, services, or corporate activities) and to make sure that the operational units of the complaint center have access to this information. In this way, the processing and problem-solving expertise of the complaint center can be increased, and the activation of the 3rd level can be avoided.

- **INDIRECT COMPLAINT-MANAGEMENT PROCESS.** In coordination with the direction of complaint management, which will be presented in the following section, some of the tasks of indirect complaint management can be assigned to the complaint center. These tasks may include subareas such as complaint analysis, complaint reporting, and complaint-management controlling. It is obvious, then, that significant key figures from evidence and task controlling, especially quality and productivity figures, must be collected directly in the Complaint

Center. This applies especially to all the complaint department-related indicators such as length of conversations, lost calls, or the observance of defined service levels.

- **PERSONNEL MANAGEMENT.** The employees who accept complaints are the most valuable resource in every Complaint Center. That is why one of the essential tasks for the management of this unit is to implement important human resources-related aspects of complaint management. Among these aspects is recruiting the right employees with the needed social, emotional, methodological, and professional competencies and making sure that all employees continue to enhance their skills on the basis of profound training concepts. Another core task pertains to the planning, the calculation, and the deployment of personnel that is needed to process the incoming customer concerns efficiently and to observe the agreed-upon service level (workforce management).

- **INFORMATION TECHNOLOGY.** Apart from personnel resources, information technology represents the second key factor for complaint centers. Mastery of the technological aspects of complaint management is thus one of the requirements for the management of complaint centers. Executives must be able to guarantee the reliable performance of complex telephone systems, software systems, and demanding hardware environments with adequate maintenance and support services. This also includes providing continuous information and training to the customer-contact personnel with respect to user-related system-technical questions as well as implementing software-technical requirements in order to optimize operational complaint processing.

If complaint centers are operated by the firm itself, a coordination of task performance is required between the departmental leadership unit in complaint management and the management of the complaint center, as well as between the departmental leadership unit in complaint management and other functional business areas such as information technology management and human resources. For reasons of efficiency, it proves advantageous to assign clearly defined personnel-related and information technology tasks to the appropriate internal departments by contract.

14.2.2 RESPONSIBILITY FOR CONCEPTUAL CONTROL BY THE DIRECTION OF COMPLAINT MANAGEMENT

The departmental leadership in complaint management is the conceptual steering part of the complaint-management department. Therefore, the relationship between the departmental leadership in complaint management and the complaint center is established in such a way that the departmental leadership in complaint management carries the expert responsibility for the entire complaint-management process and its strategic anchoring in customer-relationship management. The complaint center acts as a operational unit in accordance with the guidelines of the departmental leadership in complaint management. This applies in cases in which operational complaint handling is carried out in the firm itself or is outsourced to an external customer care center.

The conceptual-control tasks to be performed by the departmental leadership in complaint management will be briefly described below. This description follows the same structure as the presentation of the tasks of the complaint-center management, which illustrates the division of tasks between these units:

- **DIRECT COMPLAINT-MANAGEMENT PROCESS.** A key departmental leadership function is to develop and to optimize the task performance in the direct complaint-management process on a continual basis. This includes the planning of complaint-stimulation campaigns, the development of guidelines and process descriptions for all aspects of complaint acceptance, including the constant monitoring of the accessibility of complaint channels.

    The detailed and cross-functional development of the work flow for the processing of customer concerns, including the definition of the responsible departments and persons, the temporal standards for the reaction, and the contents of communication (e.g., for confirmations of receipt or intermediate replies) also take place here. In addition, the employee behavior guidelines regarding complaint reaction must be defined.

    All the guidelines and process descriptions for the handling of customer complaints together form the basis for the operational processing in the complaint center. They must be developed, discussed critically, and implemented in coordination with the responsible units there.

- **INDIRECT COMPLAINT-MANAGEMENT PROCESS.** A crucial task of the departmental leadership in complaint management is their responsibility for the indirect complaint-management process, that is, for complaint analysis, complaint-management controlling, complaint reporting, and utilization of complaint information. The relevant analytical concepts must be developed, and the various reports have to be designed, generated, and communicated to other internal customers. The task performance for the components of the direct complaint-management process should be monitored, and evidence and task controlling for the entire complaint-management system installed. In addition, decisions are to be made regarding the choice of relevant key figures of the subjective and objective task controlling and the composition of the Complaint Management Index. Likewise, the design and implementation of the cost-benefit controlling of complaint management—in coordination with the firm's controlling department—falls within this department's area of responsibility.

- **PERSONNEL MANAGEMENT.** The departmental leadership in complaint management is responsible for continually providing, sensitizing, motivating and developing the employees in the complaint-management department. Here, in cooperation with the corporate human resources department, concepts in personnel recruiting, instruction and training, the design of incentive systems, and measures for the prevention of burnout are to be developed, implemented, and evaluated. The departmental leadership has to formulate and support initiatives that aim at the empowerment of all company employees to behave in a more customer-oriented manner.

- **INFORMATION TECHNOLOGY (IT).** This task area falls within the scope of responsibility of the departmental leadership in complaint management in that the technical requirements for the implementation of the software and databases must be defined. The departmental leadership thus represents an important interface to IT experts within the firm itself and, especially when an external service provider is engaged, to IT experts in the complaint center.

The departmental leadership's central instrument for the direction and monitoring of the operational processes is the Complaint Management Index with its quality and productivity standards, which was presented in Chapter 10.2.3. The departmental leadership in complaint management has to decide on the relevant assessment dimensions and attributes, weight them, and define a standard for each attribute. The observance of these standards—and, where appropriate, a defined value from the Complaint Management Index—then becomes, in addition to the financial aspects, the subject of the agreement with the complaint center. The management of the complaint center bears responsibility for compliance with these standards. Pertinent agreements should not only be made in the case of outsourcing, but also when the complaint center is assigned internally to the complaint-management department.

Figure 14.1 shows the organization of the complaint-management department and the participation of various units in task performance.

14.3 INTEGRATION OF THE COMPLAINT-MANAGEMENT DEPARTMENT IN THE ORGANIZATIONAL STRUCTURE OF THE CORPORATION

On a company-wide level, the way has to be assessed in which the complaint-management process is linked with other corporate processes and which consequences for the institutional anchoring of the department in the overall corporate organization result from these connections.

14.3.1 RESPONSIBILITY AND LINKAGE OF THE COMPLAINT-MANAGEMENT PROCESSES WITH OTHER CORPORATE PROCESSES

The complaint-management department cannot fulfill its function as a dialogue interface to the customer if its responsibility is limited to narrowly defined tasks. The targeted reduction of communication barriers is only achievable when the department is designed to accept all customer problems and when customers perceive that this is the case. Likewise, the elimination of individual customer dissatisfaction can be fully accomplished only when the complaint-management department has the opportunity to receive and analyze all customer demands and problems and to insist on their solution.

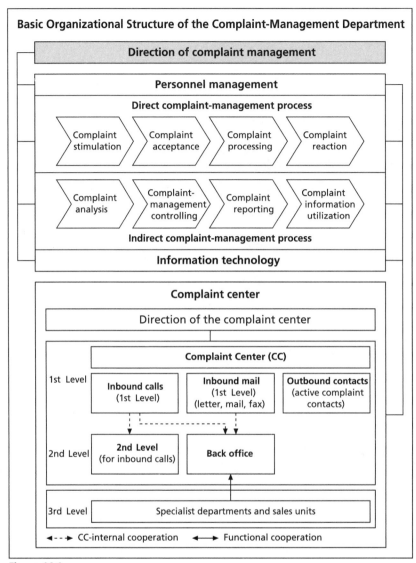

Basic Organizational Structure of the Complaint-Management Department

Direction of complaint management

Personnel management

Direct complaint-management process

Complaint stimulation / Complaint acceptance / Complaint processing / Complaint reaction

Complaint analysis / Complaint-management controlling / Complaint reporting / Complaint information utilization

Indirect complaint-management process

Information technology

Complaint center

Direction of the complaint center

Complaint Center (CC)

1st Level — Inbound calls (1st Level) | Inbound mail (1st Level) (letter, mail, fax) | Outbound contacts (active complaint contacts)

2nd Level — 2nd Level (for inbound calls) | Back office

3rd Level — Specialist departments and sales units

◄- - ► CC-internal cooperation   ◄——► Functional cooperation

Figure 14.1

Even when taking into account the internal function of making an important contribution to the customer-oriented direction of the firm, a limitation of the responsibility should be avoided. A sensitization of the firm through information, instruction, and innovative impulses requires that the work of the complaint-management department, in terms of content, be basically oriented toward the concerns articulated by customers. It is necessary to resolve these concerns because they determine the spectrum of activities for the complaint-management department.

If we accept this assessment of comprehensive customer-related responsibility, then the resulting consequences for cooperation with a multitude of other internal fields of activity and the integration of subprocesses with other corporate processes must be taken into consideration. Here we would like to point out several examples:

- Complaint stimulation measures are to be planned and implemented in cooperation with marketing, sales, and service.
- Complaint processing and reaction demands an especially close relationship with the departments that are frequently the subject of customer concerns or that often implement problem solutions, such as billing or technical service.
- A complaint reaction that is specific to a customer segment or that is individualized requires that a classification of customers according to segment affiliation and customer value be carried out on an ongoing basis through CRM or database marketing.
- Complaint analysis and reporting can take place only in a goal-oriented way when the relevant internal customers (e.g., research and development, production, quality management, marketing, sales, service) are identified, and the analyses and reports are geared toward their needs.
- The utilization of complaint information must be planned in close cooperation with quality management.
- Complaint-management controlling is to be aligned with the firm's overall system of controlling.
- Provided that the complaint-management system determines failure costs and assigns them to the departments that caused them, integration in the controlling system and intensive cooperation with the units in question is also necessary.
- Supporting and developing the infrastructure of the information technology system necessitates constant cooperation with the IT department.

Detailed process definitions and documentation, which also highlight the interfaces with other departments and the respective customer-supplier relationships, must be available for all the task modules of the complaint-management process. Service levels for the quality of internal services and institutionalized forms of participation in decision-making processes must be agreed upon. In addition, consideration must be given to the equipment of the complaint-management department with rights to influence that are necessary in order to fulfill its functions in an optimal fashion, and how this department should be integrated organizationally in the corporate hierarchy.

These rights may differ regarding the strength of influence. The right to inform affords the opportunity to forward information that has been accumulated to decision-makers. The right to consult goes beyond the right to information and allows the processing of information for initiatives and alternative suggestions. The right to monitor bestows the power to review the decisions of others with reference to their compliance with agreed-upon principles. This right experiences an increase in the right to veto, which can help prevent the implementation of others' decisions, until a higher authority solves the conflict. The right to participate in decision-making gives the opportunity to participate in intermediate and final decisions. The most far-reaching right, a right to make independent decisions, exists when a department can come to fully autonomous decisions.

The equipping of a complaint-management department with rights to influence must take place on a task-specific basis. In order to perform the tasks of the direct complaint-management process, "strong" rights such as the right to participate in decision-making and the right to make independent decisions are necessary so that the customer-related activities can be carried out in an independent and efficient manner. Task performance in the indirect complaint-management process calls for cooperation with other internal departments. For this, at least the right to inform and the right to consult are necessary. However, achieving some goals also requires the right to monitor and the right to veto, and consequently involves some interference with the autonomy of other departments, which may lead to conflicts.

In order to prevent a future occurrence of problems that have been identified, for example, complaint management should be awarded a right to monitor with respect to the consideration of its information regarding product deficits by specialist departments. Should it turn out that the responsible departments are ignoring specific indications because they are avoiding the costs of the corrective measures, the right to monitor should be linked with consequential actions. It is thus obvious that the reaction costs and the complaint handling costs for such problems should be charged to the departments that caused them.

The influence is greater when the complaint-management department is awarded veto rights. This would be wise if specialist departments are preventing complaint management from being able to achieve its goals. Such is the case when customers terminate business relationships due to the repeated occurrence of problems and in spite of a satisfactory complaint process. In cases like these, not only should the specialist departments in question be charged with the costs for dealing with the repeat complainants, but the complaint-management department should also be given veto rights in terms of the further marketing of the defective products. With the granting of a veto right such as this one, the company management makes it clear that product decisions are also made with consideration for the goals of customer retention and that complaint management is given an important role in implementing a consistent strategy of customer-relationship management.

14.3.2 THE ESTABLISHMENT OF THE COMPLAINT-MANAGEMENT DEPARTMENT AS A STAFF POSITION OR A LINE POSITION

For the hierarchical arrangement and the equipping with influence rights, there are primarily two basic alternatives available, each of which can be found in various forms: staff position or line position.

The Establishment of the Complaint-Management Department as a Staff Position

In many firms, the complaint-management department is established as a staff position that is directly subordinate to top management (see

Figure 14.2). The primary advantages of this solution are the department's functional independence and its closeness to top management. The functional independence makes it easier for the department to establish the necessary relationships with various functional areas and to carry out innovative suggestions and subsequent controls with the required autonomy and self-confidence. Its direct subordination and closeness to top management documents the high value that is attached to the complaint-management department; and since the attitude of top management is perceived by organizational units, the documented positive assessment strengthens the informal authority of the department and increases its chances for effectiveness. Moreover, this organizational classification guarantees short paths of communication for the transfer of strategic information.

The disadvantage of the staff solution, however, is that staffs have no rights of instruction and no decision-making rights over the line and cannot force other corporate units to make use of the customer-related expertise that is available. Further, if complaint management is understood in the sense presented here—as having a comprehensive field of activity—and especially if a complaint center is attached, the design as a staff no longer proves to be suitable. In this case, the work that is typical for a staff (to provide consultation to top management in its decision-making) is no longer the dominant work performed; instead, there are differentiated managerial functions to be performed, which also imply at least interdepartmental decision-making rights. Therefore, the alternative of institutionalizing complaint management as a line position should be considered.

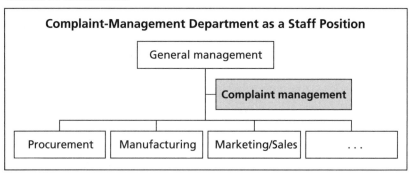

Figure 14.2

The Establishment of the Complaint-Management Department as a Line Position

If the complaint-management department is conceived as a line position, the question arises concerning assignment within the organization's hierarchy. In Chapter 1, complaint management was characterized conceptually as a key component of customer care management and as the core of customer retention and customer relationship management. It stands to reason that the organizational classification follows along the lines of this conceptual consideration. In a functional organizational structure, it would be required that below the top management level, a customer relationship unit be established in addition to the key traditional organizational units such as purchasing, production, or finance. Within this unit, the complaint-management department could be institutionalized as a line position on the same level as marketing, sales, and service (see Figure 14.3).

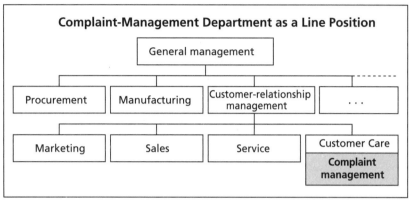

Figure 14.3

The advantages of an organizational solution such as this one are that the responsibility for achieving the defined goals can clearly be assigned to the complaint-management department and that the strategic anchoring in customer-relationship management is institutionally secured. In this way, the customer-oriented integration of customer data from marketing, sales, service, and customer care/complaint management can be achieved. Moreover, the maxim of "one face to the customer" can be realized if all customer-initiated communication is bundled in the customer care center/complaint center. A possible disadvantage of the line version is the loss of direct access to top management. It may be that the marketing and sales departments in particular gain a dominant influence in customer-relationship management due to their importance for turnover and impede a complete fulfillment of the functions of the complaint-management department. To reduce this danger, the complaint-management department must be equipped with adequate power.

The Complaint-Management Department in a Customer-Oriented Matrix Organization

For firms that make not only a functional differentiation, but also consistently implement the perspective of customer relationship management, the primary organizational structuring is made according to customer groups. Accordingly, varying organizational responsibilities are determined for different customer groups (e.g., corporate customers/private customers or private customers with varying need profiles or values). The managers then have to coordinate all the transaction-oriented activities in the marketing, sales, and service functions for these customer groups. Additionally, the responsibilities for relationship-relevant customer groups (e.g., acquisition, retention, and regain management) must be defined. For this reason, the customer-relationship manager's task of coordination extends to these measures, the result of which is a type of matrix organization in which the complaint-management department is responsible for all the complaints from all the customer groups (see Figure 14.4).

The advantage of this version is that the primary starting point is not the goals of particular functions (e.g., marketing/sales) or phases of the customer relationship life cycle (e.g., potential/current customers), but the customer or customer segment, and that the focus is on the task of coordinating differentiated instruments in a customer-oriented way.

Generally speaking, this form of matrix organization has the advantages that the customer-relationship managers achieve a high level of information through the multiple communication relationships and that innovative further developments can be expected as a result of the wide latitude for initiatives. However, every matrix organization deliberately contains overlapping competencies for the stimulation of productive conflicts. The general disadvantage is that this organizational form calls for a high degree of willingness to cooperate on the part of all

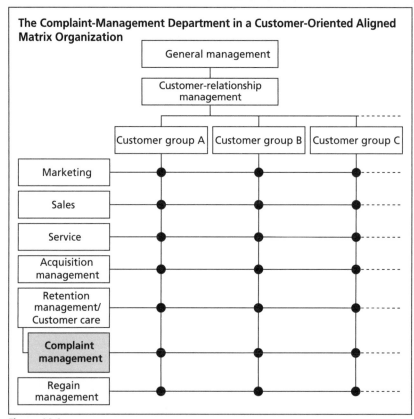

Figure 14.4

participants, which does not always exist, so that it can also come to unproductive conflicts with negative consequences for the company's performance.

For complaint management, the advantage lies in the extensive independence of this department from other functional departments. In this way, the internal significance is hardly determined by the marketing and sales functions, but by the interests of the customer-relationship managers in maintaining jeopardized business relationships. A real gain in power can arise from this situation. A disadvantage results because the type of cooperation with other departments can scarcely be defined unequivocally, since the type and extent of task achievement depend to a significant degree upon the requirements of the different customer-relationship managers, as well as upon their ability to be persuasive.

14.3.3 THE COMPLAINT-MANAGEMENT DEPARTMENT AS A PROFIT CENTER?

The potential power of the complaint-management department can be significantly increased internally if this department can successfully be designed as a profit center. The director of complaint management would then be responsible for the achievement of defined profit goals. In this way, the complaint-management department could express the relevance of its work to the firm in the most effective internal language— namely, in its profit contribution.

Whether the profit-center concept can be applied to the complaint-management department at all is certainly a controversial question. Often, this question is answered in the negative, primarily with a notice that the success of complaint management is expressed essentially by nonfinancial target figures (customer satisfaction, loyalty), opportunity categories (sales losses prevented), and benefit figures that are difficult to quantify (attitude benefits, information benefits). In the case of the complaint-management department, we are dealing with an internal service provider whose information services are not often actively demanded and even less often internally calculated. For this reason, specific revenues or profits are rarely available.

As well founded as this argument is, it nevertheless also provides starting points that would lead to a different conclusion. According to this way of thinking, a profit-center solution seems to be realistic if the complaint-management system is successful in verifying its real profit contribution, supplying relevant internal services and allocating these services internally. There is every reason to believe that a professionally managed complaint-management department is increasingly able to accomplish the above tasks.

The complaint-management department is the central contact point within the firm for dissatisfied customers. If this department is successful in preventing dissatisfied customers from switching, it secures for the firm the scarce resource of customer loyalty and the sales revenue and profits that are associated with it. The comments made regarding complaint-related cost-benefit controlling (Chapter 10.3) showed that the economic repurchase benefit of customer complaints, which arises from the successful retention of dissatisfied customers, can be verified and thus provides a solid foundation for a real profit and loss statement for complaint management. By a targeted monitoring of the causes of potential customer losses, the turnover and profit contributions can clearly be determined that complaint management actually secures for the firm. By periodically calculating these figures, the firm obtains the actual monetary profit contribution of complaint management. The challenge here is to create the data infrastructure for the detailed reporting of customer-specific lost revenues and profits, to survey lost customers on a regular basis with respect to their motives for switching, and to weight the customers lost due to dissatisfaction with their (lost) revenues and profits. Furthermore, the switching behavior of customers must be analyzed in detail. For example, the question has to be answered of whether declining rates of customer losses due to dissatisfaction can be traced exclusively to the activities of complaint management or were brought about by activities initiated by other departments, for instance, by the sales force.

The complaint-management department essentially plays the role of an internal service provider. It takes over all the tasks of direct and indirect complaint management for the firm as a whole. Successful performance of the tasks of direct complaint management—such as accepting complaints, recording the complaint information, and communicating with complainants—allows the firm to take advantage of the chance to preserve a jeopardized business relationship. It would make sense from a logical perspective, therefore, to allocate the costs arising from such activities (at market prices) to the respective departments that caused them. Nevertheless, the advantage expected to accompany this novel approach, that is, creating a strong incentive for the responsible departments to eliminate the causes of those problems, must be checked against the problems associated with allocating the costs and the difficulty of making such an allocation acceptable.

In terms of the tasks of indirect complaint management, such as performing analyses and furnishing reports, which can lead to product and process improvements, the situation must be evaluated somewhat differently. If these services are delivered only at internal prices, it might be that they are not requested by all the relevant internal groups and/or are only procured occasionally so that the advantage of information utilization is only partially realized. In order to prevent the occurrence of such a situation, it would seem to be wise to make the acceptance of a standard program of analysis and reporting obligatory for the relevant target groups, wherein content, frequency, and price are to be negotiated. For more extensive information and support services, the complaint-management department has to make innovative proposals and market them internally.

If the firm is successful in establishing the conditions necessary to determine the actual profit and in internally allocating the costs of direct complaint management and information services in indirect complaint management, organizing the complaint-center department as a profit center would appear to be appropriate.[1]

14.4 ON THE QUESTION OF OUTSOURCING COMPLAINT MANAGEMENT

Many firms go on to outsource at least part of their complaint management to external service providers. An assessment of these outsourcing decisions cannot be made in general; rather, it requires a differentiated view. In particular, it is necessary to differentiate between the strategic-conceptual tasks and the operational tasks.

The responsibility for dissatisfied customers and the responsibility for the professional steering of the complaint-management process as a whole, including its framework factors (human resources, organization, and technology), cannot be delegated externally under any circumstances. It is a fundamental task of every firm to accept responsibility for problems and failures that occur, to create the appropriate conditions to satisfy the complainants, and to introduce measures that prevent the future occurrence of problems. Another reason for arguing against outsourcing this responsibility is that complaint management represents the core of customer relationship and customer retention management, and its philosophy must originate within the firm and be lived and supported by the employees there. It is the duty of the complaint-management department to accept this responsibility and to create the appropriate basic conditions. Core competencies cannot be outsourced. Firms that count their relationships with their customers among their core competencies cannot, therefore, delegate these corporate functions to external service providers under any circumstances. Accordingly, most firms limit themselves to reflections of whether and under what conditions the operational handling of contacts with complainants can be outsourced.

This operational aspect affects the complaint center, with which the customers interact and where they experience customer orientation and quality, as the firm understands these concepts. If the firm wants to outsource the complaint center, it must fulfill a series of requirements and at the same time be certain that the risk associated with outsourcing— namely, that the firm would fail to achieve its complaint-management goals—is minimized: (1) Of central importance is that the complaint-management department leadership defines detailed targets for the procedures of processing telephone and written complaints. These targets include, for example, requirements with respect to the times for telephone conversations and reactions, the social skills of employees who

---

[1] In science-fiction novels, this situation has already become a reality. In his book *The Restaurant at the End of the Universe*, Douglas Adams (1982:10) writes of the hugely successful Sirius Cybernetics Corporation Complaint Division, "which now covers the major land masses of three medium-size planets and is the only part of the Corporation to have shown a consistent profit in recent years."

come into contact with customers, or problem solutions and compensatory benefits that are allowed. Further, the firm must determine the conditions under which complaints are to be forwarded to the 3rd level of the company. (2) At the same time, the subjective and objective quality and productivity standards described in task controlling are to be implemented in order to permit continuous monitoring with regard to compliance with the standards that have been defined. (3) In addition, the firm must see to it that its management and the service provider cooperate very closely. Here, the firm should make sure that employees in the complaint center are not only trained in system-technical, conversation-tactical and sociopsychological matters, but also are familiar with the details of the organizational structure and the responsibilities of the client and possess specialized knowledge of products and how to eliminate errors. Moreover, the firm must create framework conditions that guarantee the necessary identification with the firm and its services and above all a high degree of willingness to accept responsibility for failures that have arisen on the part of the external service provider. (4) Another important point pertains to the client's constant access to customer information generated in the complaint center, since it is precisely these data that in many firms represent an essential strategic resource for developing customer-relationship management activities and realizing competitive advantages. Providing an adequate information-technology infrastructure creates the necessary conditions for successful fulfillment of these tasks.

If the firm takes these cornerstones into account in the context of outsourcing its complaint center functions, the conditions are created for achieving the goals of complaint management, even with the help of an external service provider. At the same time, the advantages of such a delegation of operational task performance, which first relate to cost arguments, can be realized. These cost arguments involve cost savings with respect to human resources and telephone technology, and the conversion of fixed costs to variable costs and the higher degree of cost transparency that is associated with it. Further, additional expert know-how can be utilized, since professional customer care/customer interaction center providers possess extensive experience in terms of the selection, training, and directing of suitable employees.

If the external service provider does not simply feel responsible for supplying personnel and technological resources, but also sees itself in the role of actively providing ideas in areas of complaint management that have not yet been considered or that are innovative (e.g., preparation of complaint reports that are suited to the needs of particular target groups or development of new methods for complaint analysis), all the conditions exist for a successful design of the outsourcing of operational contact processing in the context of complaint management.

15

Technological Aspects of Complaint Management

Especially when there is a significant volume of complaints, the tasks of complaint management can be efficiently realized only with the use of software programs. Therefore, those in charge of complaint management must keep themselves informed about the functional performance of the programs currently offered in the marketplace and plan their implementation.

However, one must realize that appropriate programs can be effective only within the framework of a consistent strategy of complaint management and that they are not a replacement for a well-thought-out management concept.

The latter point must be stressed because especially in recent years, complaint management—primarily in the context of Customer-Relationship Management Initiatives—has been misinterpreted as a simple software project. In seeing it this way, firms overlook that a comprehensive management and leadership concept is involved. However, only when such a concept exists and when it provides the strategic framework for utilizing the software can the great potential of a complaint-management software be used to enhance efficiency and increase quality.

15.1 FUNDAMENTAL DETERMINANTS FOR THE IMPLEMENTATION OF COMPLAINT-MANAGEMENT SOFTWARE

First, the firm must review the conditions under which it would be advisable to support the processes of complaint management with a software solution. In order to answer this question, one should primarily refer to the following determinants for implementing a software solution: complaint volume, complexity of the processing procedures, extent of the product range offered by the firm, and analysis and controlling requirements. Accordingly, software support becomes essential

- when the complaint volume is so high that accepting, processing, and resolving all the complaints rapidly and efficiently is no longer possible without a software system
- when the processing procedures are complex, for example, when different organizational units are integrated in the acceptance, processing, and reaction procedures

- when the firm offers a variety of products and services that in turn can have various problems so that very differentiated procedures for recording and processing complaint information are necessary
- when extensive, multilevel, and regular analyses and reports must be performed and generated, respectively, and when the functions of complaint-management controlling must be fulfilled.

If we take into consideration that complaint management is at the core of every system of customer-relationship management, which usually requires the implementation of a software system, then we can emphasize that it is necessary and practical not just for larger firms, but also for the vast majority of medium-sized businesses, to fall back upon complaint-management software.

15.2 DECIDING BETWEEN SPECIAL COMPLAINT-MANAGEMENT SOFTWARE AND AN INTEGRATIVE CRM SOLUTION

If the conditions above exist in the firm, the fundamental decision that must be made is whether a special complaint-management software or an integrative CRM solution should be implemented. The answer to this question mainly depends upon whether complaint management is interpreted as an independent management concept (or software project) or as an integrated component of CRM. If the former is the case, it would seem reasonable to decide in favor of a software system that is specifically developed to support the complaint-management processes. However, even when the overall concept of customer-relationship management is established with the aid of comprehensive software systems, the firm may decide to implement special complaint-management software. This is always the case when a firm opts for the best possible software solution for each problem area of CRM, for example, on a special campaign management tool, a software solution for the targeted support of sales processes, or even a specific solution for the implementation of active complaint management. This type of software strategy is also designated a "best-of-breed" solution in the context of CRM.

As an alternative to the best-of-breed strategy, a firm can opt for a completely integrated solution, in which all the relevant CRM requirements are taken into consideration. The basic difference between these two software strategies is that the integrated approach guarantees uniform software implementation and thus prevents the implementation of software systems from different providers. In particular, the problems associated with having different user interfaces, as well as different database interfaces, can thereby be limited and, from this standpoint, the costs reduced. Although this advantage is frequently counteracted by the disadvantage of qualitative losses. Best-of-breed solutions are in most acses based on a better complaint-management concept and feature a greater functional range, the result of which is that they may in part provide more efficient processes and require fewer adjustments and often prove to be more cost-effective in the end. An obvious alternative, which combines the advantages of best-of-breed solutions and completely integrated solutions, can be achieved by mapping the basic functionalities of best-of-breed solutions in integrated complete solutions. Whether and to what extent such possibilities exist should be verified during the phase in which the completely integrated solutions are evaluated.

A variant that is considered and often implemented by many firms is to realize the software support of complaint-management processes with their own resources. Usually, the primary reason for considering this perspective is the seamless technical integration of new software modules into the existing system landscape. As meaningful as this variant seems to be from this point of view, such a decision is often regretted for other obvious reasons, the further the implementation proceeds (Terentis, Sander, Madden, Stone, and Cox 2002): (1) Standard software systems include a series of functionalities for the support of the complaint-management process, which are usually industry-independent and rely on diverse know-how and thus do not have to be reinvented from scratch. The expenses for firm-specific upgrades or changes in available functionalities can be reduced to a minimum. (2) Often, neither the necessary programming skills nor the corresponding capacity are available that would ensure a sound and prompt programming of the functional requirements. (3) The costs of in-house development usually exceed the licensing costs and the costs of the data-technical integration, service, and support of standard systems to a significant degree.

If in-house programming is still preferred due to strategic IT considerations, it is advisable to fall back on external expertise with respect to the definition of the detailed functional requirements of such a system and the programming of individual system components.

The general guideline for the decision regarding the software support of a software system of active complaint management should be shaped by functional, economic, and IT considerations— in this order—regardless of whether a "pure" complaint-management project or an integrated CRM project is chosen. The software must take into account the CRM approach described, which is oriented toward all the possible situations of a customer relationship, and be able to handle all the task modules of complaint management. Any concession made toward a minimum software-technical fulfillment of the functional requirements will later prove to be an erroneous decision with serious consequences that will be reflected both in additional expenditures for software adaptations and in jeopardized or lost customer relationships.

In any event, the functional perspective must drive the introduction of complaint-management software systems. The software should not determine the action alternatives and thus the corporate value contribution of complaint management; instead, it must be able to fulfill the requirements of a complaint-management concept that is strategically oriented and specifically defined for the individual firm in an optimal fashion.

15.3 CORE FUNCTIONALITIES OF COMPLAINT-MANAGEMENT SOFTWARE SYSTEMS

Complete Documentation of Complaint Information

In the context of complaint acceptance, the essential function of software solutions is to make sure that the goal of thorough, structured, and rapid complaint documentation is reached. The thorough documentation of complaint information on a software-supported basis is made possible because all the information to be documented in a complaint case is stated and predefined in specific masks of the software system, whereby the documentation of this information covers the entire complaint-processing procedure. If a complaint incident cannot be resolved during the initial contact with the complainant, the documentation of the internal handling of the complaint takes place as the complaint processing and reaction progress.

Specific data fields can be defined as "required fields" in order to support the process of documentation and to promote the discipline of documentation. Having such fields would mean that a complaint case normally could be saved only after all the information defined as "imperative" has been entered. If it is not possible for customers to provide the information essential for smooth complaint processing at the moment they are making the complaint, the program can provide for the possibility of reminding the users at the start or during the use of the application that individual data in certain complaint processes are not yet fully documented so that they can introduce other measures to obtain the data that are still needed.

An essential requirement for the thorough documentation of all the relevant complaint information is the provision of appropriate fields, which are designed in a way that is logical in terms of content and which follow the complainants' narration of the incident.

Structured Documentation of Complaint Information

The structured documentation of complaint information is essentially determined by the provision of specific options for documenting individual complaint information and by the layout of the documentation masks. It is encouraged when the complaint content and complaint-processing information are recorded in different masks, and the structure of the information to be recorded is consequentially arranged according to content and the flow of the complainants' conversation. At the same time, it should be possible to switch back and forth between the different masks easily and access the various input fields so that the information can be entered as the complainants give their descriptions, especially in the case of complaints articulated over the telephone.

The fundamental differentiation between the documentation of complaint content and complaint-processing information is important because complaint-content information must be taken directly from the customer's articulation, while complaint-processing information may be recorded after the initial contact with the complainant. A good structuring of the relevant information in the context of complaint acceptance, processing, and reaction is also a basic requirement for rapid documentation of that information.

Rapid Documentation of Complaint Information

Rapid documentation of complaint information can be accomplished by implementing complaint-management systems in which appropriate classification attributes for individual complaint data are simply and flexibly defined for like or similar circumstances and provided to employees in the form of predefined alternatives when they are in the process of recording the information. For instance, all the meaningful characteristics for customer groups, products, or problem categories are given as single-level or hierarchical lists in the appropriate fields. During the documentation of a complaint case, the applicable items can be chosen with a simple click from the respective lists so that it is not necessary to enter the information manually.

This selection process may be supported by an automated preselection of the relevant alternatives. If, for example, processors are looking for the customer group "Private Customers" during the course of categorizing complainants with respect to their affiliation with a particular target group, they can type the first letter "P," which will take them to a preselection of possible customer groups beginning with that letter.

Content relationships and dependencies may exist between the complaint information to be recorded and the respective classification attributes. If, for instance, a complaint about a specific product is lodged, the problem types that are offered as possibilities for further documentation should exclusively be those that could be related to and have been defined for that product. Similar connections between the type of problem and the corresponding solution or between the type of problem and the corresponding processing procedures would also make sense. The mapping of such dependencies between the individual complaint data in a complaint-management system implies a filter effect with regard to the alternatives available for selection and also makes it possible to manage comprehensive and complex categorization structures.

In the context of the software-technical implementation of the documentation process, the firm usually attempts to achieve rapid recording of information by including only the "really important" complaint information and/or providing the classification attributes on a very abstract level (e.g., "Product Errors" or "Employee Behavior"). When the firm does so, the quality of information suffers at the expense of rapid documentation, which limits the opportunities for customer-oriented complaint processing and for meaningful analyses and specific quality improvements. For this reason, rapid documentation such as that described above can be seen as problematic "less documentation." Therefore, during the software-technical implementation of the documentation process, conditions must be created that will provide not only rapid, but also differentiated and detailed recording of complaint information.

Documentation of Internal Complaint Handling

In the task areas of complaint processing and complaint reaction, software systems can be used primarily for steering the complaint-processing procedures, for effectively managing deadlines and communication, and for promoting a policy of rapid and consistent problem-solving.

Systematically steering the flow of complaint processing is possible to the extent that the predefined complaint-processing procedures can be initiated properly when a new case is entered in the system, either automatically, for example, depending on the respective type of problem, or manually. The "Complaint Owner" for each complaint case can be determined at the same time. When a processing procedure is initiated, the person responsible for the first processing step (the "Task Owner") is immediately informed that a processing case has entered the system, and this person also receives the temporal targets for the completion of this step of the procedure.

After the respective subtasks are completed by the "Task Owners," the case is automatically forwarded, and deadlines are set for the next subphase and for the remainder of the whole processing procedure. In this way, the firm makes certain that all the people or departments involved in the processing act according to the procedures defined and within the framework of the deadlines that have been established. At the same time that the complaint incident is being processed, the processing history is generated in chronological order as each processing step is completed.

In order to be able to guarantee completely the performance of these functions, the firm must integrate a work-flow engine in the process that will permit flexible modeling of the processes and ensure complete documentation and monitoring of deadlines, as well as ongoing status checks.

An important way to simplify the processing procedure, especially in the case of complaints articulated in writing, is to integrate a document-management system into the complaint-management software. Complaint letters, as well as additional documents submitted by the complainant, can be scanned into the system, classified under a specific complaint case, and processed further by, for example, highlighting important text passages in a different color or attaching commentary and processing notes to the document. By forwarding the complaint cases in the network along with the scanned documents directly to the person responsible for the processing, the firm can eliminate sending out duplicate or delayed customer correspondence that is related to the case, and the processing procedure can be expedited.

As far as effective deadline management is concerned, the implementation of software has further advantages. The processing times associated with the individual processing steps are translated into specific target dates, starting with the date the complaint was received. If the deadlines that have been set are exceeded, an integrated reminder system can automatically inform responsible employees about their delays when the program starts up or while the application is running. If the delay of the complaint case continues, it is possible that the case will be automatically assigned to the escalation system. When the network is adequately integrated, the persons responsible (from the Process Owner and the Complaint Owner all the way up to the company management) are informed about the temporal delay at various escalation levels and can intervene to steer the process.

Software technology can also provide services valuable for managing communication between the people or departments involved in complaint processing, and especially for managing communication with complainants. First, it is possible to send notes and processing comments as e-mail messages or telefaxes automatically generated by the system in the course of forwarding the complaint incidents to the departments located downstream in the processing procedure. In this way, the firm will be successful in expediting the flow of information and in optimizing the internal communication during the process.

Second, the firm can significantly simplify external communication with complainants. If the communication intervals for receipt confirmations, intermediate replies, and the final answer are stored in the software, it is possible to give the employees an automatic reminder when communication is necessary. Form letters and text elements that are regularly used in correspondence can be managed by the program and made available, depending on the specific complaint information in the individual case. Establishing interfaces to popular word-processing programs can further optimize written communication. Case-specific data (customer address, complainants' preferred form of address, the problem or the reference to the problematic product) can be incorporated in the letter to the customer and can aid the complaint-specific manipulation of text components. Likewise, the system should be linked to corresponding telephone software, which would make it possible for complaint-management employees to establish an immediate telephone connection with customers.

Complaint-management software can be implemented with respect to the efficient and intelligent design of the firm's problem-solving policy. Linking problem solutions or compensatory payments to defined problem types for each complaint object gives employees the opportunity to see all the previous solutions for similar cases when they are processing complaints. This method allows for consistent reactions and the rapid elimination of customers' problems. Furthermore, if the costs incurred are allocated to the solutions or compensatory payments, the firm obtains a detailed overview of the costs of disputes and the external failure costs that result from dissatisfaction.

In Spotlight 10, a specific example is used to illustrate the software-supported documentation and categorization of vital complaint content information and the key principles of the software-technical steering and monitoring of complaint processing procedures with the aid of the "Sorry!" software program.

SPOTLIGHT 10

Direct Complaint-Management Process Masks: Record, Categorization, and Processing

Customer Celia Smith directs a complaint letter to the customer service department of a leading cosmetic company. The reason for her complaint: She has been using one of the manufacturer's products to color her hair for more than five years—and has been satisfied with the results. When she used the product during a four-week vacation, however, she noticed that the blond coloring had taken on a green overtone. Indignant, she announces her intention to change brands. She encloses the bleaching product she used and a strand of her hair with the letter, in order to document the undesired tone. She demands an explanation from the manufacturer for the sudden change in results, when she used the product in the same way.

First, all the customer data are recorded using complaint-management software. The mask used for this process is logically structured in such a way that it permits a call center agent to record the relevant data easily during a telephone call.

The next step is for the employee in charge to record the facts from the customer's complaint letter in the "Record" mask. There, the customers' expectations with regard to the solution and the consequences she/he is considering are also specified and—in the case of telephone contact—any promises and agreements are documented (see Mask A).

Next, the problem is categorized ("Categorization"): The specific product is identified by making the appropriate selections in the fields "hair," "coloring," and "bleaching," and the color difference is classified—a basic requirement for the later analysis of key problems in individual product ranges and specific products in the context of a continuous quality control (see Mask B).

The actual processing procedure is then set in motion ("Processing"): Based on the work flow provided, the customer-service representative makes decisions regarding individual processing steps, each of which is assigned a specific deadline. The successive execution of these processing steps is the requirement for the completion of the process.

This integrated work flow ensures thorough documentation and monitoring of deadlines, which the processor can control with his personal processing overview ("Personal Processing Overview" Mask) at all times. Here, the processing status in each case and, where applicable, the delay for individual processes are indicated (see Mask C).

In the case at hand, the customer-service representative sends the hair and the returned product to the appropriate laboratory for testing. The result is documented according to the feedback: The

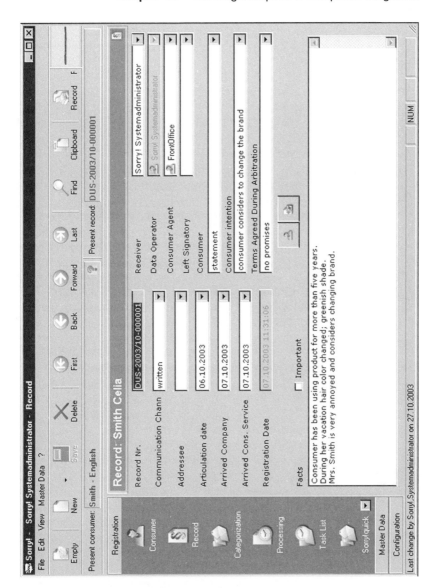

Spotlight 10, Mask A: Recording of the Facts

laboratory test showed that the green color of the hair was caused not by a defective product, but rather by copper ions in the chlorinated pool water at the resort.

The representative then decides to inform the customer of the reasons for the different color in a personal telephone call. During the conversation, he offers specific support at the same time: The customer will receive a special rinse that will eliminate the

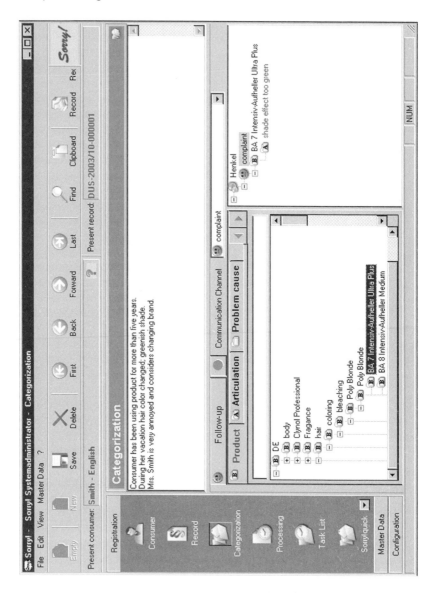

Spotlight 10, Mask B: Problem Categorization

undesired color. The customer is very satisfied with the information and the solution.

The final processing step is when the customer-service representative arranges for the shipping department to send the customer the promised rinse.

Sorry! is a product of Rödl IT-Consulting GmbH, Erlenstegenstr. 10, D-90491 Nürnberg, Germany. *www.sorry.de* and *www.roedl.com/CRM*; email: crm@roedl.de.

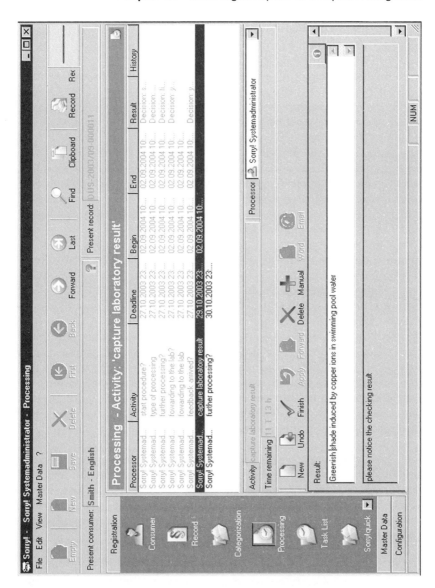

Spotlight 10, Mask C: Process Control and Documentation of Results

Analysis and Reporting of Complaint Information

The advantage of implementing a software-supported system of complaint management is not only that the relevant complaint information can be better registered and the processing procedure more efficiently steered, but also that the documented information is available for use in complaint analysis and in complaint-management controlling. At the same time, the firm can make sure that the program automatically initiates appropriate procedures for these task areas.

The frequency analyses and cross-tabulations that are part of quantitative complaint analysis can be performed within the program or be supported by appropriate third software systems, such as MS Excel, business intelligence systems, or even specific data-mining software. In either case, it is important to see that the desired analyses can be defined, accessed, and processed by users from functional departments without a great deal of effort on their part and without specific statistical or system-technical knowledge. This statement applies both to the architecture of the tables and to the desired translation of the information in the tables into graphic form. In addition, it is important that special procedures, such as the Frequency-Relevance Analysis of Complaints (FRAC), can be performed, and that problems can be prioritized from the customers' perspective. The firm must also use the opportunity it has to link logical data selections with defined frequency analyses and cross-tabulations in order to specify analyses even further. In this way, an analysis of the complaint volume, for example, can be performed separately for written or telephone articulations.

Qualitative complaint analysis can also be supported by the use of software, since the individual case descriptions and complaint histories can be accessed and planning instruments such as FMEA can be integrated. Ideally, the detailed analysis of individual case descriptions and complaint histories would also be directly initiated from quantitative complaint analysis. For instance, for each problem focus identified in a cross-tabulation for a particular product, one can go directly to the associated complainants with their respective individual case descriptions and complaint histories. On this basis, further cause analyses can be performed and/or specific follow-up measures defined for this group of complainants.

The definitions necessary for complaint reporting—in terms of the respective addressees, the analyses to be performed and the temporal rhythm at which the reports are to be generated—can likewise be anchored in the system so that analyses can automatically be performed by the program at the established times and sent out, using the appropriate distribution list.

Monitoring of the Task Performance of Complaint Management

In the context of complaint-management controlling, there are a number of other possibilities for using software. For subjective task controlling, a complaint satisfaction survey can be integrated into the software solution and, ideally, adapted and printed out as well. The data can then be entered online in the case of telephone surveys or recorded subsequently in the case of written surveys so that they can be directly linked to other complainant or complaint management data. This process supports both regular performance measurements and individual follow-up contacts in particular. At the same time, standards for the individual complaint satisfaction dimensions can be formulated, and the fulfillment of those standards can be monitored automatically.

Using the example of the "b.better" complaint-management system,

Spotlight 11 provides an excellent description of the software-supported administration of follow-up surveys to complainants.

The objective task controlling standards can be similarly stored and monitored by the system—in part automatically and in part by accessing other data. By revealing the discrepancies between actual values and target standards, the complaint-management system also provides the basis for the cause analysis that can be used to improve complaint management, in that the system takes into account the results from subjective task controlling. For purposes of cost-benefit controlling, it is possible to incorporate the necessary calculation procedures (e.g., for ascertaining

---

SPOTLIGHT 11

The complaint-management system of a sample firm has made a decision in the course of its subjective task controlling that complainants whose complaint case has been concluded in writing should be asked in the context of a follow-up survey about their satisfaction with the complaint processing one week after the answer letter is mailed.

The people responsible for making the follow-up contacts have a specific mask available to them, based on which they can specify the various customer and processing criteria that the complainants who are to be included in the follow-up survey must satisfy. Those complainants to whom the specified characteristics apply are indicated in the table in the lower section of the selection mask. (see Mask A)

In the next step, the employee responsible for administering the survey chooses the survey contents that are relevant for the chosen complainants, which are stored in the system in the form of questionnaires. In our example, the questionnaire form for Type 1 follow-up surveys is used. The tables in the lower half of the mask simultaneously provide an overview of surveys that are current or that have already been administered. (see Mask B)

When the relevant questionnaire is selected, the mask then branches off into the accompanying questions, which can be flexibly defined in the system, just like the answer alternatives that correspond to the questions. The person administering the survey registers the answer corresponding to each question in the fields provided. By saving the answers on a customer-specific basis, the employee ensures that the survey results are available in the individual customer's complaint history and for further measures of active customer care management. (see Mask C)

b.better® is a joint product of servmark management consultancy, Untere Haupt-straße 2, D-85386 Eching, Germany, email: *mail@servmark.de* and TietoEnator Consulting, Rembrandtstraße 13, D-60596 Frankfurt/Main, Germany, *www.tietoenator.de*

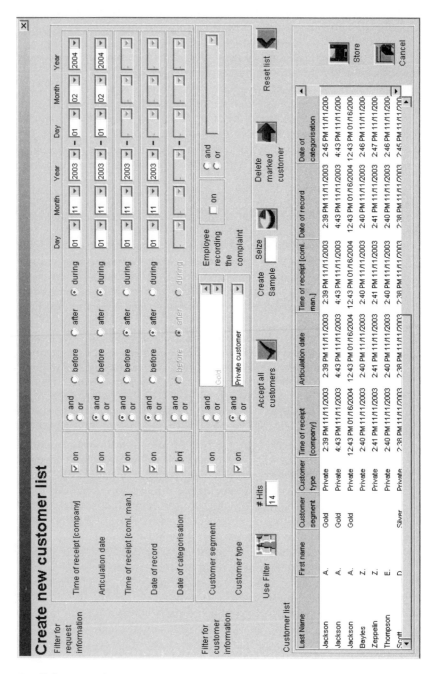

Spotlight 11, Mask A

the costs of complaint management, the individual benefit components, and the causes of customer switching) in a system such as this one.

Ideally, data interfaces to the databases would be created, which

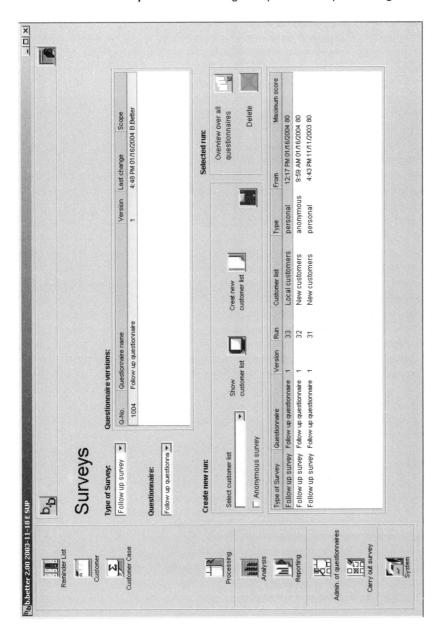

Spotlight 11, Mask B

would then register customers' actual purchase behavior. Current information regarding customer sales and profit contributions would thus be made available in the complaint-management system for purposes of cost-benefit controlling. At the same time, complainants whose purchase behavior changed significantly after a complaint could be specifically observed. In this way, it would be possible to calculate the "Return on

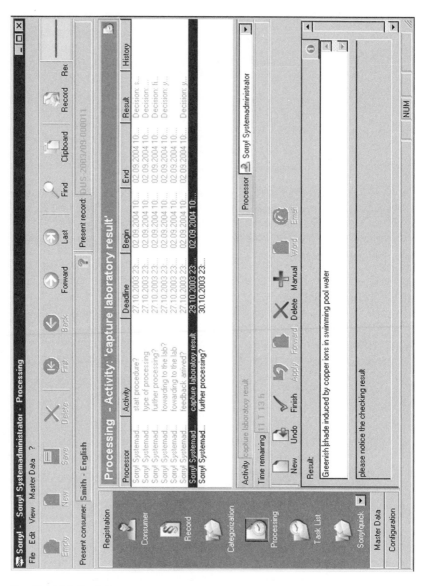

Spotlight 11, Mask C

Complaint Management" and to verify the profitability of various investments in complaint management.

Although the advantages of a software solution in performing the tasks of complaint management are undeniable, the restriction made at the beginning of this section is just as indisputable: Complaint-management software is an instrument that can make a consistent complaint-management concept significantly better and more efficient; however, it cannot replace efforts to develop and implement this concept.

16

Complaint-Management Checklist

In this last chapter, a checklist for your complaint-management system is presented (following Lash 1989; TMI 1993). With this instrument, you can get a quick overview of the extent to which the basic principles of complaint management have already been implemented and where deficits exist and action needs to be taken.

The checklist is designed in questionnaire form and follows the structure of this book. First, there are questions concerning the general importance of complaint management in the firm (Part I), followed by questions related to the individual tasks of complaint management (Parts II through IX). At the end, human resources-related, organizational, and technological aspects of complaint management are addressed (Parts X through XII). A number of statements are formulated for each group of topics, and you are asked to state your agreement or disagreement with these statements on a Yes-No Scale.

This scale is used to force you to make a decision. In many cases, corporate reality will be such that a clear agreement or a definite disagreement will be difficult for you. Instead of giving an average value in this case, however, you have to decide which tendency outweighs the other. If you feel that you cannot definitely agree with a certain statement, you should use the "No category."

Further specifications for analysis are provided below each part of the checklist.

I. GENERAL IMPORTANCE OF COMPLAINT MANAGEMENT

	yes	no
1. The goal of customer satisfaction is a top priority in our company.	☐	☐
2. Managers and employees of our company see complaints as an opportunity.	☐	☐
3. The goals and tasks of complaint management are clearly defined.	☐	☐
4. Top management takes time on a regular basis to read and answer complaints.	☐	☐

5. Complaint reports are a high priority in board ☐ ☐
   meetings.

Number of Yes Responses ☐

Score: Number of Yes Responses × 20 ☐

II. COMPLAINT STIMULATION

	yes	no
6. We want as many dissatisfied customers as possible to complain to us.	☐	☐
7. We encourage customers to complain to us when they are dissatisfied.	☐	☐
8. We make it easy for customers to complain (e.g., by offering an 800 number or service hotline).	☐	☐
9. We actively communicate the existing complaint channels to our customers.	☐	☐
10. The complaint-management resources are designed to meet the communication requirements of our customers.	☐	☐

Number of Yes Responses ☐

Score: Number of Yes Responses × 20 ☐

III. COMPLAINT ACCEPTANCE

	yes	no
11. The complaint acceptance procedures are completely and clearly defined.	☐	☐
12. All accepted complaints are forwarded to the responsible units quickly and accurately.	☐	☐
13. During complaint acceptance, the necessary complaint information is recorded completely and accurately.	☐	☐
14. There are well-structured standard forms and/or software masks for complaint recording.	☐	☐
15. Information provided by customers on the feedback site of our Internet home page is immediately recorded and processed in the complaint-management software system.	☐	☐

Number of Yes Responses ☐

Score: Number of Yes Responses × 20 ☐

IV. COMPLAINT PROCESSING

	yes	no
16. There are clear procedural definitions for complaint processing.	☐	☐
17. Responsibilities for the overall complaint-management process, as well as for individual subprocesses, are clearly defined.	☐	☐
18. There are temporal standards for the processing of complaints.	☐	☐
19. If processing deadlines are not met, an internal reminder is sent out.	☐	☐
20. Significant delays in processing are automatically brought to the attention of higher hierarchical levels.	☐	☐

Number of Yes Responses ☐

Score: Number of Yes Responses × 20 ☐

V. COMPLAINT REACTION

	yes	no
21. There are clear guidelines and codes of behavior for reacting to complaints expressed verbally, over the telephone, or in writing.	☐	☐
22. All complainants receive a receipt confirmation and a final answer and, if necessary, intermediate replies.	☐	☐
23. There are clear temporal standards for sending out reply letters.	☐	☐
24. The answers sent to customers take into account the individual circumstances of each case.	☐	☐
25. Complainants receive a fair solution to their problems.	☐	☐

Number of Yes Responses ☐

Score: Number of Yes Responses × 20 ☐

VI. COMPLAINT ANALYSIS

	yes	no
26. The complaint volume is analyzed on a regular basis with regard to quantitative criteria.	☐	☐
27. The analyses performed are differentiated (e.g., according to customer groups, products, problems, and with regard to time aspects).	☐	☐
28. There are methods used to prioritize problems.	☐	☐

29. A time series analysis of the complaint volume is performed on a regular basis. □ □

30. Important customer problems are subject to a thorough cause analysis. □ □

Number of Yes Responses □

Score: Number of Yes Responses × 20 □

VII. COMPLAINT-MANAGEMENT CONTROLLING

	yes	no
31. Our company analyzes on a regular basis how many dissatisfied customers do not complain and how many articulated complaints are not registered in the company.	□	□
32. Complainants' satisfaction with complaint handling (complaint satisfaction) is surveyed regularly.	□	□
33. Quality and productivity standards are defined and monitored for the tasks of complaint management.	□	□
34. The costs of complaint management are determined systematically.	□	□
35. The benefits of complaint management is assessed monetarily and taken into consideration when the profitability of complaint management is calculated.	□	□

Number of Yes Responses □

Score: Number of Yes Responses × 20 □

VIII. COMPLAINT REPORTING

	yes	no
36. The internal customer segments to whom complaint-relevant information should be forwarded are clearly defined.	□	□
37. There are clear definitions with regard to the contents, design, and level of detail of the reports.	□	□
38. In addition to the reports that are generated according to a clearly defined schedule, special reports are compiled if special circumstances (e.g., serious increase in important customer problems) require it.	□	□

39. Special analyses and the reports corresponding ☐ ☐
    to these analyses are made at the request of internal
    customers.
40. Authorized internal customers have access to ☐ ☐
    all the complaint information and to detailed
    analyses of that information.

Number of Yes Responses ☐

Score: Number of Yes Responses × 20 ☐

IX. UTILIZATION OF COMPLAINT INFORMATION

	yes	no
41. The information gathered as part of the complaint management process is systematically used for quality improvements.	☐	☐
42. Complaint information is utilized by specific methods (such as FMEA).	☐	☐
43. Quality improvement teams and quality circles use complaint information for systematic failure prevention and continuous improvement.	☐	☐
44. Customer panels with complainants are used to tap into the creative potential of criticizing customers.	☐	☐
45. Complaint and complaint management information are an integral part of our system of corporate customer knowledge management.	☐	☐

Number of Yes Responses ☐

Score: Number of Yes Responses × 20 ☐

X. HUMAN RESOURCE ASPECTS OF COMPLAINT MANAGEMENT

	yes	no
46. Great value is placed upon appropriate employee behavior in complaint contact situations.	☐	☐
47. Employees are trained to handle complaint situations properly.	☐	☐
48. Employees involved in complaint processing are extensively informed about the procedures, responsibilities, and technology that are part of the complaint-management system.	☐	☐
49. Customer-contact employees have ample discretion in solving customer problems.	☐	☐

50. Our incentive systems reward customer-oriented solution behavior. ☐ ☐

Number of Yes Responses ☐

Score: Number of Yes Responses × 20 ☐

XI. ORGANIZATIONAL ASPECTS OF COMPLAINT MANAGEMENT

	yes	no
51. A complaint management department exists.	☐	☐
52. There is an efficient division of tasks between centralized and decentralized complaint handling.	☐	☐
53. Competencies and responsibilities are clearly distributed between the direction of the complaint-management department and functional units (such as a Complaint Center or Customer Interaction Center).	☐	☐
54. The competencies and responsibilities of the complaint-management department are clearly regulated in relation to other organizational units.	☐	☐
55. The complaint-management department has clear targets and definite budget accountability.	☐	☐

Number of Yes Responses ☐

Score: Number of Yes Responses × 20 ☐

XII. TECHNOLOGICAL ASPECTS OF COMPLAINT MANAGEMENT

	yes	no
56. A software-supported complaint-management system has been implemented so that tasks are performed more efficiently.	☐	☐
57. The program implemented permits the quick and structured recording of information during the customer's complaint articulation.	☐	☐
58. The program implemented permits an automatic control of the processing procedures.	☐	☐
59. The program implemented contains comprehensive analysis and controlling elements.	☐	☐

60. The technology used is consistent and integrated □ □
within a comprehensive complaint-management
concept.

Number of Yes Responses □

Score: Number of Yes Responses × 20 □

Instructions for the Analysis

1. Determine the number of "Yes Answers" for each of the 12 blocks of questions and enter the number in the box provided at the end of each block.
2. Multiply this number by 20 and enter the result in the box provided below the first one.
3. Transfer the results to the appropriate lines on the result form provided below.
4. Determine the respective gap between your results and the maximum achievable result.
5. First consider the results for the "General Importance of Complaint Management." If deficits are found here, your efforts must first focus on this basic level.
6. Determine the block of questions for which the highest discrepancy value exists. This is where corrective measures to optimize your system of complaint management should begin.

Complaint-Management Checklist

Area	Maximum points achievable	Points reached	Gap
I.	General Importance of Complaint Management	100	
II.	Complaint Stimulation	100	
III.	Complaint Acceptance	100	
IV.	Complaint Processing	100	
V.	Complaint Reaction	100	
VI.	Complaint Analysis	100	
VII.	Complaint Management Controlling	100	
VIII.	Complaint Reporting	100	
IX.	Utilization of Complaint Information	100	
X.	Human Resource Aspects of Complaint Management	100	
XI.	Organizational Aspects of Complaint Management	100	
XII.	Technological Aspects of Complaint Management	100	
Total		1,200	

BIBLIOGRAPHY

Adams, D. (1982) *The Restaurant at the End of the Universe*, Ballantine Books: New York.

Adamson, C. (1993) Evolving Complaint Procedures. *Managing Service Quality*, 3 (1), 439–444.

Adamson, C. and Goodman J. (1992) *Complaint Handling*, Handout from the International Service & Quality Forum, Euro Disney, Paris.

Albrecht, K. and Zemke, R. (1985) *Service America! Doing Business in the New Economy*, Dow Jones-Irwin: Homewood, Ill.

Anderson, E W., Fornell, C. and Rust, R T. (1997) Customer Satisfaction, Productivity, and Profitability: Differences Between Goods and Services. *Marketing Science*, 16 (2), 129–145.

Andreasen, A R. and Best, A. (1977) Consumers Complain—Does Business Respond? *Harvard Business Review*, 55 (4), 93–101.

Andreassen, T.W. (1999) What Drives Customer Loyalty with Complaint Resolution? *Journal of Service Research*, 1 (4), 324–332.

Barlow, J. and Møller, C. (1996) *A Complaint Is a Gift: Using Customer Feedback as a Strategic Tool*. Berrett-Koehler: San Francisco.

Barnes, J G. (2003) Establishing Meaningful Customer Relationships: Why Some Companies and Brands Mean More to Their Customers. *Managing Service Quality*, 13 (3), 178–186.

Bearden, W O. and Mason, J B. (1984) An Investigation of Influences on Consumer Complaint Reports. *Advances in Consumer Research*, 11, pp. 490–495.

Bearden, W O. and Oliver, R L. (1985) The Role of Public and Private Complaining in Satisfaction with Problem Resolution. *The Journal of Consumer Affairs*, 19 (2), 222–240.

Bell, C.R. and Zemke, R. (1990) "Coaching for Distinctive Service," in: *Service Wisdom* (eds. Bell, C R. and Zemke, R.), Minneapolis, 164–173.

Bennet, R. (1997) Anger, Catharsis and Purchasing Behavior Following Aggressive Customer Complaints. *Journal of Consumer Marketing*, 14 (2), 156–172.

Berry, L L. and Parasuraman, A. (1991) *Marketing Services. Competing Through Quality*, Free Press: New York.

——— (1992) Services Marketing Starts From Within. *Marketing Management*, 1 (1), 24–34.

Berry, L L., Zeithaml, V A. and Parasuraman, A. (1990) Five Imperatives for Improving Service Quality. *Sloan Management Review*, 31 (4), 29–38.

Best, A. (1981) *When Consumers Complain*, Columbia University Press: New York.

Best Practices LLC (1990) *Improving Customer Satisfaction and Retention through Differentiated Service Levels*, Chapel Hill, N.C.

Bhote, K R. (1991) *Next Operation As Customer (NOAC). How to Improve Quality, Cost and Cycle Time in Service Operations*, American Management Association: New York.

Blanding, W. (1988) *The Deadly Game of Losing Customers*, Customer Service Institute: Silver Spring, Md.

——— (1991) *Customer Service Operations: The Complete Guide*, AMACOM: New York.

Blodgett, J G., Granbois, D H. and Walters, R G. (1993) The Effects of Perceived Justice on Complainants' Negative Word-of-Mouth Behavior and Repatronage Intentions. *Journal of Retailing*, 69 (4), 399–428.

Bolfing, C P. (1989) How Do Customers Express Dissatisfaction and What Can Service Marketers Do About It? *Journal of Services Marketing*, 3 (2), 5–23.

Boshoff, C. (1999) An Instrument to Measure Satisfaction with Transaction-Specific Service Recovery. *Journal of Service Research*, 1 (3), 236–249.

Bowen, D E. and Johnston, R. (1999) Internal Service Recovery: Developing a New Construct. *International Journal of Service Industry Management*, 10 (2), 118–131.

Bowen, D E. and Lawler, E E. (1992) The Empowerment of Service Workers: What, Why, How, and When. *Sloan Management Review*, 33 (1), 31–39.

———— (1995) Empowering Service Employees. *Sloan Management Review*, 36 (4), 73–84.

Brown, S W. (2000) Practicing Best-in-Class Service Recovery. *Marketing Management*, 9 (2), 8–9.

Brown, S W., Cowles, D L. and Tuten, T L. (1996) Service Recovery: Its Value and Limitations as a Retail Strategy. *International Journal of Service Industry Management*, 7 (5), 32–44.

Brymer, R.A. (1991) Employee Empowerment: A Guest-Driven Leadership Strategy, *The Cornell & Restaurant Administration Quarterly*, 32 (1), 58–68.

Buttle, F. and Burton, J. (2002) Does Service Failure Influence Customer Loyalty? *Journal of Consumer Behaviour*, 1 (3), 217–227.

Cannie, J B. and Caplin, D. (1991) *Keeping Customers for Life*, AMACOM: New York.

Carlzon, J. (1987) *Moments of Truth*, Harper Business: Cambridge, Mass.

Chase, R B. and Dasu, S. (2001) Want to Perfect Your Company's Service? Use Behavioral Science. *Harvard Business Review*, 79 (6), 78–84.

Clark, G L., Kaminski, P F. and Rink, D R. (1992) Consumer Complaints: Advice on How Companies Should Respond Based on an Empirical Study. *Journal of Services Marketing*, 6 (1), 41–49.

Cottle, D.W. (1990): *Client-Centered Service: How to Keep Them Coming Back for More*, Wiley: New York.

Davidow, M. (2003) Organizational Responses to Customer Complaints: What Works and What Doesn't. *Journal of Service Research*, 5 (3), 225–250.

Decker, A. and Meissner, H. (1999) "The Sequential Incident Technique for Innovations (SITI)—A Tool for Generating Improvements and Ideas in Service Processes," in *Service Quality and Management* (eds. Kunst, P., Lemmink, J., and Stauss, B.), Dt. Univ.-Verlag, Wiesbaden, pp. 203–222.

Dietze, U. (1997) *Reklamationen als Chance nutzen*, Verlag Moderne Industrie: Landsberg/Lech.

Durvasula, S., Lysonki, St. and Mehta S C. (2000) Business-to-Business Marketing: Service Recovery and Customer Satisfaction Issues With Ocean Shipping Lines. *European Journal of Marketing*, 34 (3/4), 433–446.

East, R. (2000) Complaining as Planned Behavior. *Psychology & Marketing*, 17 (12), 1,077–1,095.

Estelami, H. (2000) Competitive and Procedural Determinants of Delight and Disappointment in Consumer Complaint Outcomes. *Journal of Service Research*, 2 (3), 285–300.

Firnstahl, T W. (1989) My Employees Are My Service Guarantee. *Harvard Business Review*, 67 (4), 28–32.

Fisher, J E., Garrett, D E., Arnold, M J. and Ferris, M E. (1999) Dissatisfied Consumers Who Complain to the Better Business Bureau. *Journal of Consumer Marketing*, 16 (6), 576–591.

Folkes, V S. (1984) Consumer Reactions to Product Failure: An Attributional Approach. *Journal of Consumer Research*, 10 (4), 398–409.

Fornell, C. (1978) Corporate Consumer Affairs Departments—A Communication Perspective. *Journal of Consumer Policy*, 2 (4), 289–302.

Furlong, C B. (1993) *Marketing for Keeps: Building Your Business by Retaining Your Customers,* Wiley: New York.

Gierl, H. (2000) Beschwerdemanagement als Bestandteil des Qualitätsmanagements, in *Kundenorientierung durch Qualitätsmanagement: Perspektiven—Konzepte—Praxisbeispiele* (eds. Helm, R. and Pasch, H.), Deutscher Fachverlag, Frankfurt/Main, pp. 149–189.

Gilly, M C. and Gelb, B D. (1982) Post-Purchase Consumer Processes and the Complaining Consumer. *Journal of Consumer Research,* 9(3), 323–328.

Goleman, D. (1997): *Emotional Intelligence,* Bantam Books: New York.

Goleman (1998) What Makes a Leader? *Harvard Business Review.* 76 (6), 93–102.

Goodman, J A. (1999) Basic Facts on Customer Complaint Behavior and the Impact of Service on the Bottom Line. *Competitive Advantage,* June, 1–5.

——— (1989) The Nature of Customer Satisfaction. *Quality Progress,* 22 (2), 37–40.

Goodman, J A. and Grimm, C J. (1990): A Quantified Case for Improving Quality Now! *Journal for Quality & Participation,* Issue 3, 50–55.

Goodman, J A., O'Brien, P., and Segal, E. (2000) Turning CFOs into Quality Champions. *Quality Progress,* 33 (3), 47–54.

Goodwin, C. and Ross, I. (1990) Consumer Evaluations of Responses to Complaints: What's Fair and Why. *Journal of Services Marketing,* 4 (3), 53–61.

——— (1989) Salient Dimensions of Perceived Fairness in Resolution of Service Complaints. *Journal of Consumer Satisfaction, Dissatisfaction, and Complaining Behavior,* 2, 87–92.

Griffin, J. and Lowenstein, M W. (2001) *Customer Winback: How to Recapture Lost Customers—and Keep Them Loyal,* Jossey-Bass: San Francisco.

Haeske, U. (2001): *Beschwerden und Reklamationen managen: Kritische Kunden sind gute Kunden!* Beltz: Weinheim, Germany.

Halstead, D. (1993) Five Common Myths about Consumer Satisfaction Programs. *Journal of Services Marketing,* 7 (3), 4–12.

Halstead, D. and Droege, C. (1991) Consumer Attitudes Toward Complaining and the Prediction of Multiple Complaint Responses. *Advances in Consumer Research,* 18, 210–216.

Hart, C W L., Heskett, J L. and Sasser, W E. (1990) The Profitable Art of Service Recovery. *Harvard Business Review,* 68 (4), 148–156.

Hayes, B E. (1992) *Measuring Customer Satisfaction,* ASQ Quality Press: Milwaukee.

Heskett, J L., Sasser, W.E., and Schlesinger, L A. (1997) *The Service Profit Chain,* Free Press: New York.

Hochschild (1983) *The Managed Heart,* University of California Press: Berkeley.

Intelligent Intuition (2001) Customers: Your Company's "Appreciating Assets." *Trajecta Newsletter,* 3 (1), 1–4.

ISO 9001 (2000) Qualitätsmanagementsysteme—Anforderungen (ISO 9001:2000), Beuth Verlag: Berlin.

Jacoby, J. and Jaccard, J J. (1981) The Sources, Meaning, and Validity of Consumer Complaining Behavior: A Psychological Analysis. *Journal of Retailing,* 57 (81), 4–24.

Johnston, R. and Mehra, S. (2002) Best-Practice Complaint Management. *Academy of Management Executive,* 16 (4), 145–154.

Kendall, C L. and Russ, F A. (1975) Warranty and Complaint Policies: An Opportunity for Marketing Management. *Journal of Marketing,* 39 (2), 36–43.

Kingman-Brundage, J. (1992) The ABC's of Service System Blueprinting, in

Managing Services. Marketing, Operations, and Human Resources (ed. Lovelock, C.), Prentice Hall, Englewood Cliffs N.J., S. 96–102.

Klein, N. and Sasser, W E. (1994) British Airways: Using Information Systems to Better Serve the Customer, Case No 395065. Boston: Harvard Business School, S. 15.

Lam, N W W. and Dale, B G. (1999) Customer Complaints Handling System: Key Issues and Concerns. *Total Quality Management,* 10 (6), 843–851.

Lands' End (2003) Lands' End Principles of Doing Business, www.landsend.com.

Lash, L M. (1989) *The Complete Guide to Customer Service,* Wiley: New York.

Liu, B S-C., Sudharshan, D., and Hamer, L O. (2000) After-Service Response in Service Quality Assessment: A Real-Time Updating Model Approach. *Journal of Services Marketing,* 14 (2), S. 160–177.

Marketing News (1990) Burger King Opens Customer Hot Line. *Marketing News,* 24 (11), 7.

Maxham III, J G. (2001) Service Recovery's Influence on Consumer Satisfaction, Positive Word-of-Mouth, and Purchase Intentions. *Journal of Business Research,* 54 (1), 11–24.

Maxham III, J G. and Netemeyer, R G. (2002) A Longitudinal Study of Complaining Customers' Evaluations of Multiple Services Failures and Recovery Efforts. *Journal of Marketing,* 66 (4), 57–71.

Meyer, A. and Dornach, F. (2001) *Kundenmonitor Deutschland—Qualität und Kundenorientierung,* Jahrbuch der Kundenorientierung in Deutschland 2001, ServiceBarometer AG: München.

McColl-Kennedy, J R. and Sparks, B A. (2003) Application of Fairness Theory to Service Failures and Service Recovery. *Journal of Service Research,* 5 (3), 251–266.

Michel, St. (2001) Analyzing Service Failures and Recoveries: A Process Approach. *Journal of Service Industry Management,* 12 (1), 20–33.

Miller, J L., Craighead, Ch W. and Karwan, K R. (2000) Service Recovery: A Framework and Empirical Investigation. *Journal of Operations Management,* 18 (4), 387–400.

Morganosky, M A. and Buckley, H M. (1987) Complaint Behavior: Analysis by Demographics, Lifestyle, and Consumer Values. *Advances in Consumer Research,* 14, 223–226.

NIST (2003) *Criteria for Performance Excellence: The Malcolm Baldrige National Quality Award Program.* National Institute for Standards and Technology.

Oliver, R L. (1980) A Cognitive Model of the Antecedents and Consequences of Satisfaction Decisions. *Journal of Marketing Research,* 17 (11), 460–469.

———— (1997) *Satisfaction—A Behavioral Perspective on the Consumer,* Irwin McGraw-Hill: Boston.

Osborn, A F. (1953) *Applied Imagination.* Charles Scribner's Sons: New York.

Parasuraman, A., Zeithaml, V A., and Berry, L L. (1985) A Conceptual Model of Service Quality and Its Implications for Future Research. *Journal of Marketing,* 49 (4), 41–50.

———— (1988) SERVQUAL: A Multiple-Item Scale for Measuring Consumer Perceptions of Service Quality. *Journal of Retailing,* 64 (1), 12–40.

Plymire, J. (1991) Complaints as Opportunities. *Journal of Services Marketing,* 5 (1), 61–65.

Rafiq, M. and Ahmed, P K. (1998) A Customer-Oriented Framework for Empowering Service Employees, *Journal of Services Marketing,* 12 (5), 379–396.

Reichheld, F F. and Sasser, W E. Jr. (1990) Zero Defections: Quality Comes to Services. *Harvard Business Review*, 68 (4), 105–111.

Richins, M. (1983) Negative Word-of Mouth by Dissatisfied Consumers: A Pilot Study. *Journal of Marketing*, 47 (4), 68–78.

Richins, M L. and Verhage, B J. (1985) Seeking Redress for Consumer Dissatisfaction: The Role of Attitudes and Situational Factors. *Journal of Consumer Policy*, 17 (1), 29–44.

Ritz-Carlton Hotel Company (1999) *Application Summary for the 1999 Malcolm Baldrige National Quality Award.*

Ross, I. and Oliver, R L. (1984) "The Accuracy of Unsolicited Consumer Communications as Indicators of 'True' Consumer Satisfaction/ Dissatisfaction," in: *Advances in Consumer Research*, (ed. Kinnear, T C.), Provo, 11, 504–508.

Russ, T. (1999) *Qualitaetsmanagement in der Bankunternehmung*, Lang: Frankfurt/Main.

Rust, R T., Subramanian, B. and Wells, M. (1992) Making Complaints a Management Tool. *Marketing Management*, 1 (3), 41–45.

Scheerer, H. (1994) Kundengefühle sind Tatsachen, *Harvard Manager*, 16 (2), 9–13.

Schneider, B. and Schechter, D. (1991) "Development of a Personnel Selection System for Service Jobs," in *Service Quality* (eds. Brown, S., Gummesson, E., Edvardsson, B., and Gustavsson, B.), Lexington Books, Lexington, Ky., pp. 217–235.

Servicebarometer (2003) Kundenmonitor Deutschland 2003, www.servicebarometer.de/kundenmonitor/2003.

Sewell, C. and Brown P B. (1992) *Customers for Life*, Bantam Doubleday Dell: New York.

Shostack, G L. (1987): Service Positioning Through Structural Change, *Journal of Marketing*, 51 (1), 34–43.

Singh, J. (1990) A Typology of Consumer Dissatisfaction Styles. *Journal of Retailing*, 66 (1), 57–99.

——— (1988) Consumer Complaint Intentions and Behaviors: Definitional and Taxonomical Issues. *Journal of Marketing*, 52 (1), 93–107.

——— (2000) Performance Productivity and Quality of Frontline Employees in Service Organizations. *Journal of Marketing*, 64 (2), 15–34.

Singh, J. and Pandya, S. (1991) Exploring the Effects of Consumers' Dissatisfaction Level on Complaint Behaviors. *European Journal of Marketing*, 25 (9), 7–21.

Singh, J. and Widing, R E. (1991) What Occurs Once Consumers Complain? A Theoretical Model for Understanding Satisfaction/Dissatisfaction Outcomes of Complaint Responses. *European Journal of Marketing*, 25 (5), 30–46.

Smith, A K., Bolton, R N., and Wagner, J. (1999) A Model of Customer Satisfaction with Service Encounters Involving Failure and Recovery. *Journal of Marketing Research*, 36 (3), 356–72.

——— (1998) An Experimental Investigation of Customer Reactions to Service Failure and Recovery Encounters—Paradox or Peril? *Journal of Service Research*, 1 (1), 65–81.

Spector, R. and McCarthy, P D. (2000) *The Nordstrom Way*, 2nd ed., Wiley: New York.

Stamatis, D H. (1995) *Failure Mode and Effect Analysis: FMEA from Theory to Execution*, ASQ Quality Press: Milwaukee.

Stauss, B. (2000) Perspektivenwandel: Vom Produkt-Lebenszyklus zum Kundenbeziehungs-Lebenszyklus. *Thexis – Fachzeitschrift für Marketing*, 17 (2), 15–18.

—— (2002) The Dimensions of Complaint Satisfaction: Process and Outcome Complaint Satisfaction Versus Cold Fact and Warm Act Complaint Satisfaction. *Managing Service Quality*, 12 (3), 173–183.

Stauss, B. and Friege, C. (1999) Regaining Service Customers. Cost and Benefits of Regain Management. *Journal of Service Research*, 1 (4), 347–361.

Stauss, B. and Weinlich, B. (1997) Process-Oriented Measurement of Service Quality Applying the Sequential Incident Technique. *European Journal of Marketing*, 31 (1), 33–55.

Sterne, J. (2000) *Customer Service on the Internet*, 2nd ed., Wiley: New York.

Susskind, A M. (2000) Efficacy and Outcome Expectations Related to Customer Complaints About Service Experiences. *Communication Research*, 27 (3), 353–378.

TARP (1979) *Consumer Complaint Handling in America: Final Report*, Washington, D.C.

—— (1988) The Benefits of Tollfree Telephone Numbers and the Pitfalls of System Rollout, Working Paper, Washington, D.C.

—— (1997) *Using Complaints for Quality Assurance Decisions*, TARP home page www.tarp.com/pdf/complaints.pdf, 1–21.

Tax, S S. and Brown, S W. (1998) Recovering and Learning from Service Failure. *Sloan Management Review*, 40 (1), 75–88.

Tax, S S., Brown, S W., and Chandrashekaran, M. (1998) Customer Evaluations of Service Complaint Experiences: Implications for Relationship Marketing. *Journal of Marketing*, 62 (2), 60–76.

Terentis, J., Sander, F., Madden, M., Stone, M., and Cox, D. (2002) Customer Service, Complaints Management and Regulatory Compliance. *Journal of Financial Regulation and Compliance*, 10 (1), 37–54.

TMI (1993) *A Complaint Is a Gift. From Complaint to Satisfaction*, Hillerod, Denmark.

Vavra, T G. (1995) *Aftermarketing*, Irwin Professional: Homewood, Ill.

Venkatesan, M.V. (1993) "Empowering Employees," in *The Service Quality Handbook* (eds. Scheuing, E E. and Christopher, W F.), AMACOM, New York, pp 259–266.

Walther, G R. (1994) *Upside-Down Marketing*, McGraw-Hill: New York.

Warland, R H., Herrmann, R O. and Willits, J. (1975) Dissatisfied Consumers: Who Gets Upset and Who Takes Action? *Journal of Consumer Affairs*, 9 (4), 148–163.

Wei, C P. and Chiu, I T. (2002) Turning Telecommunications Call Details to Churn Prediction: A Data Mining Approach. *Expert Systems with Applications*, 23 (2), 103–112.

Whiteley, R C. (1993) *The Customer Driven Company: Moving from Talk to Action*, Addison-Wesley: Reading, Mass.

Wirtz, J. and Tomlin, M. (2000) Institutionalizing Customer-Driven Learning Through Fully Integrated Customer Feedback Systems. *Managing Service Quality*, 10 (4), 205–213.

Zeithaml, V A. and Bitner M J. (2003) *Services Marketing*, 3rd ed., McGraw-Hill: Boston.

Zemke, R. (1993) "The Art of Service Recovery. Fixing Broken Customers— And Keeping Them on Your Side," in *The Service Quality Handbook* (eds. Scheuing, E E. and Christopher, W F.), AMACOM, New York, pp 463–473.

INDEX